BORN A SLAVE

Rediscovering Arthur Jackson's African American Heritage

by
David W. Jackson

Civil War Sesquicentennial Edition

The Orderly Pack Rat
2015

Library of Congress Control Number: 2015906537

Jackson, David W. (1969-)
  Born a Slave: Rediscovering Arthur Jackson's African American Heritage
    328 p.   cm.
 Includes bibliographical references, illustrations and index.

ISBN-13: 978-0970430816 (The Orderly Pack Rat)
ISBN: 0-9704308-1-7

First Edition, April 2015. *Civil War Sesquicentennial Edition.*
Revised, December 2015.

1. African Americans—Biography. 2. Slaves—United States—Biography.
3. African American families. 4. Slavery—Virginia. 5. Slavery—Missouri.
6. Slaveholders—Virginia. 7. Slaveholders—Missouri. 8. Kanawha County
(W.Va.) —History. 9. Franklin County (Mo.) —History. 10. Holt County (Mo.)—
History. 11. Interracial marriage—United States. 12. Racially mixed families—
United States. 13. Deatley family. 14. Jackson family.
I. Jackson, David W. (1969-). II. Title.

Published by:
The Orderly Pack Rat
Greenwood, Missouri
david.jackson@orderlypackrat.com
orderlypackrat.com

Table of Contents

Dedication

To Grandpa, Roy Weldon Jackson.

You have always been like a father to me.
I'm eternally grateful for the years we have had together.

You are 97. I'll soon be 47.
"We are buddies . . . forever."

BORN A SLAVE

Preface

My Jackson family has identified as Caucasian for the last five generations. But, after 30 years of genealogical research, I re-discovered a family secret. My great great grandfather, Arthur Jackson, was born an African American slave in Virginia in 1856.

Arthur grew up and *married* a white woman. When she died unexpectedly after four years of *marriage*, Arthur *married* her sister, who became my great great grandmother, Ida May (Anderson) Jackson. Now I know why I was never able to locate a record for either *marriage*. Once I proved Arthur was African American and that he and his wives were considered interracial, I realized they were *never legally allowed to marry*. Interracial couples weren't extended the freedom to marry in the United States until the definition of marriage was broadened by the Supreme Court in 1967, decades after my great great grandparents had died.

By studying Arthur Jackson's life and exploring his enslavement and ancestry, I have also researched and documented an extensive, meticulous *histiogeneography*™ including his slaveholding family, Mr. and Mrs. Richard Ludlow Jackson, Sr., and Lucinda Edwards (Deatley) Jackson.[1]

In the preface to my first book published in 2000, which made available for the first time the letters and diary of two maternal ancestors—cousins of Abraham Lincoln—who experienced the California Gold Rush between 1850-1852, I wrote, "the letters that are available tell the first-hand story of two pioneers who participated in an extraordinary saga that ranks today as perhaps the *largest, voluntary,* overland mass migration in world history."[2]

How ironic that a decade later I would prove in 2010 that my direct, paternal ancestry involved another kind of mass migration—the African slave trade—and that my slave ancestor was ultimately set free by President Lincoln. "The slave trade from Africa to the Americas was the *largest, forced* migration in human history."[3] Shockingly, slavery is still a reality around this globe. "According to Anti-Slavery International, there were more than 200 million slaves in the world in 1999."[4] The International Labour Organisation (ILO) and FreeTheSlaves.net estimate 21-36 million people in slavery today (2015).[5]

I have casually thought how ideal it would have been if Arthur might have written about his experiences as a slave. Original, insightful narratives written by African Americans about their first-hand experiences of slavery in American history are fascinating and valuable. Solomon Northup's book, *12 Years a Slave*, was most recently immortalized in a major Hollywood motion picture in 2013.

Incidents in the Life of a Slave Girl, by Harriet Jacobs, is one of the first books to describe the sexual abuse and torment that female slaves endured. It might easily have been the story of Arthur's mother, or grandmothers. *Incidents* became one of the most influential works in its time.

Our Nig: Sketches from the Life of a Free Black, by Harriet Wilson, believed to be the first novel published by an African American in North America, is a historical fiction based on her life growing up in indentured servitude in New Hampshire.

Narrative of the Life of Frederick Douglass, An American Slave, is, perhaps, one of the most important autobiographical works ever written by an American. In his shadow was contemporary, "William Wells Brown, traditionally regarded as the first African American man of letters and the founder of African American literature in Missouri."[6]

And, the Slave narratives from the Federal Writers' Project of the Works Progress Administration (WPA), collected between 1936 and 1938, contain more than 2,300 first-person accounts of slavery in America. These were microfilmed in 1941 and now digitized and available online after years as the 17-volume, *Slave Narratives: A Folk History of Slavery in the United States from Interviews with Former Slaves*.

With these few examples at hand—and there are many more of their kind—I had to accept that Arthur Jackson never learned to read or write. And, he died before the WPA slave narrative project was initiated . . . not that there was much likelihood that Arthur would have been included.

Rather than to document his birth into slavery, Arthur . . . and his wife and children . . . hid, denied, and lied about their racial truth. They successfully allowed this fact about our family's race and ethnicity to die with living memory.

My Jackson clan has not given much if any thought about American slavery—let alone their connections to it—in generations. No living descendants of Arthur and Ida Jackson had a clue about this family secret that I 'unshackled' with this publication. But, it is a real-life American family story based in fact. And, I feel we should humbly claim this heritage with honor.

I try my best to imagine the life Arthur and Ida Jackson struggled through as an interracial couple to make this world a better place for their descendants. No, they didn't champion or spearhead a civil rights movement. In actuality, they did the opposite. To quote a maxim shared with me by a wonderful friend and mentor, Kathy Tuohey, I have to believe, *"they did what they did at the time that they did it, because at the time it seemed to be the thing to do."*

Arthur and Ida raised their family in rural northeastern Kansas roughly between 1890-1910, and moved to Kansas City, Missouri, about 1913, where they lived together until Arthur died in 1931. They created a family that was perceived by others initially as a mixed-race family when living in Kansas near a Native American Indian reservation. Eventually, and especially after they moved to Kansas City, they ended up somehow 'passing for white.'

With each successive generation this reality about race and ethnicity intentionally died. In fact, Arthur and Ida's grand- and great grandchildren were ironically raised in a culture of prejudice and racism. They would never have imagined—and some, I suspect, will never accept—that the genes passed down through their paternal Jackson line contain African blood. It most certainly does. This is the DNA we have inherited.

Dr. Dorothy Witherspoon in her lecture and book by the same title, *Researching Slave Ancestry*, said, "Spirit guides us." I believe this, too. Arthur's soul must be calling me from beyond. I have pursued his life story since I was 11 in 1980. My Grandpa Jackson and I spent hours together running microfilm and researching our genealogy. We went to cemeteries and funeral homes. Eventually, my Grandma Jackson and I did the same for her side of our family, and I pursued similar pursuits with my maternal grandparents.

Rare fragments of information about Arthur uncovered through the years kept me going. The last five years of immense discovery are a reward for 30+ years of patience, persistence, and diligence in recovering Arthur Jackson's truth.

"Slavery was and remains one of the central elements in our conflicted national history. We are all products of that history, and we must all reckon with our past."[7]

That reckoning must first happen on an individual basis with an ever-present awareness that our nation continues to face and struggle with inequality and bias on many levels.

That reckoning must also result in positive action leading change forward.

"The life of the slave holder was extremely complicated and can be very sensitive subject matter for slave owning descendants and the descendants of those formerly enslaved. If you discover in your research that slavery was a part of your family history, you automatically are faced with decision as to how deeply you want to explore the relationships between these two groups of people."[8]

I have recognized and reckoned with my past and reconciled it with my present. Beyond DNA, I have found at least one life experience common to myself and my great great grandfather. Arthur Jackson was never allowed to legally marry the person of his heart's desire. Until recently, I, too, had been forbidden to legally marry the person of my heart's desire. Unlike Arthur, however, I have lived to see this change. The U.S. Supreme Court this summer determined that two loving, tax-paying American citizens—regardless of gender—may legally marry. The spirit guiding the Court in 1967 to allow marriage—regardless of race— surely influenced a right and just decision for equal civil marriage for gays and lesbians across the United States.

This book is a tribute to Mr. and Mrs. Arthur Jackson and Ida (Anderson) Jackson.

This book is also a testament to my desire for *true* unification and unconditional equality among all of my fellow countrymen and women. All we have to do is look to the past and empathize more with the varied and diverse lives of our ancestors to gain a greater respect for those with whom we share this planet today.

In the 1997 Academy Award nominated motion picture, Amistad, there is a scene, "A Call to the Ancestors," when the lead African character, Cinque, says, *"I will call into the past, far back to the beginning of time, and beg them to come and help me.... I will reach back and draw them into me. And they must come. For* <u>*at this moment I am the whole reason they have existed at all*</u>*."*[9]

Let us each call upon our endless cast of ancestors that the spirit of equality, universal peace, mutual respect and unconditional love will envelop and guide each future generation.

Thank you for following me on this journey to rediscover a family secret that began with Arthur Jackson, who was . . .

. . . Born a Slave.

David W. Jackson
    Kansas City, Missouri
        Revised December 10, 2015

BORN A SLAVE

1

A Packrat is Born

I was born on Valentine's Day in 1969. For the most part, my childhood was "normal" and relatively happy. In 1972 my brother, Nathan, was born. Then, our parents, Reginald Wayne and Marcia Ann Jackson divorced in 1975. Each parent re-married and life for our 'modern family' expanded and evolved.

David W. Jackson
high school graduation, 1987

Confession. While "normal" (whatever *that* is), I was a different sort of child. I preferred to sit inside and listen to my elders talk—even if I had no idea what they were saying—rather than go outside and play with other kids. Grandma Campbell said that when I was from three- to five-years-old, if she could not find me, she knew to look out in the back yard or next door because I would likely be found with "Mrs. O," her elderly next door neighbor. "Mrs. O" [Mildred (Cassell) O'Flaherty] would often sit in her lounge chair, shaded by the large trees in her backyard. I would sit beside her, and just listen to her talk. We would watch her bird bath and bird feeders. Sometimes, I would knock on her door and we would sit inside where she gave me butterscotch candy. She kept my attention by repeating my name often, and she asked me questions. I would have to go under a hypnotist's spell to try and recall exactly what wisdom she imparted to me; but, it seems to me that she talked about loving nature and appreciating and respecting all living things. I speculate this because ever since I can remember I've had a heartstring for the welfare and security of defenseless living beings (defenseless against human animals, that is). Mrs. O, in her 80s, also reminisced about her ancestors.

In 1980, I began studying my family's history at age 11. My great grandfather, Lester Campbell, passed away that summer. His sister had died the month before and hers was my first funeral. Also that spring, the 1980 U.S. Census was mailed to our home and my mother was filling in all the answers one weekend. I became intrigued seeing some of the genealogy she had started as a hobby some years before. I immediately caught the genealogy bug.

I embarked writing this particular family story in April 2010, when, after 30 years nearly to the month, I had a major breakthrough in my Jackson genealogy. I had uncovered a fascinating family secret that is testament to the rich, diverse culture and heritage of United States history.

By fitting this family history puzzle piece that has eluded me for three decades … three quarters of my life … I've never been more deeply affected by the legacy passed down to me by my ancestors.

This *histiogeneography*™ reveals the discovery by his great great grandson, that his direct, paternal ancestor, Arthur Jackson, was born a slave. The exploration continues with a detailed illustration documenting the white family to whom Arthur was enslaved. It chronicles Arthur's life, speculating his childhood in bondage and his early adulthood as a freedman. It traces his experience in an interracial marriage and their biracial family, who eventually passed for white. And, we glimpse Arthur's ancestry, with clues and leads to his African roots.

16

2

Catching the Genealogy Bug

I checked-out and followed the advice of all the "how to" genealogy books that my local public library carried in 1980. Little did I know then that we were on the doorstep of the Information Age. The personal computer would soon begin to infiltrate American homes. And, a decade later when I was in college, the World Wide Web would begin connecting and expanding our knowledge beyond imagination. But, in those early days of my genealogical pursuits, I found information the old fashioned way.

The resounding advice in every published instruction guide I read was to gather all you can from living ancestors post haste. I did it. I interviewed them all. I assembled "stuff" that they had each collected over their lifetimes. I was fortunate that I descend from a long line of packrats. I was also blessed that many of my direct and indirect ancestors were still living at that time (my parents, all four grandparents, and two sets of great grandparents...not to mention countless cousins in every direction, some of whom I would track-down and meet along the way).

Most people who become interested in genealogy do so after they retire. They lament that by then it is often too late to rely upon ancestors to provide personal life stories like those I was able to gather. Still, much information can be assembled with diligence.

I've been blessed and lucky to know my grandparents, who in many ways were more like parents. All four have said I 'should have been theirs.' And, at the time of this publication, both of my grandfathers are still living.

BORN A SLAVE

3

Who Are My People?

The number one question most people ask when you tell them you are studying your family's history is, "How far back have you gotten?" They are usually referring to the one surname by which you go by, not recognizing that your ancestry includes four surnames of your grandparents, and that the number of surnames grows exponentially going back in time (8 great-grandparents; 1,024 8th-great-grandparents, etc.).

**Roy Weldon Jackson
World War II**

With regard to my Jackson ancestry (my father's paternal line), my Grandfather Roy Weldon Jackson didn't know much beyond the names and personal remembrance of his own grandparents (my great great grandparents), Arthur Jackson and Ida May (Anderson) Jackson.

Roy's father, Jabez Jackson, was one of six siblings—children of Arthur and Ida—who grew to adulthood. They each married . . . some twice, three or four times. Three had children. Jabez's male descendants solely carry on this line of the Jackson surname. Roy said he was lucky to know what little he did because he found his Jackson elders to be unusually secretive about the family's history. One sibling lied about her age until the day she died. Roy saw names and dates altered in the family Bible. Jabez used nicknames such as "Jack," "Davis Roy," "Javis," or "Javies" (phonetic variation of Jabez). "Jarvis," was the name his brother, Reginald "Reg," selected for Jabez's death certificate and headstone.

Roy added, *"the Jacksons . . . were drunks."* This definitely applied to his father, Jabez. Roy said, *"While Dad was lazy, he was not a "crook." He just couldn't, or wouldn't hold a job. When sober, he was very likable. One time when Nancy and I were still dating, he came by and had been drinking. I needed to put him on the streetcar just to get rid of him. Well, he only had a nickel and I wasn't going to give him the whole fare ($.10), so I borrowed a nickel from Nancy so he could make his fare. She often joked that she married me so she could get her nickel back! I let Dad know when our daughter, Virginia Lee, was born, however, that he wasn't of any use to us and to stay away... and he did."* According to another grandchild of Arthur and Ida Jackson, Mary (Johnson) Bentley, Jabez would also show up begging for money at his brother Reg's workplace, *The Kansas City Star.* Reg would give him money and usher him off as fast as he could to avoid embarrassment. To show how desperate he once was, Jabez, while visiting his sister, Dollie (Jackson) Johnson, drank the rubbing alcohol that was in her medicine cabinet.

The men in the family drank, some more than others. Depression or other mental instability was also a factor. Two of Arthur and Ida's children committed suicide; one (Jabez) died early from alcoholism; and, a fourth died months after being released from a 17-year admission in a state hospital.[10]

To be sure, Roy and cousins of his generation worked during their lives to successfully 'raise the bar' for the Jackson clan, to lead their families into the American middle-class, and to make good on the family name.

4

Introducing Arthur Jackson and Ida May (Anderson) Jackson

Roy wrote about his grandparents:

"I was born August 13, 1918. My parents Jarvis [Jabez] and Grace (Clifford) Jackson, who had been married in 1916, divorced when I was about one year old. My paternal grandparents, Arthur and Ida (Anderson) Jackson raised me until Grandpa Jackson died in 1931 when I was 12 years old.

Grandma, Grandpa and I lived on Boone Street (called 42nd Terrace today) at the south edge of the old Westport area of Kansas City. Grandpa Jackson

21

was a landscape gardener and worked for wealthy homeowners along Ward Parkway south of the Country Club Plaza. My father lived a couple houses up the street, which is where he lived when he married Florence Wolverton, and had their child, Virginia Lee.

Dad and two of my Uncles worked with Grandpa at landscape gardening ... Uncle Ed and Uncle Ollie drove the truck. I often worked with them too, and I remember customers complaining that they were working me so hard and at such a young age. I was from 10 to 12 years old then. I remember they had a large barrel with a pump hooked to a hose and my job was to manually pump the contraption to keep the pressure up on the hose so that the men could spray whatever it was they were spraying up into the trees. I got $1 a day when I worked with them."

Every once in a while for very short periods, Roy lived with his father or mother—who had separated right after he was born in 1918—but, they were never in a position to provide a proper space or living situation for their son.

So, Grandpa Roy was shifted from home to home and from school to school. Grandpa counted and noted that before he turned 16, he moved 18 times and attended eight Kansas City, Missouri, elementary schools before dropping out of Central Junior High School half-way through ninth grade in 1935. That's as far as Grandpa's formal education went. As you will see, he was 'on his own' at an early age.

In the summer of 1929, at age 11, Roy returned to his Grandpa and Grandma Jackson's home at 414 Boone (renamed West 42nd Terrace in the early 1930s).

This bungalow was situated on the northern edge of the Steptoe neighborhood in an area of Kansas City, Missouri, known as Westport (formerly Westport, Missouri, before it was incorporated into the City in the late 1890s).

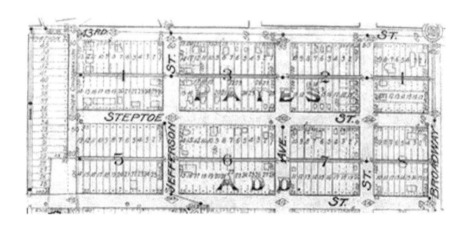

Above: Pate's Addition included Steptoe Street (today, 43rd Terrace) that ran 4 blocks west of Broadway to Summit.
***Plat Book of Jackson County, Missouri*, 1911.**

**Left: 414 Boone Street, Kansas City, Missouri, 1940.
Courtesy Missouri Valley Special Collections, Kansas City Public Library, Kansas City, Missouri**

Steptoe (technically, Pate's Addition with Steptoe Street as its main east-west thoroughfare, which is 43rd Terrace today (2015)) is a historic African American neighborhood. "Longtime   Steptoe residents called their community 'a little island' and talked about having white, Jewish, German, Italian, Hispanic and Swedish people for neighbors."[11]

Most homes in Steptoe have been razed as 'progress' has forced the area to evolve. While vanishing with each passing year, some remnants of Steptoe still exist as of 2015.

Local Kansas City historian and preservationist, JoeLouis Mattox, initiated study and scholarship on Steptoe in 2004 with a feature periodical article, "Taking Steps to Record Steptoe, Westport's Vanishing African American Neighborhood," in the *Jackson County Historical Society JOURNAL*. Since then, Mattox has entertained press coverage including, "Remembering Steptoe," by Andre Riley with the *Independence* (Mo.) *Examiner*; broadcast interviews including, "Remembering Steptoe," with Sylvia Maria Gross on KCUR (89.3FM); and a DVD documentary by Rodney M. Thompson, in partnership with St. Luke's Health System, "A Step Above the Plaza."

This was Arthur, Ida, and Roy Jackson's neighborhood.

I think about my Grandpa Roy at age 11 in 1929 . . . the same age I was when I started digging into my family's history in 1980:

> *"Boone was a short street with a large field behind our house and a coal yard next door where I used to play with other neighborhood kids. I woke up each morning for school to the clock my Grandfather got when he worked grading and laying track on the Missouri Pacific Railroad.*

> *"I had to be at school around 8:45 a.m. Grandma would get me up and feed me breakfast. I had a three or four block walk to Allen School at that time. I can't recall, but I may have come home for lunch.*

"When Nancy and I bought our first house on Walrond, I got this clock from Aunt Hazel's attic and we cleaned it up, hung it on the wall in our bedroom and wound it up.

"The clock ticked so loud that we had to stop the pendulum; there wasn't any other place in the tiny house that would have made it any better, so for years it hung on the wall in silence."

"When we moved to our present home in 1964, the clock was relegated to the garage wall.

"One summer in the early 1980s when David and I were really getting into genealogy, I took the clock to have its mechanism cleaned and we brought the clock inside and hung it in the kitchen. I wind it every Sunday night and it's ticking right now [July 2006].*"*

When the Antiques Roadshow® (PBS) came to Kansas City, without looking for a serial number, they said "The E. Ingraham Company" name was used as early as 1885, the year the company's founder, Elias Ingraham, died. This timeframe fits Arthur's life and work on the Missouri Pacific Railroad.

Grandpa kept the clock wound until 2009 when his house was broken up and he, at age 91, went to live in a nearby nursing home. I now proudly display my great great grandfather Arthur Jackson's Ingraham Regulator clock in my home. I admit, however, it is not ticking right now for the same reason Grandma and Grandpa discovered in their early married life together.

David W. Jackson holding his Great Great Grandfather Arthur Jackson's clock at the Antiques Roadshow® Kansas City, Missouri, 10 August 2013

BORN A SLAVE

5

Jabez Jackson and his daughter, Virginia

Grandpa Roy Jackson said that his father, Jabez, was a clown and was always joking and playing games.

"For entertainment, the Jacksons attended dances and played music. Grandpa [Arthur] played the violin...."

Mary (Johnson) Bentley, a granddaughter of Arthur Jackson, remembered her grandpa playing the tune, *"Buffalo Gals, Won't You Come out Tonight?"* which is a traditional blackface minstrel.[12]

"He simultaneously tapped one toe and the other heel to keep time. And, his feet were big. I think they said he wore something like a size 13 shoe."

Jabez "Jarvis" Jackson (right) with an unidentified friend, Swope Park, Kansas City, Missouri, ca. 1920

Roy continued:

> "*Grandma* [Ida] *always used to get mad at Grandpa* [Arthur] *because he'd go outdoors and hang out, and even play music with 'the coloreds' in the neighborhood.*

> "*...Dad* [Jabez] *could play lots of instruments: the guitar, mandolin, even the piano. He was what you might call the 'life of the party.' He could play the violin upside down, or put the bow under his leg to play it.*

> "*I guess it was at one of these dances that he met my mother in 1916. As it turned out my Grandpa Clifford* [Roy's mother's father] *had met or knew Grandpa Jackson when they worked on the railroad.*

> "*Maybe he also met Florence this way, too? He and Florence Wolverton were married and baby Virginia Lee was born on June 4, 1930.*

> "*I probably only saw my sister once because shortly after she was born Florence separated from my Dad and I think she even left town.*

> "*Then, Grandpa Jackson died in 1931 and Grandma and I were out of a home. (Years later I was given a little beaded baby bracelet—which I still have— that had been Virginia's, and Nancy and I decided to name our first daughter Virginia Lee after my sister).*"

Roy's father, Jabez, and his second wife, Florence (Wolverton) Jackson, lived at 418 Boone, a couple doors up the street from his parents, Arthur and Ida Jackson, where Roy lived with his grandparents.

Jabez and Florence had a daughter in June 1930 and named her Virginia Lee Jackson, my Grandpa Roy's half sister.

The couple soon separated and Florence moved away when Virginia was a baby. She never kept in touch.

Sixty years later when I was in college in the early 1990s, I sought Virginia with the intention of reuniting her with her half-brother.

After some detective work and genealogy, I found one of Florence's aged brothers living in Colorado.

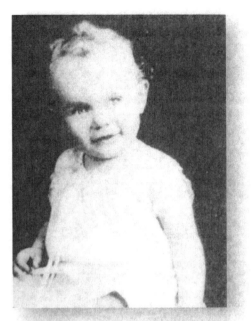

Virginia Lee Jackson, daughter of Jabez "Jarvis" and Florence (Wolverton) Jackson, 1930

Charlie Wolverton put me in touch with his niece, Virginia.

Virginia and her half-brother, Roy, started a genial correspondence catching-up on their lives apart over more than a half a century. She and Grandpa Roy remained pen-pals until 2009 when he moved to a nursing home. I continue to keep them each apprised of one another.

My great grandfather, Jabez Jackson, as mentioned previously, went at times by "Jack," "Davis Roy," "Javis," "Javies," or "Jarvis" Jackson. From all accounts he was jovial in his youth; but, quickly devolved into alcoholism that may have been instigated by depression. His was a tortured life that ended at age 57. Jabez's grandson, Reg, my father, was a lively youth; but, he returned from Vietnam "a different person." Of course the war traumatized him, and he may never have fully "returned home." But, he may also have inherited some of the mental illness and/or depression that seemed to plague Arthur and Ida Jackson's children.

BORN A SLAVE

6

Two Years of Stability Before...

Arthur, Ida, and their grandson, Roy, moved from 508 West 46th Street to 414 Boone (later, West 42nd Terrace in Edward Prices' Addition) by September 1929, when Roy transferred from Troost Elementary (at 5914 Troost Avenue) to Allen Elementary School (located at 42nd and Waddell; 706 West 42nd Street).[13]

Allen School, courtesy Kansas City Public Library, Missouri Valley Special Collections, Kansas City, Missouri.

Roy, at age 11, got his first job as a bicycle delivery boy for Crown Drug Store, located on the northwest corner of Westport Road and Broadway in Westport.

Parkview Drug Store, where Roy was a bicycle delivery boy, was located on the corner at the far left of this view, the northwest corner of Westport Road and Broadway. This was the view looking north from that intersection on June 7, 1948.
Courtesy Kansas City Public Library,
Missouri Valley Special Collections, Kansas City, Missouri.

Roy also had fun in those early days before the pinch of the Great Depression started to sting. He played marbles and "shot craps" with neighborhood boys. They also played, "War," as Grandpa called it:

"My friends and I [who were all white] *would line up our defenses using whatever we could salvage into a fort along the tracks of the railroad bridge that once crossed Broadway at 43rd Street.*

"The black kids would do the same. I had a shield that was a boiler lid that had a handle, and I could deflect the oncoming 'bombs.'

"The black boys would hurl stones our way. We would return 'fire' with lumps of coal that we'd scavenged from the [Wiedenmann & Simpson] *coal yard that was virtually in our back yard* [this was just west of where the Embassy Suites Hotel stands in Westport today in 2015].

"After the 'war' ended, the black kids would pick up the coal we'd hurled their way, and take it home to use for heat and cooking."

Streetcar Bridge over Broadway at 43rd Street, Kansas City, Missouri, as it appeared in 1985 (since demolished)

Above: Streetcar bridge at 43rd Street from below, 1977. Courtesy Kansas City Public Library, Randy Storck, photographer

Below: Office of the Wiedenmann & Simpson coal yard, 1940. Courtesy Missouri Valley Special Collections, Kansas City Public Library, Kansas City, Missouri

In the photo opposite and below, you can see the coal company's office building. The coal yard was behind, and beyond you can see a glimpse of the neighborhood along Boone (or, West 42nd Terrace) where Arthur, Ida, and grandson Roy lived at the edge of the Steptoe neighborhood of Westport.

Their immediate neighborhood may also be seen on the Sanborn Fire Insurance map below. This is a view as the block appeared in 1931, the year Arthur died.

Behind the house at 414 Boone—on the north—is the Wiedenmann & Simpson coal yard with its office along West 42nd Street. Today, though this entire block has been surfaced as a parking lot for the Saint Luke's Hospital complex, there remain some very old elm trees that once shaded the homes lining the north side of Boone Street, including Arthur and Ida's house.

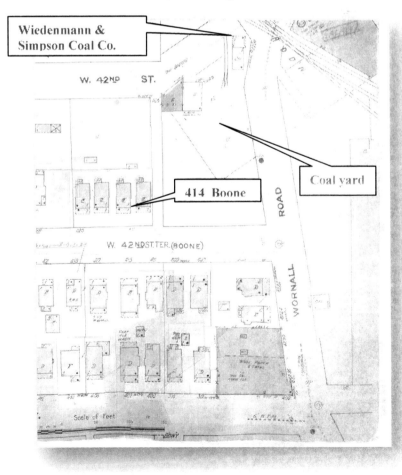

BORN A SLAVE

7

Shiftless As Great Depression Begins

Roy, at 12½-years-old, became shiftless once again after his grandfather, Arthur Jackson, died suddenly but peacefully at his home in Westport on the morning of February 5, 1931.

39

Roy clearly remembered having looked out the window to see his grandfather sitting on the porch at just the moment that Arthur's head tilted to one side and rested gently on the side of the house. Thinking his old grandpa had dozed-off, Roy went out to check on him to discover Arthur had at that moment peacefully passed. It was in the dead of winter. Arthur's death certificate says his cause of death at 7:45 a.m. was chronic myocarditis with general arteriosclerosis as a contributory factor. Arthur was a month shy of turning 75-years-old.[14]

Roy said his grandfather Arthur usually wore a vest and had a gold pocket watch. *"Grandpa said I could have that watch when he died,"* said Roy. As it turns out, Arthur had taken the timepiece to a watchmaker to get it fixed, and nobody knew which shop. Grandpa always regretted not inheriting his promised timepiece. Maybe that's why he grew up and always had a durable wristwatch that he was emphatic about keeping perfect time. Even in his 90s, Grandpa looks down at his Timex wristwatch and makes sure it's still ticking and keeping perfect time.

Upon Arthur's death, Roy and his grandmother, Ida Jackson, were both shiftless and found refuge between different relatives' homes (though rarely together again in the same home).

Roy continued to work hard and earn his own spending money. *"Between the ages of 14-16, I delivered on a bicycle delivering for Crown Drug Store for 10 cents an hour and worked seven days a week just to get by. At times I paid for my own board and a sleeping room at a buddy's home. I'm lucky to have gotten through*

to 8th grade. At age 16 I joined the CCC, mostly to have a home." Roy's Civilian Conservation Corps recollections are included in a memoir section at the end of this work.

Roy said, *"Aunt Hazel* [(Jackson) Levine] *was one that I could always count on. She and a family friend, Betty Weinstein, helped me and Nancy get off on the right foot when we set up housekeeping in 1939. I returned the favor and helped Hazel in her later years by taking her to her doctor's appointments and the like. In fact, her doctor, Dr. Moore, became our family doctor and has remained so all these years."*

Ida (Anderson) Jackson died 17 years after her husband, Arthur, in 1948. Before her death, she told Roy that his grandfather, Arthur Jackson, was related to Dr. Jabez North Jackson, a prominent Kansas City doctor. Specifically, Ida said that Dr. Jackson and Arthur were "half brothers."

Roy wasn't too interested and didn't think much about it at the time. He was busy raising his family, serving in the Navy in World War II, and starting what would become a 37-year career at the Sheffield Steel Corporation (later, Armco Steel) in Kansas City's historic Blue Valley.

On her deathbed, Grandma Ida Jackson motioned for Roy to come closer. He sensed that she was desperate to tell him something important. However, when he leaned in close to her mouth, *"All I could hear was her breath and her lips smacking. I couldn't hear a word she tried to tell me."* He was always uncomfortable by that situation in not having been able to hear what he felt was her, "dying wish, or confession."

And, of course, he never forgot that . . . not ever knowing what Grandma had tried to tell him.

Grandpa Roy and I made pact years ago to depart one another's company each time as if it were our last. We *know* the breadth and depth of our love and affection for one another . . . no deathbed confessions or testimonies needed.

BORN A SLAVE

8

Remembering a Family Tradition

About 20 years after his Grandma Jackson died, Roy clipped a couple of *Kansas City Star* newspaper obituaries for relatives of Dr. Jabez North Jackson. His second wife, Florence, died in 1967; and a daughter, Virginia, died in 1969.

Remembering his grandmother's story, Roy tried in the late 1960s to document the connection between his grandfather, Arthur Jackson, and Dr. Jabez North Jackson.

Roy thought surely there was some truth to the story, especially given the identical and unusual Christian names used in both families. Roy's father's name was also **Jabez** Jackson (although he usually went by one of several nicknames, usually Jarvis). Jabez/Jarvis named his daughter, Roy's half sister, **Virginia**. The doctor's mother, aunt, and daughter were named Virginia. Roy had even named his eldest daughter, Virginia, born in 1941, after his half sister, born in 1930. **Dollie, Edgar,** and **Walter** were other names in both families. Yet another coincidence is that both Jabez Jacksons married a woman named Florence.

Arthur was a poor landscape gardener.

Dr. Jackson, of course, was quite prominent.

Not having success at finding any corroborating evidence or connection, Roy gave up on his grandmother's story as fiction.

In 1980, Grandpa shared this history with me, and gave me the aforementioned obituaries for me to "give it a try." I collected quite a bit of material about Dr. Jabez North Jackson and his ancestry. However, I was unable to document Grandma Jackson's family tradition that Arthur and Dr. Jackson were "half brothers." I, too, filed that research away as a fable.

Through the 1980s and 1990s, Grandpa (and Grandma) Jackson and I continued to study and research together all of our other ancestral lines with success. We spent lots of time reviewing microfilm and even taking trips to cemeteries and meeting and visiting with long-lost cousins. We even worked to mark and/or restore the grave sites of some of our ancestors. Grandpa and Grandma were supportive in my endeavors, and they enjoyed the surprises and discovery process of learning about our family history they had never known.

9

Discoveries and Questions about Race

Grandma Ida Jackson's assertion about our family connection to Dr. Jabez North Jackson seemed even more unbelievable when I uncovered early on in my genealogical pursuits some peculiarities about Arthur and Ida Jackson.

In all early records about the couple, Arthur was listed as either "black" or "mulatto" (i.e., antiquated pejorative meaning 'mixed race'), and his wife, Ida, was listed as "white." Their children (my grandfather's father, Jabez, and his siblings) were always enumerated by the door-to-door census taker as "mulatto."[15] Clearly, they appeared to be a biracial family.

The only documents listing Arthur as white are when he was between the approximate ages of 60-75 in the 1920 and 1930 U.S. Census returns. His February 1931 death certificate also lists him as "white." His doctor, Frank B. Henderson, who had attended Arthur since December 16, 1930, operated from the Waldheim Building, Suite 803, in downtown Kansas City. (See Appendix: "Arthur Jackson Age, Race & Literacy in Historical Documents.")

When I shared this curiosity with Grandpa Roy, he refuted that his grandfather was black. *"Grandpa was a landscape gardener and had dark skin from the sun. If anything, he was part Indian."* It is true that Native-Americans were often listed in census returns as "black."

Grandpa relayed a memory when he was living with his grandparents as a child. One day, Roy met an older man who was introduced as Arthur's half brother named Dennis. This man, Grandpa said, *"looked just like the Indian on a buffalo nickel."* Grandpa always assumed this brother's name was "Dennis *Jackson*;" but, he could easily have had another surname if Arthur and Dennis shared the same mother, who remarried. And, given the 'tall tales' that Grandpa was used to hearing, he figured Dennis might not have been a brother at all.[16]

Still, even from his childhood memory, Grandpa remembered that Dennis, *"was from Hiawatha and had gone to college, maybe on a Federal grant; he got a government check."*[17] I guess my Grandpa Jackson, like myself, was good at listening to his elders as a child. Dennis must have made an impression. With little else about Dennis to go on, I have not yet been able to find anything about this mystery 'relative.'

A letter to Grandpa's cousin, Mary (Johnson) Bentley, by Dulcie (Rosecrans) Jackson, the widow of Grandpa's Uncle Edgar Walter "Ed" Jackson, confirms Grandpa's memory . . . and reiterated his grandmother's "fable." Dulcie's recollection was written 50+ years after her husband's death:

> *"Mr. Jackson* [Arthur] *had a half brother named Dennis Jackson that used to visit them once in a while. He was from Hiawatha, Kan. I don't know if he lived on the Indian reservation or not. I do know he got a government check.*
> *"There was a Dr. Edgar Walter* [actually, Walter Emmet] *Jackson and Dr. Jabez Jackson, half brother, I believe."*[18]

Setting these revealing indicators about race and ethnicity aside, Grandpa and I continued to focus on other aspects of our Jackson genealogy.

10

Birthplace

With regard to Arthur Jackson's birthplace, Grandpa Roy told me, *"Grandpa said he was born in Charleston."*

We never found any remote connection to the obvious Charleston, South Carolina.

Arthur relayed on several of the U.S. Census returns that he was born in Missouri. We went on the presumption that Arthur must have been born in Charleston, Mississippi County, Missouri.

On countless visits to the National Archives over several summers, Grandpa and I used printed indexes, then looked on microfilm to find every person named Jackson in the 1850, 1860 and 1870 U. S. Censuses for Missouri in counties stretching from the southern "boot heel" (where Charleston, Missouri, is located) up the Mississippi and Missouri River valleys to Holt County where we knew the Anderson family to have been by the mid-1880s.

We also sought endlessly to try and find the marriage record of Arthur and Ida Jackson. Grandpa said, *"Grandma always wore a thick, gold wedding ring. It was like a big statement she was making: 'See. WE ARE MARRIED.'"* We wrote letters to every Recorder of Deeds in every county in the tri-state area (Missouri-Kansas-Nebraska) requesting the marriage record for *"ANY Anderson woman marrying ANY man named Jackson."*

In each attempt at census or marriage record we struck out, reinforcing Grandpa's belief that his parents, grandparents and other relatives were, *"a bunch of liars."*

As you will see in the study that follows, Arthur was, indeed, born in Charleston.

Arthur Jackson was born in 1856 in Charleston, Kanawha County, Virginia, which is today (2015) in West Virginia.

11

Arthur and Ida Sitting in a Tree

The earliest document we had for Arthur in 1980 was a family Bible page where he was recorded as having married Melissa E. Anderson, a sister of Ida May Anderson, October 25, 1884.

Map of the tri-state area of with emphasis on Holt County, Missouri; Richardson County, Nebraska; and, Doniphan and Brown Counties, Kansas. Later, the Jacksons moved to Kansas City, Jackson County, Missouri

49

The Anderson family, a white family from Ohio, was living in northwestern Missouri when Arthur Jackson would have met Melissa in Holt County.

Other than the Bible entry for their elusive 1884 marriage, the earliest public record found identifying *an* Arthur Jackson of appropriate age and race was an 1885 Nebraska State Census for a waiter in Omaha, Douglas County (*without* a bride).[19]

The next record placed Arthur in White Cloud, Doniphan County, Kansas, on October 20, 1887. A "White Cloud" column in the *Weekly Kansas Chief*, published at Troy, Kansas, announced:

> *"Mr. Arthur Jackson lost a two hundred dollar horse, last week, the cause of its death being change of food."*

His luck got worse. The November 10, 1887, issue stated:

> *"Arthur Jackson has again been in luck—bad luck— to the tune of another dead horse. This makes five equines that he has lost within a year."*

The December 8, 1887, *Weekly Kansas Chief* provided an even more somber event:

> *"Arthur Jackson still keeps right along in his streak of bad horse luck. The announcements of the death of equine Nos. 1, 2, 3, 4, and 5, were duly noted, and now comes word from Horton, that while Mr. J was working upon the "dump" at Mission Creek, his last span of horses tumbled off into the deep water, and perished. What with Mrs. J. stricken helpless with paralysis, and the losses of seven horses while engaged in railroading, one would think such an array of misfortunes, to a poor man, would be quite overwhelming."*

Mrs. J. at this time, remember, was Melissa E. (Anderson) Jackson. The *Weekly Kansas Chief* reported on April 12, 1888:

> *"Mrs. Jackson, wife of Arthur Jackson, who resides on the farm of Mr.* [Giles A. and Eliza (O'Banion)] *Briggs, died very suddenly, last week, while sitting in her chair. She had been suffering from partial paralysis for some months, and the presumption is that her death was caused by a second stroke. It is noteworthy that she had been trying the 'faith cure.'"*

Arthur and Melissa did not have any children in their four-years together.

But, here's another interesting twist. Arthur '*married*' Melissa's sister, Ida May Anderson, five months after Melissa's death. The Anderson-Jackson family Bible shows the marriage date as September 18, 1888.

Grandpa Roy hypothesized that Melissa's younger sister, Ida, likely came to care for her ailing sibling, and that possibly Ida and Arthur 'hit-it-off' during that time.

Ida told her grandchildren that she met their grandpa in Argentine, an area just north of downtown Kansas City, Missouri, on the north side of the Missouri River. If this is true, they had to have met years prior to Arthur marrying Melissa, since neither Arthur Jackson nor the Andersons *lived* anywhere close to Argentine. This recollection remains a mystery.

Then I got to thinking about it. Arthur was perceived to be black and his spouse white, by at least five different census takers between 1895 and 1930. They were, then, considered by casual observers as an interracial couple, and would not have been able to legally marry. Interracial marriage wasn't legalized in the United States, in fact, until the 1967 Supreme Court case, Loving v Virginia.

That explains why we never located a marriage record. In Kansas, however, where Arthur and Ida lived, the state's anti-miscegenation law of 1855 had been overturned in 1859, before Kansas even became a state.[20] So, there is a chance that cohabitation was at least more acceptable where they lived near the Iowa, Sac, Fox Indian reservation.

Still, what must their lives have been like? How common was interracial marriage back then? Surely it was a challenge, and I can only fathom the obstacles and prejudice they might have faced.

One of the most well known African American leaders of that time, Frederick Douglass, a writer, social reformer and statesman—whose mother was a slave and whose father was her white master—married a white abolitionist and suffragist after his first wife's suicide death in the early 1880s. Their marriage "was the subject of scorn by both white and black Americans, but the couple was firm in their convictions."[21]

Arthur and Ida's early domestic years were spent living in areas that were rather diverse. Specifically, they lived in northeastern Kansas near the Great Nemaha reservation of the Sac and Fox Nation, in Doniphan and Brown Counties. Because of that proximity to other minorities, and the post-Civil War influx of African Americans, an interracial couple in that area was not uncommon, and may have been more accepted.

When Arthur and Ida moved to Kansas City by 1913, they lived in or near areas that were racially segregated; but, in neighborhoods very near the understood but unmarked 'racial line.' As will be seen, their family "became white."

Arthur and Ida (Anderson) Jackson's Children

Name	Birth date	Birth place
Mary E.	1889	White Cloud, Doniphan Co., KS
Edgar Walter	1 Sep 1891	White Cloud
Jabez "Jarvis"	7 Apr 1896	White Cloud
Hazel Mae	21 May 1899	White Cloud
Dollie Frances	8 Dec 1902	Hiawatha, Brown Co., KS or NE
Reginald Brewster	19 May 1905	Hiawatha or Rulo, Richardson, NE
Oliver Wadsworth	3 Oct. 1908	Hiawatha or Rulo, Richardson, NE

His grandchildren knew that their Grandpa Arthur Jackson had worked for the Missouri Pacific Railroad at one time.

As will be seen, other Jackson family members were involved with the Missouri Pacific Railroad, so his connection or employment by the railroad has substantiation.

Arthur also must have had a hog farm "close to the Missouri River." Two of his granddaughters, Mary (Johnson) Bentley and Dorothy (Johnson) Rittermeyer, remembered a story that their grandparents *may* have lived over the Kansas state line into Nebraska, and that their hogs once were stricken with a cholera epidemic.

As will be seen, Arthur gained knowledge and experience at raising hogs in his youth in Franklin County, Missouri.

Arthur and Ida Jackson never owned a home; but, rather rented. Bentley and Rittermeyer said they remembered their Grandmother Ida Jackson say that Arthur had once gotten a government land grant with a big house . . . but, that an Indian Agent later claimed

Chief White Cloud

When I asked what their Grandpa looked like, my Grandpa Roy Jackson and his cousins, Mary Bentley and Dorothy Rittermeyer, said that their Grandpa Arthur Jackson had red hair in his youth, and even as an older man, had a reddish mustache.

to have *'head rights.'*" They relayed that this event happened, *"when Chief White Cloud was living."*[22]

One of Arthur and Ida's homes when their children were young was described by Bentley, as, *"a shack with a dirt floor that was shared with chickens."* Chickens might seem an odd bedfellow; but, they help control bugs like fleas, ticks, mites, and even roaches. They were poor, to be sure.

Sons of Arthur and Ida May (Anderson) Jackson, Reginald Brewster "Reg" Jackson (left), and Oliver Wadsworth "Ollie" Jackson (right)

Two of Arthur and Ida's sons, Reginald "Reg" and Edgar Walter "Ed," had curly, wavy, red hair. Reg may have had reddish hair; but, his World War II discharge papers show his hair color as "gray." Other siblings were said to have had dark brown hair that was both tight and curly (Ollie), or wavy (Hazel and Dollie).

Above: Hazel Mae (Jackson) Levine; Left: Hazel and Dollie Frances (Jackson) Johnson, daughters of Arthur and Ida May (Anderson) Jackson

Ed and Reg had blue eyes like their mother, Ida Jackson.

Daughter, Dollie (Jackson) Johnson, had slightly darker skin, according to her daughters. Each sibling had an 'olive' complexion.

Reg and his sister, Hazel, had deep voices, and Hazel, according to a niece, had an unusual, archetypal southern 'drawl.'

Right: Edgar Walter "Ed" Jackson, son of Arthur and Ida May (Anderson) Jackson

BORN A SLAVE

12

After 30 Years, a Clue Out of the Blue

With the approaching 30th anniversary (Summer 2010) of when I started genealogy, I got a telephone call in April 2010 from a long-lost cousin, Justine Conway, researching Ida Anderson's ancestry.

Justine suggested I look at an Arthur Jackson that she had found in the 1880 Census of Holt County, Missouri (where the Anderson family lived at that time). I followed her lead and found:

1880 Census, Bigelow Township, Holt Co., Mo.
Richard L., Jr., Laura, Lucinda, and Arthur Jackson

Name	Race	Gender	Age	Relationship	Birthplace
Jackson, Richard L.	White	Male	35	head of household	Virginia
Jackson, Laura	White	Female	23	wife	Ohio
Jackson, **Edgar**	White	Male	1	son	Missouri
Jackson, Lucinda	White	Female	68	mother	Virginia
Jackson, Arthur	Black	Male	21	hired farm laborer	Virginia
Thomas, Matthew	White	Male	23	nephew	Virginia

I became somewhat excited when I noticed that this Arthur Jackson (black), born about 1859, was living with a white family: Richard L. and Laura Jackson; their 1-year-old son, Edgar; and, Richard's mother, Lucinda Jackson.

The child named Edgar intrigued me because it is not that common of a name . . . and Arthur and Ida's eldest son was named Edgar Walter Jackson.

Jacksons of Holt County, Missouri

I proceeded to learn more about Holt County, and about Richard L. Jackson, and his mother, Lucinda Jackson.

Holt County was part of the Platte Purchase, and became a separate county in Missouri in 1841. It was named in honor of Dr. David Rice Holt, a member of the State Legislature from Platte County, who died while a representative, December 7, 1840.[23]

One reference connected these Jacksons to Andrew P. Jackson (11 May 1820-26 Dec 1878), son of S. B. and Rachel (1798-) Jackson, who, in 1845, founded Jackson's Point in Holt County. This is "a region of country where Davis Creek enters the Missouri bottom."[24] In 1853,[25] Jackson abandoned the village to participate in the California Gold Rush. Jackson's Point was re-named Worth Point, and is today Mound City, Missouri, where the town's founder, Andrew P. Jackson, returned. He later died the day after Christmas in 1878, and is buried in the old city cemetery.[26]

Though I did not find the Jacksons ten years earlier in 1870, Lucinda Jackson was enumerated in the 1860 Franklin County, Missouri, Census, where she lived with her husband, Richard L. Jackson, Sr., their family, and about a dozen African slaves.

Something Sounds Familiar: A Revelation!

Recalling that I had seen Richard and Lucinda's names before, I looked back through all my old notes. I found my 30-year-old research from 1980 on Kansas City's pre-eminent Dr. Jabez North Jackson . . . following up on Ida Jackson's "fable" that she once relayed to her grandson, Roy.

Do you know what I found written at the top?

Dr. Jabez North Jackson was a grandson of Richard Ludlow Jackson and Lucinda Edwards (Deatley) Jackson, who had moved from Virginia to Missouri.

I had spent the weekend researching the doctor's ancestry—*again, after 30 years*—this time, however, I was following the trail of my great great grandfather, Arthur Jackson.

Grandma Ida Jackson was right after all, God love her.

We are 'related' to Jabez North Jackson's family. Ida had omitted the fact that her husband, Arthur, had been born a slave into Dr. Jackson's grandparent's household. That is, she intentionally failed to reveal to Roy that we are descended from the slave side of that Jackson family.

This is the family secret they tried to forget and intentionally squelch all those years . . . the secret Ida most likely tried to impart on her deathbed to her grandson, Roy, in 1948.

Spirit Guides Us

I proceeded to research Dr. Jabez North Jackson's descendants, and found that our family and Dr. Jackson's family have both been living in and around Kansas City since 1913.

The first descendant of Dr. Jackson's that I discovered was one of his grandsons, Jabez Jackson "Jim" MacLaughlin, who lived in the Kansas City area, minutes from where I resided. In a twist of fate, Mr. MacLaughlin was involved with the Jackson County (Mo.) Historical Society (JCHS) in the 1960s, and helped the nonprofit organization to save, restore and adaptively reuse the famed John B. Wornall House into a house museum. Forty years later, I, too, was employed by JCHS and was dedicated to its mission as a staff member between 2000 and 2014. Small world?

When Mr. MacLaughlin and I initially connected by telephone I explained how I had located him, and encapsulated my long-lost, distant relationship to his Jackson family. He said he had not thought about his ancestors owning slaves. I responded that in my genealogical pursuits since 1980, I had not focused on my ancestors as slaveholders, though it is a certainty. I admitted, too, that I had not fathomed being a slave's descendant. Mr. MacLaughlin later wrote to me:

"Thank you for your note and for passing along the link to your story posted on the Smithsonian web site. That is an interesting story. It must be a peculiarly American story, how the lives of our ancestors seem to have been intertwined through the years.

"And now we find ourselves in the same town. I wonder if your family and mine maintained their acquaintance in those early days here in Kansas City.... Thank you for making the story richer."[27]

I'm sure our ancestors never imagined the great great grandson of a slave owner might connect more than a century later with the great great grandson of one of their family's slaves.[28]

One day in 2010, shortly after this breakthrough, a researcher visited the JCHS Archives where I served as archivist. He was investigating the Wiedenmann surname. One branch of the Kansas City Wiedenmann family were business owners in Westport. I relayed that my family lived in Westport in the 1930s and shared my Grandfather Jackson's recollection of playing in and around the Wiedenmann coal yard. In our dialogue about genealogical pursuits, I shared that I recently proved that my earliest known Jackson forefather had been born a slave, and that it all came about through a family tradition that our family was related to a once-prominent Kansas City doctor, Jabez North Jackson. His eyes widened and he said that his friend and law partner was a descendant of Dr. Jackson. *"Who is your law partner?"* I asked. *"Jim MacLaughlin,"* he replied. Small world?

Also in 2010, I read an obituary for a gentleman whom I had met in 2005 and admired for his passion for local history and its preservation. He had contacted and invited me to his stately home south of the Kansas City Country Club Plaza to retrieve and transfer to JCHS a donation of historical materials. As I stood in awe at his beautiful living room, he relayed that his house had been the private home of Kansas City real estate pioneer, J. C. Nichols. Only recently did I discover that the second owner of the Nichols home had been Dr. Jabez North Jackson. Small world?

In 2012, I worked with the Kansas City Museum's educational programming director to conduct trolley tours of sites pertinent to Kansas City lumber baron, Robert A. Long. One of the stops was a hospital (today, adaptively reused as condominiums), partially funded by Long, where Dr. Jabez North Jackson had delivered the Grand Opening remarks almost 100 years before. Small world?

In Spring 2013, I mentored an intern at the Historical Society who was close to attaining her B.S. in Historic Preservation from my alma mater, Southeast Missouri State University. She went home to St. Louis for a weekend and afterwards I asked her about her trip. *"Where in St. Louis does your family live?"* She answered, *"I tell people I'm from St. Louis because they've never heard of my hometown, Labadie, Missouri."* My eyes widened. I could hardly believe that she lives in the neighborhood—one quarter mile—from where my great great grandfather, Arthur Jackson, lived as a slave in the 1860s! Small world?

Then, in October 2013, a gentleman approached me after a lecture I delivered for the Historical Society. He asked me if my Jackson ancestors were from Kansas City. I said they had lived in Kansas before coming to Kansas City; but, that my earliest-known Jackson ancestor had been born in Virginia and was raised in eastern Missouri near St. Louis. *"Where near St. Louis?"* he asked. I answered, *"Franklin County,"* and he said, *"My Jackson ancestors were from Franklin County, too."* His ancestors were Richard L. and Lucinda Jackson, Sr.! We spent the next two hours talking about kindred family history. I'm pleased that he and I are becoming better acquainted.

Amazingly, he and his family still own some of their Jackson ancestors' land in Franklin County, Missouri . . . also the ancestral homeland of Arthur Jackson.[29] Small world?

I strongly believe Dr. Dorothy Witherspoon's maxim that, "Spirit guides us!"[30]

Dr. Jabez North Jackson
grandson of Richard Ludlow and
Lucinda Edwards (Deatley) Jackson, Sr.

BORN A SLAVE

13

Time Traveling

"Identifying the owner of a slave is very difficult. Sometimes collateral research (whole families including spouses and in-laws) can lead to the name of the slave-owning family. If you are able to identify the owner of your [slave] ancestor, you might be able to find records pertaining to the slave owners as well as to the slaves (such as plantation records, wills naming slaves, etc.).

"Searching for slave ancestors always requires a thorough investigation of the white slave-owning family in all records. You should also investigate the slave owner's extended family including his spouse's family." [31]

After 30 years of patience and persistence, I had finally rediscovered Arthur was an African American slave. I had proven his connection to his slaveholding family. I then proceeded to follow the advice above and learn all I could about Richard Ludlow Jackson and Lucinda Edwards (Deatley) Jackson, Sr.— their descendants and ancestors—in order to uncover additional context clues about my great great grandfather, Arthur Jackson.

I hoped to learn more about what his youth might have been as a slave; how the Civil War and emancipation affected him and his family; his young adulthood during Reconstruction; and, his courtship and married life. Of course, I also dreamed the impossible dream of discovering who Arthur's parents may have been; or, at least wondering at what point in his life they may have separated . . . and if and when he may have learned of their demise.

The evidence linking Arthur Jackson to the slave owning family of Richard and Lucinda Jackson is unmistakable.

It is also clear that Arthur Jackson, when freed from bondage in 1865, took the surname of his slaveholding family with whom he was born into, grew-up with, and apparently lived with (at least off and on) until his early adulthood.

14

African American Surnames and Family Units

Slaves' first names were generally assigned by their parents, who almost always named children after their own, known kin. "Slave owners were more likely to assign names to newly arriving Africans than to those who were born on U.S. soil."[32] Sometimes slave mothers "would ask the white folks to assist in the selection. On the other hand, negro mammies occasionally named white babies."[33] African Americans have a strong matriarchic culture.[34]

When it comes to surnames, however, many researchers tracing African lineage in America find confusing, seeming unfathomable, and sometimes impossible naming patterns. This is because former slaves at the time of Emancipation had the freedom to adopt, assume, or randomly pick their preferred surname (and some used multiple surnames depending on circumstances). "Even before Emancipation, many enslaved black people chose their own surnames to establish their identities."[35]

A main consideration in all of the possible options is <u>not</u> to assume that slave families were created, or remained nuclear; that is, they did not always cohabitate in a traditional social unit.

A high percentage of children were separated from their parents in childhood due to the slave trade. "*I seen some slaves sold off dat big auction block and de little chillun sho' would be-a cryin' when dey takes deir mothers away from dem.*"[36]

But, consider a slave mother who was afforded the opportunity to live with and raise—individually or communally—her own children. The biological father(s) of her child(ren) *may* have been owned and/or lived on nearby farm(s)/plantation(s). These relationships were sometimes called "abroad marriages."[37] They may have met through communal gatherings, like a barn raising or harvest social. *"An old fashioned corn-shucking took place once a year...which afforded pleasant amusement for the out-door negroes for miles around. On these occasions, the servants, on all plantations, were allowed to attend by mere invitation of the blacks where the corn was to be shucked. As the grain was brought in from the field, it was left in a pile near the corn-cribs. The night appointed, and invitations sent out, slaves from plantations five or six miles away, would assemble and join on the road, and in large bodies march along, singing their melodious plantation songs."[38]*

"When a girl became a woman, she was required to go to a man and become a mother. Master would sometimes go and get a large hale hearty Negro man from some other plantation to go to his Negro women. He would ask the other master to let this man come over to his place to go to his slave girls. A slave girl was expected to have children as soon as she became a woman. Some of them had children at the age of 12- or 13-years-old."[39] This would also mean that unrelated males with whom she did cohabitate *may* or *may not* have been biologically related to the children with whom he lived...and he was likely the biological ancestor of children on other farm(s)/plantation(s).

"One [former Missouri slave when questioned on the subject of marriage] said that he and his wife liked one another, and as they both belonged to the same master they 'took up' or 'simply lived together,' and that arrangement was the custom and nothing was said."[40] Another former slave, "stated that his parents belonged to different persons, and by the consent of both, were married by the squire.... The slave marriage was never recognized by the law, consequently a statue was passed in 1865 required a legal marriage of all former slaves in the State." The law read:

"In all cases where persons of color, heretofore held as slaves in the State of Missouri, have cohabited together as husband and wife, it shall be the duty of persons thus cohabitating to appear before a justice of the peace of the township where they reside, or before any other officer authorized to solemnize marriages, and it shall be the duty of such officer to join in marriage the persons thus applying, and to keep a record of the same." [41]

Children born by slaves became the property of the mother's master, and might likely carry her surname...oftentimes the name of the mother's master.[42] *"De chillen allus [always] b'long to dey mama's marster."*[43]

All of this would mean that the biological father(s) and mother(s) of slave children quite likely had different surnames. So, which surname, if either, might the children grow up to assume and introduce to the free world as their own?

There existed as many possibilities as there were individuals facing this decision. "There was a lot more consciousness and pride in American history among African Americans and enslaved African Americans than a lot of people give them credit for. They had a very strong sense of politics and history," says Adam Goodheart, a professor at Washington College."[44]

A fair percentage of former slaves "felt proud of the family whom they had served and spoke of them as "my white folks."[45] One former slaveholder alluded to the fact that many "Missouri slave holders were not such through choice. They inherited their negroes and felt duty bound to keep them."[46] Another stated, "that his father left him a number of slaves to who he was fondly attached and whom he considered as a family trust."[47] This appears from evidence gathered thus far to be the kind of relationship between Arthur and his master, Richard L. Jackson, Sr.

Some African slaves may have been biologically related to their white masters, too. Without excuse or judgment, the obvious explanation for this interbreeding was likely the result of rape. One can only fathom the infinite, complex and sometimes intimate relationships between these ancestors.

For personal reasons, slaves may well have chosen the surname of their beloved master, "to perpetuate the fine old name."[48]

Conversely, "slaves would take the name of someone besides their owner, if they did not like him."[49]

Dr. Dorothy Witherspoon in her book, *Researching Slave Ancestry,* added that slaves sometimes kept the surname of their long-time slave owning family, the surname of their earliest-known ancestor, or the surname of their original master, so that they might have the promise of one day re-connecting with separated family members.

A slave that had been sold or otherwise removed from his or her biological/natural family, may have assumed the new slave master's surname . . . and may possibly have re-claimed after emancipation his or her *original* master's surname. But, it is an oversimplification that *most* enslaved blacks bore the last name of their master. "Only a handful of George Washington's [124] slaves did, for example, and he recorded most as having just a first name, says Mary Thompson, the historian at Mount Vernon."[50]

If a slave ran away, it is logically he or she may have chosen a fictitious name so as to assume a new identity to try and avoid being discovered.

Name reversals were another possibility (ex. "Johnson Alfred" becoming "Alfred Johnson").

If a slave mother later re-married, she likely, as with most married women, took the name of her new husband. Her children, once emancipated, may have retained her maiden name, the surname of their biological/natural father, or a random surname.

A differing opinion worth considering is that slaves, "did not usually take the surname of their most recent owner but sometimes took the given name of their father . . . of an earlier owner, a prominent local citizen, or a prominent American (such as Washington or Lincoln). For this reason, it is usually not profitable to try to match black surnames with those of plantation masters. One should try instead to trace a freed slave to his or her mother. The slave mothers' owner usually had a different surname than the freedman."[51]

While a statistic showing how many slaves or freedmen and women may have taken their mother's slave owner's surname has not been found, out of 20 respondents quoting 65 enslaved ancestors, 57.0% took the name of the most recent slave owner; 26.1% took the name of a previous slave owner; and, 16.9% had a surname of unknown origin[52]

To compound all of this is the problem of surname usage, spelling, pronunciation, and reporting necessitating researching all possible variations of the surname's spelling.

While being cognizant of the above complexities, ascertaining the name(s) of a slave ancestor may not end up being so profound or unreal. "Most slaves seem to have had surnames they knew and were known by among other slaves. When you read former slaves' narratives, you really get a sense that the slaves had coherent family structures, surnames and all."[53] This was especially the case on large-scale plantations where there was less close communications and living arrangements with owners; where absentee ownership may have existed; or, where multi-generational slave communities had formed and surname usage was encouraged for continuity.

The U.S. Census Bureau in 2000 collected data and cultural information to formulate a list of the 1,000 most common American surnames. Jackson was ranked 18th overall, with a total 666,125 people. Among the African American population, Jackson was number five.[54]

Jackson Fifth Most Common Surname in the U.S.

	Surname	% Black	# Blacks with Surname	% White
1	Washington	89.9%	146,500	5.2%
2	Jefferson	75.2%	38,600	18.7%
3	Booker	65.6%	23,000	30.1%
4	Banks	54.2%	53,900	41.3%
5	Jackson	53.0%	353,200	41.9%

BORN A SLAVE

15

One Jackson Family's Chronology

In addition to chronicling the history and migration of the Richard Ludlow and Lucinda Edwards (Deatley) Jackson, Sr., family, I uncovered little-known details about slavery, particularly about slavery in Missouri, where the family moved in 1859.

My search continued back to 1850 in present-day West Virginia (Kanawha County), thence to Westmoreland County, Virginia. Still further back, I found 1770s references to several adjacent counties in Maryland and the "Northern Neck" of Virginia. There, Richard L. and Lucinda Jackson, Sr., and their ancestors amassed quantifiable real and human property.

The human property included my direct ancestor, Arthur Jackson, and his unnumbered forbearers. Since Arthur was only about 9-years-old when emancipated in 1865, Arthur's mother was one of the slaves in the Jackson household. I also discovered in the final stages of preparing this biography for publication, that Arthur had a half sister who lived in this slave family. They shared the same mother who may well have had some connections to Richard Ludlow Jackson's parents, William and Catherine (Ludlow) Jackson of Fredericksburg, Spotsylvania County, Virginia.

Judging from common African American slave social and mating patterns, it is probable that Arthur's father, and the father of his half sister, were two different male slaves on a nearby plantation(s) in Kanawha County, Virginia.

Arthur remained close to his former master's family after Emancipation. He grew up and lived with and/or near them through 1905. And, Arthur's children and grandchildren bore strikingly identical names to those of "his white family."

I can only imagine what oral traditions or memories might have been passed down to Arthur as a child, which he took to his grave. How far back was his knowledge of his ancestry? "In 1865, many freedmen could remember an African ancestor, but perhaps could not remember their African names."[55]

The following, detailed chronology starts on Thanksgiving Day in 1828, with the marriage of Richard Ludlow Jackson to Lucinda Edwards Deatley.

My initial purpose in constructing this *histiogeneography*™ was to determine the exact migratory path of this couple, particularly ascertaining their precise whereabouts during Lucinda's childbearing years, and comparing various sources for each of her children's birthplaces. I also sought to discover more about the birth dates and birth places of the slaves they acquired through purchase, inheritance, or natural increase between 1828 and 1863. I hoped, too, to discover when, and possibly why, they migrated from Kanawha County, (West) Virginia, to Franklin County, Missouri in 1859.

This journey of discovery eventually included my great great grandfather, Arthur Jackson, who was in 1856 and into this family, born a slave.

1828:

Richard Ludlow Jackson, a Captain in the War of 1812,[56] married Lucinda Edwards Deatley on Thanksgiving Day, November 24, 1828, in Westmoreland County, Virginia, where Lucinda had been born on February 11, 1811, "in the vicinity of the birthplace of General George Washington and General Robert E. Lee."[57] They had met at 'Shiloh Church.' At the time of their marriage, Richard was 31 and Lucinda was 17.

Richard was born July 9, 1797, in Fredericksburg, Spotsylvania County, Virginia.[58] Richard's parents, William H. Jackson and Catherine (Ludlow) Jackson, emigrated from Scotland to Spotsylvania County, where William "became a well-to-do farmer."[59] In 1783, one William Jackson of Spotsylvania County owned three slaves.[60] And, there is evidence that one William Jackson became the guardian of two boys between 1781 and 1799.[61]

Lucinda's parents were Colonel James E. Deatley and Lucy (Edwards) Deatley, Sr. [The surname is also sometimes written DeAtley, de Atley, or even Deatly. Deatley is used throughout.]

James E. Deatley was a Revolutionary War patriot.

Lucy was James Deatley's third wife, married on January 4, 1797, in King George County, Virginia. Lucy's father, James Edwards, was also a Revolutionary compatriot.

About Westmoreland County, Lucinda Jackson said in later life. *"It is one of the prettiest counties in the world. It lies within a neck of land from Fredericksburg with other counties between the Rappahannock and Potomac."*[62]

"Known variously as 'the garden of Virginia' and 'the Athens of the New World,' the Northern Neck is a 61-mile peninsula bracketed by [those] rivers and the Chesapeake Bay."[63] Francesca Henle Taylor, Genealogy Volunteer, Westmoreland County, Virginia, notes on her website: *"Drive down Virginia Route 3,*

which leads to Virginia's tidewater country on the Potomac, turn off the side roads, and you drive clean out of the 20th century. Westmoreland County, Virginia, is rural still, innocent of roadside advertising, populated by farming folk and horses."

1829-1830:

The young couple's first child, a male, was born between 1829 and 1830.[64] This young son died between 1830 and 1840.

1830:

Richard L. Jackson was enumerated in the Westmoreland County, Virginia, U.S. Census. In that year, only the heads of households were named in the enumeration, with each member of the family identified by gender and age. Included in the household with Richard, Lucinda and their infant son were listed along with two female slaves, one under 10 (b. ca. 1820-1830), and another between 10-23 (b. ca. 1807-1820).

It may be presumed that when Lucinda was married, she was given a personal servant by her father as a "wedding present," a common practice in that era and region. The older, female slave (possibly Hannah), then, *may* then have had a daughter with her.

1833:

Richard and Lucinda's second child, Virginia Catherine Jackson, was born on October 25, 1833, in Charles County, Maryland.[65]

1834:

Richard and Lucinda's third child, John Wesley Jackson, was born November 6, 1834, in Charles County, Maryland.[66]

Slavery in the British West Indies was abolished in 1834. "The United States Congress [had] declared that participation in the slave trade is equivalent to piracy" in 1820,[67] and had abolished the trans-Atlantic slave trade more than a decade before, in 1808.[68]

1838:

Richard and Lucinda's fourth child, Lucy Christina Jackson, was born Christmas Day, 1838, in Charles County, Maryland.[69]

1840:

Richard and Lucinda's fifth child, Thomas B. Jackson, was born March 14, 1840, in Charles County, Maryland.[70]

Again, in this U.S. census year, only the heads of households were named. Richard L. Jackson's family consisted of seven white, free individuals enumerated in the Charles County, Maryland, U.S. Census. Shockingly, Richard and Lucinda's slaveholdings in 1840 soared to a total of 40 slaves!

A typical American slave family in front of a rather atypical slave dwelling. Most slave quarters were less substantially constructed, generally log cabins or frame structures, built cheaply of perishable materials, in much the same way as the houses of poorer white Virginians.

That they owned only two slaves in 1830 when in Westmoreland County, Virginia, and, as will be seen, five slaves in 1850, when they lived in Kanawha County, Virginia, it has not been ascertained how or why this significant increase was reported in 1840.

How and why they were acquired and released may never be known. The only explanation yet hypothesized is, that, perhaps Richard's father, William H. Jackson, and/or his mother, Catherine (Ludlow) Jackson, died and left the abundant number of slaves to their son. Lucinda also had received from her father one female slave and her child(ren).

The family was enumerated thus:

1840 U.S. Census, Charles County, Maryland
Richard and Lucinda Jackson

Free White Persons - Males - Under 5:   1 (Thomas B., under 1-year-old)
Free White Persons - Males - 5 thru 9:   1 (John Wesley, 6)
Free White Persons - Males - 40 thru 49:   1 (Richard L., 43)
Free White Persons - Females - Under 5:   1 (Lucy Christina, 2)
Free White Persons - Females - 5 thru 9:   1 (Virginia Catherine, 7)
Free White Persons - Females - 10 thru 14:   1 (Unknown)[71]
Free White Persons - Females - 20 thru 29:   1 (Lucinda, 29)

Slaves - Males - Under 10:	8	
Slaves - Males - 10 thru 23:	4	14 Males
Slaves - Males - 24 thru 35:	1	
Slaves - Males - 36 thru 54:	1	
Slaves - Females - Under 10:	13	
Slaves - Females - 10 thru 23:	8	26 Females
Slaves - Females - 24 thru 35:	3	
Slaves - Females - 36 thru 54:	1	
Slaves - Females - 54 thru 99:	1	

Persons Employed in Agriculture: 0
Free White Persons - Under 20:   5
Free White Persons - 20 thru 49:   2
Total Free White Persons: 7
Total Slaves: 40

More than half (21 out of 40) of Richard and Lucinda Jackson's slaves were under ten-years-old . . . and <u>none</u> of the slaves were involved in agriculture. These statistics certainly require further speculation and study.

Lucinda's father, James E. Deatley, owned 35 slaves in 1840 (see the enumeration below).

In 1841, Deatley would make out his Last Will. And, in 1843 when he died, Lucinda stood to inherit 1/7th of his slaveholdings (five+ slaves).

Therefore, between 1840 and 1850, Richard and Lucinda Jackson either sold or manumitted some 40 enslaved individuals (the 40 slaves listed in the 1840 Census included at least two they'd had since 1828; and, five+ inherited from her father in 1844). They only owned 5 slaves by 1850.

1840 U.S. Census, Westmoreland County, Virginia
James Datly [sic.]

Free White Persons - Males - Under 5:   1
Free White Persons - Males - 30 thru 39:   2
Free White Persons - Males - 90 thru 99:   1

Slaves - Males - Under 10:   11
Slaves - Males - 10 thru 23:   2   16 Males
Slaves - Males - 24 thru 35:   2
Slaves - Males - 36 thru 54:   1

Slaves - Females - Under 10:   7
Slaves - Females - 10 thru 23:   2   19 Females
Slaves - Females - 24 thru 35:   6
Slaves - Females - 36 thru 54:   4

Persons Employed in Agriculture: 12
Free White Persons - Under 20:   1
Free White Persons - 20 thru 49:   2
Total Free White Persons: 4
Total Slaves: 35

1841:

Lucinda was in possession of a slave of her father's named Hannah, "and increase," (i.e., child/ren) when her father's Last Will and Testament was made on January 15, 1841.

Richard and Lucinda Jackson migrated west with their young family . . . and slaves . . . to Kanawha County, Virginia.[72]

1842:

Richard and Lucinda's sixth child, Richard Ludlow Jackson, Jr., was born on September 13, 1842, in Charleston, Kanawha County, (West) Virginia.[73]

Charleston is the County Seat of Kanawha County. Charleston should not be confused with Charlestown, which is in Jefferson County, Virginia. West Virginia was created from northwestern Virginia during the Civil War (January 20, 1863). Charleston has served as the state capital of West Virginia since 1877.[74]

It was by 1842 that, "England, the United States, France, Denmark, Holland and Spain had all passed laws against the trans-Atlantic slave trade."[75] As was noted earlier, in 1820, "The United States Congress declared that participation in the slave trade is equivalent to piracy."[76]

Even with formal declarations and laws, "the slave trade from Africa to the Americas was only legally dead, however, and African slaves continued to be shipped across the Atlantic for another 38 years."[77]

Slavery in Kanawha, Western Virginia

"The western part of West Virginia was situated on the 'Border' and although it is probable the majority of the people of the South-western and Southern West Virginia emigrated from Virginia and brought with them their sectional prejudices and slave property, yet it is a fact that many persons from Ohio also settled there and helped to settle those counteracting influences."[78]

"Although most people in western Virginia were engaged in farming and livestock operations in which slavery was not economical, there were parts of the region which did use slave labor. In addition to the small farms, the South Branch, Greenbrier, Monongahela, and Kanawha Valleys also consisted of larger farms of tobacco and other cash crops which used slaves.

"In 1860, there were 490,308 slaves (approximately 30% of the total population) in eastern Virginia belonging to 48,308 slaveholders, averaging over ten slaves per owner. In western Virginia (including Eastern Panhandle counties), 18,451 slaves (4% of the total population) belonged to 3,820 slaveholders, or less than 6 slaves per owner. It is important to note that in both regions most slaveholders owned fewer than five slaves.

"Most slaves from present-day West Virginia lived in the Eastern Panhandle counties, but a substantial slave population existed in the Kanawha Valley." [79]

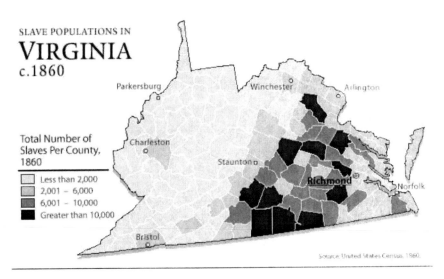

http://www.slaveryinamerica.org/geography/slave_census_VA_1860.htm

"Due to the decline of plantation agriculture in the 1800s, slavery was no longer as profitable in the east and slaves were frequently hired out or sold.

"The salt industry was driven by poor white transients and slave labor, often leased from eastern Virginia. This was the first significant introduction of slavery into western Virginia because salt was the first major industry to develop. In fact, by the 1800s, slave labor was rarely used in areas that did not rely heavily upon industry....

"Of the slaves in the Kanawha Valley, half were owned or hired by salt firms. Forty percent of these slaves were used to mine coal for the salt works because they could be hired from their owners for much lower wages than white laborers demanded. These slaves were usually leased and insured rather than bought due to the risk of death or injury in the coal mines."[80]

"Coal was used to fuel the salt furnaces of the Kanawha Valley, and by 1860 twenty-five companies were engaged in coal mining in West Virginia.... These companies advertised for hired slaves at $120 to $200 a year. Women and children were also employed in the mines. Approximately 2000 slaves were employed in coal mining. A system of slides, tramways and rail moved the coal to barges for export to Louisville, Cincinnati and the lower south."[81]

"The failure of slavery to become as vital and profitable to the western Virginia economy led many to the opinion that the existence of slavery actually harmed the economy and discouraged immigrants from settling in the region."[82]

"In the early 19th century new settlers on their way to the Missouri territory would pass through the Kanawha valley to the Ohio River and often remained there, attracted by the low cost of land and money made by leasing their slaves to the local salt makers."[83]

As will be seen, the Richard and Lucinda Jackson family remained in Kanawha County until 1859.

After the Civil War erupted in 1861, the northwestern portion of Virginia separated from Virginia, and Kanawha County became a part of West Virginia.[84]

1843:

Lucinda Jackson's father, Revolutionary War patriot, Colonel James E. Deatley, Sr., who had been in the War for seven years, died on December 29, 1843, at the age of 94 in Westmoreland County, Virginia. Deatley was buried in the Deatley family cemetery at Locust Hill (now Oak Grove, an unincorporated community in the Washington Parrish of Westmoreland County, Virginia; another source located the cemetery at Poplar Hill).[85]

Deatley's estate of 593-acres, then known as *Fairview*, adjoined the estate of Lawrence "Law" Washington, relative of General George Washington, whose birthplace was only ten miles distant.[86] "Washington was born . . . near a bend of . . . Pope's Creek, and so in other nearby towns were James Madison and James Monroe. Among other early colonists who got their start in life on the Northern Neck were the brothers Richard Henry Lee and Francis Lightfoot Lee, both signatories of the Declaration of Independence, and their descendant, Confederate General Robert E. Lee."[87]

According to a February 15, 1844, account of sales of Deatley's real and personal property by Law Washington, the entire 593-acre plantation was sold on March 14 to James H. Noel for $2,373.50 (or roughly $4/acre).[88]

Deatley's home, *Fairview*, stood until at least March 1929, when one Thomas Deatley died in Washington, D.C., and was "brought to the old Deatley home here for internment."[89]

Deatley's Last Will and Testament dated January 15, 1841, specifically named 35 slaves (with unnamed and unnumbered "increase," or, children) that were "to be equally divided between" his seven children (five sons and two daughters). Specific provisions for six-plus slaves (underlined in the following listing) were bequeathed in separate clauses.[90]

James Deatley's Significant Slaveholdings at his Death

James E. Deatley's slaves are listed on the facing leaf.

In the left column, names are presented as they were listed in Deatley's 1841 Last Will and Testament (in the likely case that the order had some significance to slave family structure).

The names in the right column are re-arranged alphabetically.

Duplication in several of Deatley's slaves' Christian names (in **bold**) indicate they belonged to different and distinct slave family lines.

Names in the right column without a numeral indicate that they were listed in a February 1844 accounting by the Westmoreland County Court, likely born or acquired since Deatley's Will was written.

Similarly, names with an "X" were in the Will but not in the 1844 enumeration, when an assessed value was also attributed to each slave.

Those names underlined are slaves specifically bequeathed to a certain heir, including Lucinda Edwards (Deatley) Jackson.

The author thanks Francesca Henle Taylor, Genealogy Volunteer, Westmoreland County, Virginia, for locating and sharing Deatley's Will and estate papers for this study.[91]

<u>1841</u> <u>Slaves in Will of</u> <u>James Deatley</u>	<u>1844</u> <u>Alphabetical Slave</u> <u>Inventory</u>	
1 Janney	Addison	$50
2 Mary	1 Aggy	$125
3 Battle	2 Ann	$100
4 Caroline	3 Battle	$440
5 Rosetta	4 Billy	**X**
6 Aggy	5 **Caroline**	$375
7 Harriet	6 **Caroline-Hannah's dau**.	$350
8 George	7 Celia	$225
9 Spencer	8 **Charlotte & ch**	$375
10 Henry	9 **Charlotte & ch**	**X**
11 Sally	10 Daniel	$200
12 <u>Hannah & ch</u>	11 Davy	$100
13 Mary	12 <u>Ellen</u>	**X**
14 Martha	13 Ellick	$300
15 Rose	14 Fanny	$350
16 Fanny	15 Frank	$450
17 Ellick	16 George	$350
18 John	17 **Hannah**	$300
19 Daniel	18 **Hannah & ch**	$350
20 Winney	19 Harriet	$375
21 John	20 Henry	$350
22 Celia	James	$75
23 William	21 Janney/Jenny	$100
24 Ann	22 **John**	$300
25 Frank	23 **John**	$300
26 Tom	24 Martha	$125
27 Davy	25 **Mary**	$300
28 Billy	26 **Mary**	$125
29 Reubin	27 Reubin	$250
30 Winney	28 Rose	$300
31 <u>Hannah</u>	29 Rosetta	$150
32 <u>Caroline-Hannah's dau</u>.	30 Sally	$375
33 <u>Ellen</u>	31 Spencer	$300
34 <u>Charlotte & ch</u>	32 Tom	$350
35 <u>Charlotte & ch</u>	33 **William**	$150
	William	$400
	34 **Winney**	$30
	35 **Winney**	$50

83

In the three year interval between the signing of the Will (Jan 1841) and James Deatley's death (Dec 1843), his slaveholdings understandably changed somewhat.

In his Will, the slave named Ellen was specifically bequeathed to Deatley's granddaughter, Mary Deatley.

Two slaves, both named Charlotte, and their offspring, were specifically bequeathed to Deatley's sons, Henry and William, who were already living by that time in Kentucky.

Two slaves, both named Hannah, and their offspring (one named Caroline), were specifically noted in Deatley's 1841 Will as being in the possession of his daughters, Mary Arnold, and Lucinda Jackson.

Mary Arnold, had possession of Hannah, and her daughter, Caroline.

Lucinda had possession of, "a negro woman Hannah and increase." As before stated, it may have been Hannah who was given as a wedding gift to Lucinda when she married in 1828 and enumerated in the 1830 Census. It was a common practice at that time and region to bestow personal servants in such a manner.

1844:

Lucinda stood to inherit from her father around five, possibly six slaves sometime in 1844.

Her husband, Richard Ludlow Jackson, purchased from the Deatley estate on February 15, 1844, a bed for $8, and one set of castors for $2, for a $10 total outlay.

"Deeds were one means of transferring ownership of slaves. Recording of slave sales was not required in Virginia, however, so very few deeds for slave sales exist. Some deeds have survived in collections of family papers. Occasionally slave sales are recorded as part of land deeds or estate settlements. Slaves are not named in personal property tax records after 1810."[92]

Lucinda Jackson inherited a 1/7th share in the disbursement of James Deatley's slaves and 593-acre estate, *Fairview*, in 1844.

1845:

Richard and Lucinda's seventh and youngest child, James Polk Jackson, was born, April 16, 1845. While one source said he was born in Stafford County, Virginia, most other source documents, including those about his siblings (like his brother's 1842 birth), indicate the Jackson family was already residing in Kanawha County.[93]

A mulatto, female, slave child was born about this year in the Richard and Lucinda Jackson household.[94]

1847:

A black, male, slave child was born about this year in the Richard and Lucinda Jackson household.

A Trustee's Deed, Bill of Sale for personal property, was filed with the Kanawha County Recorder of Deeds. Richard L. Jackson sold personal property (i.e., human property?) to Betty W. Lovell.[95]

1848:

A black, female, slave child was born about this year in the Richard and Lucinda Jackson household.

In the Kanawha County Circuit Court, Elizabeth A. Capehart sued Richard L. Jackson and Henry Bailey/Bayly for debt.[96] There were other court cases involving the Jacksons, as noted individually below. This was the earliest file located. As court data was gathered, it became highly probably that the "debt" involved in many of the cases that would follow, were the result of Jackson "hiring-out" slaves from nearby plantation owners.

Dr. Diane Mutti Burke discusses this working arrangement, citing other authors' and statisticians' analyses:

"Slaveholders were well compensated for the hire of their slaves. Harrison Trexler calculated the yearly hiring rate for male slaves was one-seventh to one-eighth of their sale price, whereas female slaves' hiring rates were much less, sometimes as low as one-sixteenth of their value due to the loss of labor and the expense of the care of small children who oftentimes accompanied them."[97]

Trexler, in his 1914 detailed study on the subject, *Slavery in Missouri: 1804-1865*, wrote:

"Many slave-owners naturally had more of such labor than they could utilize. Negroes inherited by professional men and other townsmen often had little work except as household servants. The excess hands were therefore hired to those needing their services. These slave-masters retained their slaves either because they thought the investment was paying, or in order to preserve the family dignity, which was largely based on slave property. Widows were unable to alienate their slaves if there were other heirs, and consequently hired them out as a means of income. The slaves of orphans and of estates in probate were annually hired out by the court, bond being necessary 'for the amount of hire'[98]

The data on the court cases that follow was abstracted from microfilmed court indices. The original case files, not yet investigated one-by-one, will reveal more specifics.

1850:

Richard and Lucinda Jackson and family appeared in the August 5, 1850, Population Schedules of the U.S. Census, District No. 29, Kanawha County, Virginia.

Beginning in 1850, names of all free persons are given, with age, gender, race, occupation, value of property, and state of birth.

1850 U.S. Census, Kanawha County, Viriginia
Richard L. and Lucinda Jackson, Sr.

Jackson, Richard [Sr.]	53 [b. 1797]	VA
Jackson, Lucinda [Deatley]	38 [b. 1811]	VA
Jackson, Virginia	17 [b. 1833]	MD
Jackson, John [Wesley]	16 [b. 1834]	MD
Jackson, Lucy	12 [b. 1838]	MD
Jackson, Thomas [B.]	9 [b. 1840]	MD
[moved from MD to VA 1840-42]		
Jackson, Richard [Jr.]	7 [b.1842]	VA
Jackson, James P.	5 [b.1845]	VA
Jackson, George (unrelated laborer) 23		Germany

	40 [b.ca. 1810] black male
Their 5 slaves	20 [b.ca. 1830] mulatto female
	[moved from MD to VA 1840-42]
	5 [b.ca. 1845] mulatto female
	3 [b.ca. 1847] black male
	2 [b.ca. 1848] black female[99]

The Population Schedules reveal Richard Jackson did not own real estate.[100] Kanawha County land records confirm this fact. He never purchased or sold real estate while living in the county.

However, the Agricultural Schedules list 170 acres of improved land and 180 acres of unimproved land. If he rented land, one can see renting improved land; but, why rent unimproved land, unless he intended to improve it.

Beginning in 1850, enumerators collected information about agricultural production in separate, Agricultural Schedules. In 1850 and 1860, the Census Bureau enumerated farms with a production value of $100 or greater. In 1850, the agricultural schedules contained 50 questions.[101]

The 1850 Agricultural Schedules of Kanawha County, Virginia, document that Richard Jackson and his family and five slaves had produced 1,500 bushels of Indian corn. Notably, they did not produce any cotton or tobacco.

They also grew 600 bushels of oats; 400 bushels of wheat; 100 bushes of flaxseed; and, 5 tons of hay.

Incidental productions included 50 bushels of sweet potatoes; 20 bushels of Irish potatoes; 3 bushels of peas and beans; 300 pounds of butter (totaling $75 of produce of market gardens); and, $87 worth of homemade manufactures.

The family was supported by five horses; 2 working oxen; 5 milch cows; and 21 other cattle in the year ending June 1, 1850.[102]

Statistics about their slaves was recorded on separate Slave Schedules.

Western Virginia's slave population peaked in 1850 with 20,428 slaves. Kanawha County had 1,902 male slaves and 1,238 female slaves, for a total of 3,140 slaves.[103]

Ten years later in 1860—and one year following the Jacksons' westward migration to Missouri—Kanawha County only had 1,234 male slaves and 950 female slaves, for a total of 2,184 slaves.[104]

Sometime in 1850, Richard L. Jackson sued James S. O. Brooks for "Trespass on the Case in Assumpsit."[105]

1851:

A Trustee's Deed Bill of Sale for personal property was filed with the Kanawha County Recorder of Deeds. Richard L. Jackson sold some personal property (possibly human property) to Richard C. M. Lovell.[106]

Richard L. Jackson was also involved in four Kanawha County court cases in 1851:

Plaintiff(s)	Defendant(s)	Cause
R. L. Jackson (use of)	John P. Hale	
R. L. Cobbs	George M. Morrison, surety	Debt-salt[107]
Milton Parker	R. L. Jackson	Trespass on the Case on Assumpsit[108]
Lucy Chilton	R. L. Jackson Henry Chappell	Debt *hire of a negro*[109]
James Clarkson	R. L. Jackson	Debt[110]

1852:

A mulatto, female, slave child was born about this year in the Richard and Lucinda Jackson household. [This daughter may well be Mary "Mollie" Jackson Pryor/Prior, the half sister of Arthur Jackson, who would be born four years later.]

Kanawha County court cases involving Jackson continued:

Plaintiff(s)	Defendant(s)	Cause
Milton Parker	R. L. Jackson, and Coal River Navigation Co.	Garnishes[111]
Daniel Coakley, adm. Nathaniel H. Haas, decd.	R. L. Jackson, and Richard C. M. Lovell	Not specified[112]
Moses F. Ward, adm. of Fleming Cobbs	R. L. Jackson	Debt-Attachment[113]
Abraham Wright	R. L. Jackson	Debt[114]
Milton Parker	R. L. Jackson	Not specified[115]
Milton Parker	R. L. Jackson, and Coal River Navigation Co.	Garnishes[116]

1853:

A black, male, slave child was born about this year in the Richard and Lucinda Jackson household.

Richard and Lucinda's eldest daughter, Virginia Catherine Jackson, married George W. Thomas, son of Thomas Matthew and Ann C. (Ward) Thomas, on November 3, 1853, in Kanawha County, Virginia.[117]

A review of Kanawha County Court and Circuit Court indices reveal the following cases involving Richard L. Jackson in 1853:

Plaintiff(s)	Defendant(s)	Cause
Commonwealth	R. L. Jackson	Fine-Contempt[118]
Commonwealth	R. L. J. and William Tucker	Contempt[119]
R. L. J. for Moses F. Ward	John J. Brown Landon C. Moseley, surety	Not specified[120]
Henry Chappell	R. L. J. George W. Thomas, surety	Debt on bond[121]

1854:

A Trustee's Deed Bill of Sale for personal property was filed with the Kanawha County Recorder of Deeds. Richard L. Jackson sold some personal property (likely human property) to Abraham Wright.[122]

Richard was only involved in one court case in 1854 when he sued James S. O. Brooks for costs in a Circuit Court case.[123]

1855:

Richard L. Jackson was involved in two court cases in 1855:

Plaintiff(s)	Defendant(s)	Cause
R.L.J.	Jesse Hudson Aylett Thornton	Trespass on Case-Trover[124]
R.L.J.	William H. Webb	Trespass on Case-Assumpsit[125]

<u>1856 [Arthur Jackson was born on March 4]</u>:

A mulatto, male, slave was born about this year in the Richard and Lucinda Jackson household (recalling that slaves' ages were routinely estimated).

The baby appears—unnamed, but by race, gender, and approximately four-years-old—in the 1860 Slave Schedules of the U.S. Census for Charleston, Kanawha County, (West) Virginia.

This child was author David W. Jackson's great great grandfather, Arthur Jackson, born on March 4, 1856.

George and Virginia Catherine (Jackson) Thomas had a daughter, Anna "Annie" P. Thomas, born on October 6, 1856.

Arthur Jackson's mother, like the slave girl above, may have served "her white family" as a personal servant, nurse and/or nanny. All the while she raised at least two children (Arthur and Mary "Mollie") from two partners.

At the time of Arthur's birth, Richard and Lucinda's six children were aged 11, 13, 15, 18, 22 and 23-years-old. One can only speculate how the Jackson children interacted with their family's slaves.

Arthur's 26-year-old mother was about the same age as Richard and Lucinda's older children. She may have been a personal servant, nanny, and/or nurse to the younger ones.

It is possible that the white and black youths on the Jackson farm (and also the Thomases nearby) might have felt familial bonds, and may have treated one another as "play" siblings. As will be seen some twenty years later, Annie (Thomas) Isbell, her siblings, and their descendants lived in northeastern Kansas, and mingled very close to Arthur and his family, supporting the fact that some former slaves continued close relationships with their former masters long after emancipation.

Certainly events of the times would test the bonds between the Jacksons and their slaves. Already since 1854, the westernmost border between Missouri and the new Kansas Territory was smoldering as abolitionists fanned the flames of freedom. The nation was on the brink of a titanic struggle that would directly affect young Arthur and his Jackson family . . . black and white.

Richard L. Jackson (R. L. J. below) was directly involved in 11 court cases in 1856. And, he was surety in one case when his 22-year-old son, John Wesley Jackson, and his new son-in-law, George W. Thomas, were sued by Samuel Herron for debt in the Kanawha County Court.[126]

The three were involved in several Kanawha County court cases between 1856 and 1858, as noted below.[127]

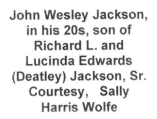

John Wesley Jackson, in his 20s, son of Richard L. and Lucinda Edwards (Deatley) Jackson, Sr. Courtesy, Sally Harris Wolfe

The 1856 Kanawha County Circuit Court cases involving Richard L. Jackson and his son-in-law, George W. Thomas:

Plaintiff(s)	Defendant(s)	Cause
J.S . & J. J. Yarnell	R. L. Jackson George W. Thomas, surety	Debt on bond[128]
A. Gout	R. L. Jackson George W. Thomas, surety	Debt on bond[129]
Nathan Gardner	R. L. Jackson George W. Thomas, surety	Debt on bond[130]
Hall and Robertson	R. L. Jackson George W. Thomas, surety	Debt on bond[131]
R. L. Jackson for Jacob Mahan	Edward Kenna and Benjamin S. Thompson	Debt[132]
A. [G]out	R. L. Jackson George W. Thomas, surety	Debt on bond[133]
Nathan Gardner	R. L. Jackson	Trespass on Case- Assumpsit[134]
James E. Richardson (use of) Nelson Mahan	R. L. Jackson and David J. W. Clarkson	Debt[135]
Jesse Hudson	R. L. Jackson and wife	Trespass on Case[136]
John W. O'Bannon	R. L. Jackson	Debt[137]
James E. Richardson	R. L. Jackson and David J. W. Clarkson	Not specified[138]
R. L. Jackson (use of) Jacob Mahan	Benjamin S. Thompson Charles L. Capehart, surety	Not specified[139]

1857 [Arthur turned 1 in March]:

George W. and Virginia Catherine (Jackson) Thomas had a son, Matthew L. Thomas, born on February 5, 1857.[140]

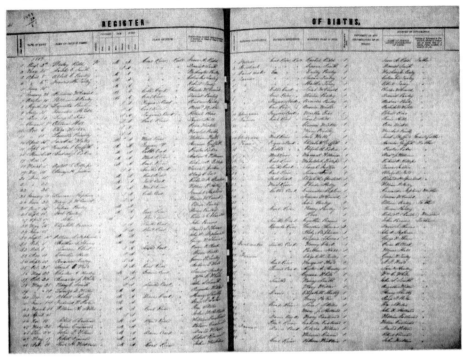

**Birth record of Matthew L. Thomas, February 5, 1857.
Courtesy Recorder of Deeds,
Kanawha County, West Virginia**

[In 1880, Matthew L. Thomas, age 23, lived with his uncle, Richard Ludlow Jackson, Jr., in the same household where their former slave, Arthur Jackson, was also staying in Holt County, Missouri. Matthew's brother, William Andrew Thomas, and his wife, Cordelia (Rowland) and family, soon thereafter settled in White Cloud, Doniphan County. After William died, Cordelia married Samuel V. Lear. They continued to live there, in close proximity to Arthur Jackson, for a number of years, and remained there long after Arthur moved to Kansas City.]

Kanawha County court cases involving the Jacksons and George W. Thomas continued in 1857:

Plaintiff(s)	Defendant(s)	Cause
Calvin Spredlin	John W. Jackson	damages, aka. "Trespass on the Case in Assumpsit."[141]
William Wilson and Samuel Gilland	Richard L. Jackson and John W. Jackson (with George W. Thomas as surety)	debt on bond[142]
Isaac Seasoal	John W. Jackson	debt[143]
James Mitchell	Richard L. Jackson (with George W. Thomas as surety)	debt on bond[144]
Mrs. R. W. Tompkins, executrix of William Tompkins, deceased	John W. Jackson (with his father, Richard L. Jackson as surety)	debt on bond[145]
George A. Goshorn	John W. Jackson (with his father, Richard L. Jackson as surety)	debt on bond[146]
Austin Sheperd	George W. Thomas and R. W. Mays (with John W. Jackson as surety)	debt[147]
George A. Goshorn (use of), Martin-Morell	George W. Thomas (with Richard L. Jackson as surety) and Company	debt[148]
Milton Parker	George W. Thomas and John W. Jackson	debt[149]
William Whittington	George W. Thomas (with John W. Jackson as surety)	debt[150]

1858 [Arthur turned 2 in March]:

Kanawha County Court cases involving the Jackson continued. *The Kanawha Valley Star* newspaper reported on March 2, 1858, that "no County in the State of Virginia ever had as much litigation in it in any four months, as Kanawha has had in the last four months.... On the 22nd of October last, the Circuit Court commenced its session and lasted seven weeks," with 98 old law issues and six new suits. "On the 15th of last month (Feb.) the County Court...commenced its quarterly term. On the law docket of this Court there were 97 old issues and 300 new suits on office judgment to be tried." Three different courts of Kanawha County were in session 13 weeks between October and February.[151]

The Jacksons were involved in 14 Circuit Court cases in Kanawha County in 1857 and 1858:

Plaintiff(s)	Defendant(s)	Cause
John W. Jackson sued for George W. Thomas	David J. W. Clarkson	debt[152]
John W. Jackson, or George Bender	Lewis Hazlett and Andrew H. Beach, doing-business-as Hazlett and Beach	debt[153]
John W. Jackson	Kanawha Cannel Coal and Mining and Oil Manufacturing Company	Trespass on case of Assumpsit[154]
Richard L. Jackson	John Slack, administrator of E. Kenna	debt *involving a negro.*[155]

1859 [Arthur turned 3 in March]:

A black, female, slave child was born about this year in the Richard and Lucinda Jackson household.

After having lived in Kanawha County, Virginia, for 15-17 years, since 1842 or 1844, the Richard L. and Lucinda Jackson family emigrated to Franklin County, Missouri, in 1859.[156]

George W. and Virginia Catherine (Jackson) Thomas and family, including their slaves, joined the migration.

The Jackson family traveled by steamer and settled on a farm just south of the Missouri River, near Labaddie (today, Labadie), Boles Township, in the northeastern corner of Franklin County, Missouri.[157]

Richard L. Jackson's main occupation was that of farmer. However, another source provided that Jackson "was a physician but would not practice except among his neighbors."[158]

Upon arrival in Franklin County, Jackson's son, John Wesley Jackson, began the study of medicine under the proprietorship of Dr. George Johnson and Dr. J. L. Mathews.

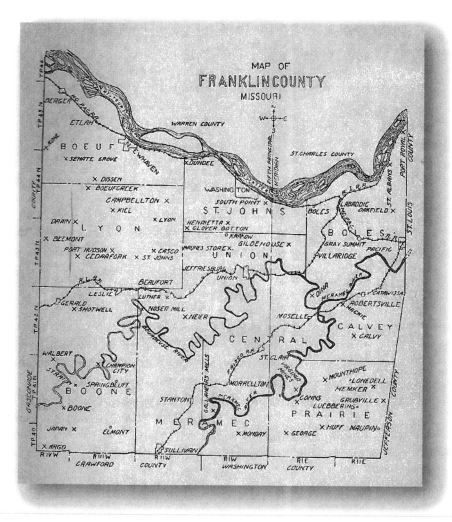

Why Move to Franklin County, Missouri, in 1859?

The aforementioned court cases, mostly involving debt, could provide some clue or reason for the Jacksons deciding to move. Was it political fervor in Kanawha County that drove the Jacksons to move away? Was the "Black Code" becoming too odious for the Jacksons to withstand? Or, did Richard Jackson, then in his late 60s, wish to retire and "go west," possibly to more fertile or picturesque country? Perhaps a life nearer to St. Louis might have allured them, as potential prospects for his children's futures?

Without ever knowing, it is also possible that Richard Jackson foresaw the coming war, and desired to move his family and slaves to slightly more neutral, perhaps safer, less vehemently controlled territory. Still, Missouri was no safe haven.

The Missouri Supreme Court had decided the Dred Scott case in 1852. And, two years later in 1854, the Border War between the Missouri and Kansas Territorial border began to fester between slave owners of western Missouri and free-soilers/abolitionists of eastern Kansas. The John Brown incident at Harper's Ferry took place in October 1859, in the midst of the Jackson's migration west to Missouri's Little Dixie.

Did they move because of the possibility that their slaves might run away?[159] "The Point Pleasant-Parkersburg Route of the Underground Railroad aided slaves escaping the interior of West Virginia could follow the Kanawha River to Point Pleasant."[160] Slave narratives recount the baying of blood hounds at night along the Ohio River, trying to follow the scent of escaped slaves, and the crack of firearms as white people, employed by the plantation owners, attempted to halt the Negroes in their efforts to cross the Ohio River into Ohio, or to join the Federal army.[161]

It doesn't seem probable that Richard and Lucinda Jackson's slaves desired to escape given that after Emancipation, the former African American 'servants' stayed with 'their white family' . . . at least for a time, before separating and moving on with their lives (see the 1868 Missouri State Census results below).

Franklin County may have been chosen because of its proximity to St. Louis and/or the Missouri River's navigation.

"The [Mississippi and Missouri] river counties were the home of slavery in the early days. Half of the slaves in the state were owned in counties that border on the Missouri River. The element that predominated in politics in those days is today in many counties the ruling influences. The counties along the Mississippi above St. Louis had more slaves than those along the river south of St. Louis. They were settled earlier and were more prosperous. The counties along the river were settled first because they had the means of transportation. They also had the level, fertile river lands where farming was profitable and slaves would be worked to the best advantage."[162]

How the Jackson's Migration Impacted Arthur's Parents

"A very bitter experience which the slave might at any time be forced to undergo was his removal to a strange region far from his wife or children or old associations."[163]

This may well have been the case for Arthur's parents. If his father had lived on a separate, nearby plantation, then his father likely was left behind when Richard and Lucinda Jackson moved from Kanawha County, Virginia, to Franklin County, Missouri, sometime in 1859.

For Arthur's descendants, this means the paternal, African bloodline flows from a male slave who lived on a Kanawha County, Virginia, plantation near the Jacksons at least in 1855 when Arthur was conceived.

If, by chance, Arthur's father was from the Thomas Matthew and Ann C. (Ward) Thomas plantation, then there is a possibility that Arthur's biological father *may* have migrated, too, when Ann's son, George W. Thomas, moved with his wife, Virginia Catherine (Jackson) Thomas, to Franklin County, Missouri, in 1859. This speculated connection has only been speculated.

Another possibility to consider is that Arthur's father was within the contiguous Richard L. and Lucinda Jackson family that had migrated from the eastern seaboard.

Ancestry.com DNA testing reveals present-day connections between Arthur's male descendants and at least one male descendant with nearly matching DNA also participating in the Ancestry.com DNA project. That participant's earliest, direct, male, Jackson ancestor has also been tracked to Charles County, Maryland, where Richard and Lucinda Jackson had also resided. This indicates that common male "Jackson" progenitors as slaves, at one time in the late 1700s to early 1800s, co-mingled together in the exact same county, and perhaps on the same plantation.

1860 [Arthur turned 4 in March]:

The U.S. Census enumerator visited the Jacksons between June 7 and 9, 1860, at their home in Boles Township, Franklin County, Missouri. The U.S. Population and Slave Schedules revealed:

1860 U.S. Census, Franklin County, Missouri
Richard L. and Lucinda Jackson, Sr.

Jackson, Richard [Ludlow, Sr.]	63[b. 1797]	VA
Jackson, Lucinda [Edwards]	50[b. 1811]	VA
Jackson, John [Wesley]	23[b. 1834]	MD
Jackson, [Lucy] Christina	20[b. 1839]	VA [MD]
[moved from MD to VA 1840-42]		
Jackson, Thomas [B.]	18[b.ca. 1842]	VA
Jackson, Richard [Ludlow, Jr.]	17[b. 1843]	VA
Jackson, James P[olk]	14[b.ca. 1846]	VA

Their 12 slaves lived in two slave houses:

40 [b.ca. 1820]	black	female
[moved from MD to VA 1840-42]		
19 [b.ca. 1841]	mulatto	female
16 [b.ca. 1844]	black	male
14 [b.ca. 1846]	black	male
13 [b.ca. 1847]	mulatto	male
13 [b.ca. 1847]	black	female
12 [b.ca. 1848]	black	female
12 [b.ca. 1848]	black	male
8 [b.ca. 1852]	mulatto	female
7 [b.ca. 1853]	black	male
4 [b.ca. 1856]	mulatto	male
1 [b.ca. 1859]	black	female

There were 1,601 slaves belonging to 293 slaveholders in Franklin County in 1860.[164] Slaves comprised 9.1% of the total population (18,087) in Franklin County.[165]

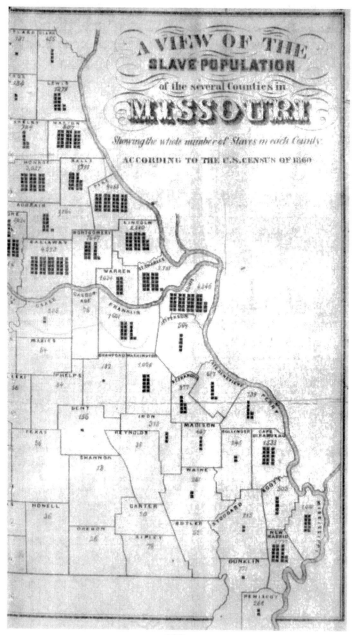

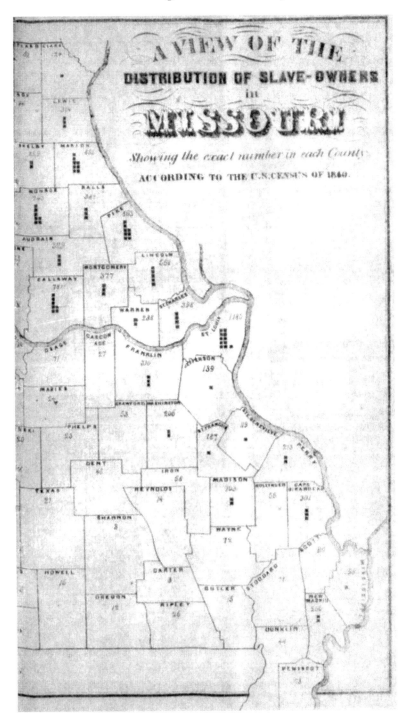

"Figures taken from Census returns give some idea of the rapid growth of slavery in Missouri prior to the Civil War."[166]

However, a "decrease is found in the counties along the Missouri from its mouth to the boundaries of Callaway and Cole— St. Louis, St. Charles, Franklin, Warren, Montgomery, Gasconade, and Osage—which in this decade [between 1850 and 1860] fell from 11,732 to 11,597 slaves."[167] In Franklin County alone, the percentage of slaves to the total population decreased from 13.8% in 1850.[168]

Overall, "[as] the slave trade grew, demand exceeded supply and values rose. The price of slaves, which was also based on the work that slaves could do, reached a peak in Missouri during the period immediately preceding the Civil War. In 1860, top male slaves brought about $1,300 each, and female slaves about $1,000."[169] There is absolutely no evidence that Richard L. and Lucinda Jackson were in the business buying, selling, or even breeding slaves.[170] These figures are applicable, however, in determining the potential value of their slaves.

With regard to the Jackson's enslaved human property, some assumptions should be addressed. Contrary to popularly held misconceptions, "slavery in Missouri was not a monolith; it was, in fact, a varied collection of complex social and economic relationships that occasionally worked to the benefit of the slaves."[171] "The great plantation of the Mississippi and Louisiana type with its white overseer and gangs of driven blacks was comparatively uncommon in the State...."[172] "Mr. George F. Shaw of Independence, formerly of Franklin County, said that there were few overseers in the latter county, as general farming was the rule."[173] "From [all available figures] Missouri was a State of small slaveholdings."[174] An adult slave typically acted as a foreman to manage other slaves.[175]

"The old slave masters without exception declare that the system was patriarchal in Missouri and that the bond between the owner and the owned was very close. The small number of slaves held by the vast majority of the masters was one reason for this condition. When the young Virginian or Kentuckian and his Negroes emigrated to far-off Missouri, they suffered in common the pangs of parting, and together went to develop the virgin soil amid common dangers and common hardships. Thus there undoubtedly grew up an attachment that the older communities had long since outgrown.

"This condition of fellowship between master and man, made possible by deep respect on the part of the slave, continued on to the Civil War in many rural communities. 'The Missouri slave holders,' said Mr. Robert B. Price of Columbia, 'were not such through choice. They inherited their Negroes and felt duty bound to keep them.' Colonel J. L. Robards of Hannibal stated that his father left him a number of slaves to whom he was fondly attached and whom he considered as a family trust. Mr. E. W. Strode of Independence claims that the Negro was closely united to the master's family. Mr. Strode stated that his grandfather required in his Will that the slaves be kept in the family, and that they were so held till the Civil War. 'The children of the master,' said Mr. Strode, 'played and fought with the slave children with due respect, there being no need for race distinction.'"[176]

Missouri also did not have the stereotypical cotton plantations that typified the Deep South. In fact, the climate was not conducive to cotton growing. There was, however, "possibilities for slave labor in tobacco and hemp production, as well as in the cultivation and production of grain and live stock. This caused an influx of slaveholders and their chattel into Missouri. A majority of these slaveholders came from the worn out lands of Kentucky, Tennessee, North Carolina, and Virginia." [177]

Indeed, Richard L. Jackson was a tobacco planter, at least partially. "In the tobacco regions of the State," reported former Lieutenant-Governor R. A. Campbell of Bowling Green, Pike County, Missouri, "there was no task system for the slaves. They were expected, and in many instances required, to do a reasonable day's work…. And, Missouri law forbade a master to work his slaves on Sunday, except in regular housework or labor for charity. Field work was thus forbidden on Sunday. The penalty for the master was one dollar for each negro so employed."[178]

The 1860 Agricultural Schedules show Richard Jackson and his family and slaves had produced 12,000 pounds of tobacco.[179]

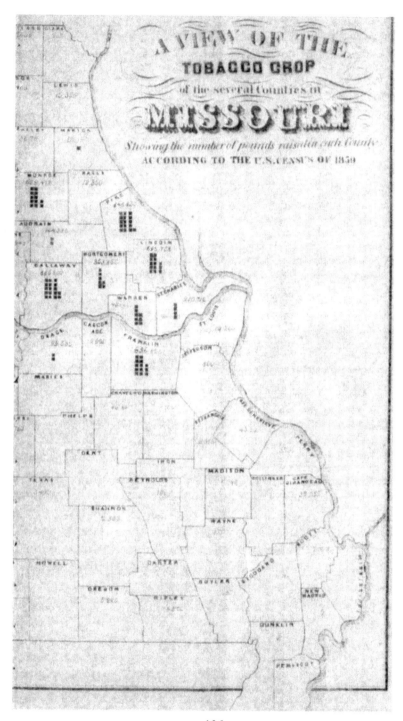

They also grew 2,000 bushels of Indian corn; 100 bushels of oats; 2 tons of hay; and, raised 107 head of swine.[180]

Incidental productions included 75 bushels of Irish potatoes; 100 pounds of butter; and, $20 in orchard products.

The family was supported by five horses; 1 mule; 2 milch cows; and two other cattle in the year ending June 1, 1860.[181]

The 1860 Population Schedules show that Richard L. Jackson, Sr., owned $7,000 in personal property, a figure calculating his household effects; but, reflecting most likely his chattel slaves.[182]

In the preceding decade, Richard and Lucinda's slave family appears to have naturally increased in size with four children between 1850 and 1860.

The elder 'couple' (who may not have been a familial couple) disappear from the roster in that decade. Although, it is possible the 20-year-old mulatto female in 1850 is the same 40-year-old black female in 1860.

But, the elder male slave (possibly the father of at least some of the children) did not appear to migrate. There is the possibility that he did not survive, or was sold and left behind in Kanawha County.

In any event the Jacksons also acquired between 1850 and 1860 an additional four slaves who, judging from their ages, could not have been part of their 1850 slave family unit.

While a nuclear family unit is visible in 1850, by 1860 the additional adolescents infer that a second 'family' had joined them, and might possibly have been living in the second of two slave quarters identified in the Census.

One of the 'siblings' from the conjoined family might be Dennis, the supposed 'half brother' of Arthur Jackson that his grandson, Roy, remembered meeting as a child.

And, Arthur's half sister, Mary "Mollie" Jackson (Pryor/Prior) Sharp, must be reconciled within this Jackson household in 1860. Her calculated birth in 1855 match most closely to the 8-year-old mulatto female (b.ca. 1852). That she, too, was identified as a mulatto gives credence that her (and Arthur's) mother was the 19-year-old mulatto female.

Slaveholding Comparison, 1850-1860
Richard L. and Lucinda Jackson, Sr.

1850 (5 slaves)	1860 (12 slaves)
40 [b.ca. 1810] black male	
20 [b.ca. 1830] mulatto female	
	40 [b.ca. 1820] black female
5 [b.ca. 1845] mulatto female	19 [b.ca. 1841] mulatto female
	16 [b.ca. 1844] black male
3 [b.ca. 1847] black male	14 [b.ca. 1846] black male
	13 [b.ca. 1847] mulatto male
	13 [b.ca. 1847] black female
2 [b.ca. 1848] black female	12 [b.ca. 1848] black female
	12 [b.ca. 1848] black male
	8 [b.ca. 1852] mulatto female
	7 [b.ca. 1853] black male
	4 [b.ca. 1856] mulatto male
	1 [b.ca. 1859] black female

Was Arthur Jackson "black" or "mulatto?"

The 1860 Census is the closest record of birth for the author's great great grandfather, Arthur Jackson, then a four-year-old slave infant underlined above in what appeared to be a two-family unit on the Richard L. and Lucinda Jackson farm. Arthur's half sister, Mary "Mollie" Jackson (Pryor/Prior) Sharp, would have been a year or two older. The most likely match is the 8-year-old mulatto female, who is also underlined above.

Though the distinct slave family units were not separated in the Census, the author tried to separate the two in the comparison above with **boldface Arial text** shading.

Presuming Arthur's attribution as a "mulatto" is accurate, then one of Arthur's parents or ancestors may likely have had Caucasian ancestry. According to DNA testing, Arthur's direct, paternal, male ancestral line is uninterrupted for generations to Africa. As stated above, Arthur's father *might* have been a slave from a nearby farm, with a different surname.

Arthur and Mollie's mother, therefore, is most likely to have been the 19-year-old mulatto female in the slave family <u>underlined above</u>. She may or may not have carried the Jackson surname; but she was with the family since she was a child. That she was mulatto would mean that she most likely had a Caucasian father. It was much more common for a mulatto child to have a white father—usually a slave master—than to have a white mother, which was not generally accepted.

It might also be hypothesized that the two elders from the 1850 and single elder from the 1860 Census could have been Arthur and Mollie's grandparents, only if presuming that this was, indeed, a nuclear family. Understanding that slave ages were generally estimated, it is also possible that the 20-year-old female in 1850 might actually be the 40-year-old female in 1860. She is *italicized* in the comparison above.

A Real Property Quandary

Beyond personal property, there is an unanswered mystery with regard to Richard and Lucinda Jackson's real property.

The 1860 Population Schedules show that Richard L. Jackson did not own any real estate.[183] The 1860 Franklin County tax rolls confirm this,[184] as does a study of Franklin County deeds. There is no record in the Franklin County Recorder of Deeds office documenting that Richard or his wife, Lucinda, ever purchased or disposed of real property in Franklin County, Missouri.[185]

However, the 1860 Agricultural Schedules revealed that Jackson claimed 100 acres of improved land, and 150 acres of unimproved land worth a total cash value of $5,000 (and $200 in farming implements and machinery).

The 250 acres is a mystery.

Perhaps he was merely renting the land.

It should be remembered that the 1850 Population Schedules also document that Jackson did not own any real property; but, that the Agricultural Schedules listed 350 acres.

Richard and Lucinda's sons, John W., Thomas B., and James P. Jackson, each purchased and disposed of land in Franklin County between 1865 and at least 1876.[186]

And, John W. Jackson and his heirs retained ownership of some property, which they continue to own to this day (2015).

A Look at the Thomas Family

It is worth illustrating the George W. and Virginia Catherine (Jackson) Thomas family. Virginia was the only offspring of Richard and Lucinda Jackson who was out of the home at this time.

Though George Thomas did not own any real property in Franklin County, Missouri, in 1860, he claimed $3,900 in personal property, including four slaves.[187]

Back in Kanawha County, Virginia, in 1860, George Thomas' mother, Ann C. (Ward) Thomas—a widow since her husband, Thomas Matthew Thomas died in 1840—was living alone. Her real estate holdings totaled $10,000, and her personal estate of $5,000 included eight slaves.[188]

Ten years earlier in 1850, when George was still living at home at age 21, his mother, then age 45, owned 19 slaves.[189]

Slaveholding Comparison, 1850-1860
Ann Thomas, and her son, George Thomas[190]

1850 (Ann owned 19)		1860 (Ann owned 8; George 4)		
70 [b.ca. 1780]	black female			
50 [b.ca. 1800]	black female	68 [b.ca. 1792]	black female (Ann)	
36 [b.ca. 1814]	black female			
31 [b.ca. 1819]	black male	46 [b.ca. 1814]	black male (Ann)	
30 [b.ca. 1820]	black male	42 [b.ca. 1818]	black male (Ann)	
30 [b.ca. 1820]	mulatto female			
30 [b.ca. 1820]	black female			
		41 [b.ca. 1819]	black male (Ann)	
29 [b.ca. 1821]	black male	40 [b.ca. 1820]	colored male **(George)**	
		35 [b.ca. 1825]	black male **(George)**	
20 [b.ca. 1830]	black female			
16 [b.ca. 1834]	black female			
15 [b.ca. 1835]	black female	25 [b.ca. 1835]	colored female **(George)**	
12 [b.ca. 1838]	black male	22 [b.ca. 1838]	mulatto male (Ann)[191]	
6 [b.ca. 1844]	black male			
5 [b.ca. 1845]	mulatto female			
3 [b.ca. 1847]	black male			
2 [b.ca. 1848]	black female			
1 [b.ca. 1849]	black male			
1/12 [b.ca. 1850]	black female	10 [b.ca. 1850]	black	female **(George)**
1/12 [b.ca. 1850]	black male			
		6 [b.ca 1854]	black	male (Ann)
		6 [b.ca 1854]	black	female (Ann)
		3 [b.ca 1857]	black	male (Ann)

There is a remote chance that Arthur and/or Mollie's biological father may have visited the Jackson plantation from the Thomas plantation in Kanawha County. He would have done so at the same time George Thomas was courting Virginia Catherine Jackson. And, it should be remembered that Virginia Jackson bore a daughter a little over six months after Arthur was born. The potential matches for Arthur/Mollie's father in the Thomas family are underlined in the comparison above; the most likely aged slave double underlined (although he was attributed as mulatto).

Thomas descendants also have later geographical connections to Arthur Jackson and his family:

1) Matthew Thomas and Arthur lived together when Matthew was staying at his uncle Richard Ludlow Jackson, Jr., in the 1880 Holt County, Missouri, Census.

2) Thomas descendants lived in White Cloud, Doniphan County, Kansas, as early as 1875, and lived very near Arthur in White Cloud between at least 1895-1905.

3) Arthur's first grandchild by his son, Jabez Jackson, was named Virginia…possibly after Virginia Catherine (Jackson) Thomas, who died by 1875 in Holt County, Missouri. (Another namesake might be Virginia's sister-in-law, Virginia Carter North, who married her brother, John W. Jackson, and died in Kansas City in 1917, just a few years after Arthur and his family migrated to the City.)

Virginia (North) Jackson, wife of John W. Jackson, courtesy Sally Harris Wolfe

4) Arthur supposedly had a ½ brother named "Dennis Jackson" from Hiawatha (near White Cloud). If this is true, then, perhaps, one (or, both) of Arthur's parents may have migrated there, too.

"Even though the support for slavery in Franklin County was on the wane, voters were evenly split in 1860 between the Democrats who supported slavery and other parties including the Republicans who were opposed to the practice. However, the Democratic Party was divided between those who favored further compromise on slavery-related issues in order to preserve the Union and those who were pro-slavery secessionists.... When the question of secession or preservation of the Union was weighted, the pro-Union voices in Franklin County had a clear majority. As a result the representatives that were selected to represent Franklin County at the state supported preservation of the Union and predominantly were in favor of a neutral stance in the state."[192]

1861 [Arthur turned 5 in March]:

"After the initial power struggle over the slavery question, Franklin County itself was largely spared the ravages associated with the large scale battles [in the south]."[193] To protect local communities from guerrilla warfare that typified the fighting throughout Missouri, some men joined local Home Guard and Enrolled Missouri Militia [EMM] units. "Squads were drilling in different parts of Franklin County as early as January, 1861."[194]

Civil War erupted in Missouri in May 1861 when a Federal raid captured Confederate-led, local militia at an arsenal at Camp Jackson at the southern edge of St. Louis. The next month, "Two hundred and fourteen muskets were sent out by Capt. Lyon [from St. Louis] to Washington, Mo., on the night of June 11, and with them were armed two companies, commanded, respectively, by Capt. Wilhelm and Capt. Maupin. The former company, upon receiving their muskets, immediately took possession of Washington, [Missouri], and the latter marched to Union, [Missouri]. Upon approaching the town, Capt. Maupin took the precaution to place guards on every road leading out of Union, and then marched into town, the glistening bayonets of his 100 men making a brilliant spectacle."[195]

Through the summer, action continued southwesterly to Springfield, west towards Lexington in Lafayette County, southwest, and falling back to Rolla and Sedalia. Near the end of the year, "a different cast of characters became involved in Missouri's fighting. General Ulysses S. Grant crossed the Mississippi River and attacked Confederate troops stationed at Belmont in southeast Missouri. After initial success General Grant was forced to retreat to Cairo, Illinois. Winter weather ended campaigning in the state for the year."[196]

It should be noted again that warfare along the Missouri and Kansas border had been raging since 1854, some five years before the Jacksons moved from western Virginia to eastern Missouri.

From this time on, Franklin County was comparatively peaceful during the Civil War, except during Sterling Price's 1864 raid."[197]

Meanwhile, in 1861, in a dispute over secession, fifty western counties broke off from Virginia to form the "restored government of Virginia," which remained loyal to the Union. Kanawha County, Virginia, where the Jacksons had migrated from, became part of the state of West Virginia, which was admitted to the Union in 1863.[198]

General Orders No. 135
Establishment of the Department of the Missouri

War Dep't, Adjutant General's Office
Washington, September 19, 1861

1. By direction of the President, the States of Missouri, Arkansas, Kansas, and the bordering Indian Territory, will constitute the Department of the Missouri, and will be commanded by Major General S. R. Curtis; headquartered in St. Louis.

2. Western Virginia is attached to the Department of the Ohio; headquartered in Cincinnati.

By Order of the Secretary of War:
E.D. TOWNSEND, *Assistant Adjutant General*[199]

A Window into Arthur's Childhood

"Nuclear [slave] families should … be viewed as the exception rather than the rule. Housing did not accommodate such an arrangement anyway. Slave families often shared one cabin, common meals, and because of the nature of their enslavement, common supervision of children. Slave life was far more communal than can be imagined today…. The slave family should be, therefore, viewed as an extended family where children were reared by parents, grandparents, aunts, and uncles for a good portion of their youth."[200] Those parental figures that were not necessarily biologically related were part of an extended family of "fictive kinship" often called—to this day—"play-mothers," "play-aunts," etc.

"Some of the colored people fared good en' some of dem fared bad in slavery time. Some of dem had good owners en' some of dem had bad ones. Thank de Lord, I didn't get much of it 'cause I won' but nine years old when freedom come."[201] This could easily have been an observation and statement of Arthur Jackson. *"I wasn't big enough to tote water to the field when war started, but I driv up the cows and calves and helped 'tend Massa's chillen. I was only eleven year old when the niggers was freed."*[202] Simon Gallman *"was about twelve years old when dey made me go to de field to work. Befo' dat and after dat, too, I worked around de barn and took care of de stock."*[203]

Questions about slaves' housing, food, clothing, playtime, and work remain unanswered, as does the treatment and interaction between everyone on the Jackson farm. "The daily work of enslaved men, women and children in Missouri varied with their owners and the seasons."[204] Everyone wishes they had listened more attentively or recorded their parent's and grandparent's stories. And, I surely wish Arthur had had the invitation to record his life, born a slave.

Without specific anecdotal evidence of Arthur's slave experience, the narratives shared by other former slaves might apply to his situation, and those with whom he lived among on the Jackson farm. As stated above, conditions varied not only regionally, but also from owner to owner, plantation to plantation. "Although Missouri slaves were generally worked from sunup to sundown during the week, they were often allowed [Saturday and] Sunday afternoons to themselves."[205]

The author found a few narratives from the locality where the Jacksons lived in (West) Virginia and Missouri, where Arthur was born and lived as an infant slave.

Nan Stewart was born in Charleston, West Virginia, in February 1850. *"Marse an' missus, mighty kind to us slaves."* Her owners were Mr. and Mrs. Harley and Maria (Sanders) Hunt; he was a magistrate in Charleston. She remembered seeing slaves auctioned off *"to niggah tradahs way down farthah south."* Slaves were also by the year for $900.[206]

Eli Davison was born in 1844 in Dunbar, West Virginia, a slave of Will and Elsie Davison, who are said to have had three plantations. In 1858, Mr. Davison divided his slaves, left his wife with half, and moved (with Eli) to Madison County, Texas, where after Eli was sold.[207]

Lizzie Grant, a slave from Kanawha County, West Virginia, was born in Dunbar, West Virginia, in 1847, and was owned by Ellis Grant, cousin to General Ulysses S. Grant. She recalled:

> *"I was about 17 years old when I was given to my young Maser, me and the man that I called my husband. So our young Maser put us to live together to raise from just like you would stock today. They never thought anything about it either. They never cared or thought about our feeling in the matter."* Grant made her marry, *"as we were going to raise him some more slaves. Maser said it was cheaper to raise slaves than it was to buy them, and I guess it was for they did not lose so much when we was free by the government."* *"Our home life as slave children was hell, as we never had any playtime at all. From the time we could walk Mistress had us carrying in wood and water and we did not know what it was to get out and romp and play like children do now. Our quarters was pretty good, they were built out of bark logs and all the cracks were*

117

dobed with mud to keep out the cold and rain. Our beds they were built down on the ground in one corner of our quarters out of moss, shucks and grass. Yes we kept real warm in there all the time as we had a big rock fireplace built to keep us warm. We kept plenty wood as that and water was about all we got free. As slaves we done all kinds of work such as, hoe tobacco, pull and dry it then, we out rails for fences, and just anything that Maser had to do as it did not make any difference to him, he worked men or women slaves just alike. The women cooked and washed dishes while the men tended to the stock that Maser owned. Maser would give us a nickel or dime once and awhile and we bought candy and things like that when he would give us any money, but that was seldom ever, maybe once or twice a year."[208]

"I was but a lad in slavery days," says Mr. Dean D. Duggins of Marshall, "but my recollections of the institution are most pleasant. I can remember how in the evening at husking time the negroes would come singing up the creek. They would work 'till ten o'clock amidst singing and pleasantry and after a hot supper and hard cider would depart for their cabins. The servants were very careful of the language used before the white children and would reprove and even punish the master's children.[35] *"How well I remember those happy days!" wrote Lucy A. Delaney. "Slavery had no horror then for me, as I played about the place, with the same joyful freedom as the little white Children. With mother, father, and sister, a pleasant home and surroundings, what happier child than I!"[209]*

I like to think my great great grandfather Arthur Jackson's remembrances of his youth were as pleasant. He got along with his owners and their children, especially since he lived with or near them—at least off and on—into his 20s. The daily life of slave children is presented, in their own words, in volume five of Donna Wyant Howell's multi-volume work, *I Was a Slave: True Life Stories Dictated by Former American Slaves in the 1930's.*

1862 [Arthur turned 6 in March]:

Early in 1862, Civil War action continued with advances from Rolla south to Arkansas. "Numerous skirmishes marked the period from March to late summer in the state. There were a series of small forays into the central portion of the state to recruit men and obtain horses...."[210]

About 600 citizens of Franklin County joined the rebel army, to whom befell the usual fortunes of war. All who returned home, after the cause for which they fought was lost, have accepted the situation with various degrees of gracefulness, and many of them are well satisfied that it was lost, and are good citizens as any in the county."[211]

"In October an important psychological and historical moment occurred when African Americans, mustered into military service as the 1st Kansas Colored Infantry, engaged in their first combat action. The skirmish at Island Mound, while not a crucial military action, answered a key question to many political and military leaders about the African Americans fighting qualities."[212]

How did the Civil War affect the Richard and Lucinda Jackson family? The next year would begin to reveal their how their lives transpired during this tumultuous time.

One historical record, the 1862 Franklin County tax assessments, list exactly where Richard L. Jackson and family resided within Franklin County:

Section 31, Township 44, Range 1 East.[213]

Interestingly, no slaves were listed. Richard paid $1 Poll tax; $.88 State tax; $.19 Mill (military) tax; and, $.03 for Lunatic Asylum tax.[214]

Sometime in 1862, Jackson's son, Dr. John Wesley Jackson, became associated in business with his former tutor, Dr. George Johnson, in Franklin County.

1863 [Arthur turned 7 in March]:

Abraham Lincoln issued the Emancipation Proclamation on January 1, 1863.

As will be seen, however, it did not free slaves in every state. Missouri's slaves—Arthur included—were under servitude for another two years.

"The early months of 1863 were characterized by small [Civil War] engagements throughout the state.... While the main Confederate army remained occupied in Arkansas throughout the year. Colonel Jo[seph Orville "Jo"] Shelby raided the central portion of the state. His raid that began on September 22, and was highlighted by the large amount of property destroyed and supplies captured.... Despite the guerrilla uprisings the year concluded with the Federals solidly in control of Missouri, but their leadership saw Union troop strength dwindle to support activities in other theaters of combat."[215]

That Richard and Lucinda Jackson migrated from Virginia and owned slaves, one might assume that they would have sympathized with the South during the Civil War. Of course, they must have had strong feelings and ties to their cultural heritage. However, their political leanings contradicted the status quo and commonly held stereotypes that 'all' northerners supported the Union and 'all' southerners sided with the Confederacy.

Three of the Richard and Lucinda Jackson's eldest sons registered for the Federal, or Union draft in July-August 1863. John Wesley Jackson was 26; Thomas B., 22; and, Richard, 20. John's listed profession was doctor; his brothers were farmers. All said they were born in Virginia.[216]

Dr. John Wesley Jackson was graduated from the St. Louis Medical College in 1863 (his brother, James, would graduate there in 1868).[217] The next year, John W. Jackson entered the Union Army as a surgeon, and his brother, Thomas B. Jackson, enlisted with the Enrolled Missouri Militia.[218]

An "order to enlist men to fight in the war under the United States Colored Troops division was issued May 22, 1863 (War Department General Order 143). Several units had already been raised, trained, and had seen battle. Those units in New Orleans, South Carolina, and Kansas whose formation had preceded this official order were eventually incorporated into the USCT."[219] Of course, there are "many fascinating cases of men who acted as scouts, spies, and laborers for the Union effort without being enlisted."[220]

COME AND JOIN US BROTHERS

Creation of the U.S. Colored Troops

GENERAL ORDERS
No. 143
WAR DEPARTMENT
ADJUTANT GENERAL'S OFFICE
Washington, May 22, 1863

I --   A Bureau is established in the Adjutant General's Office for the record of all matters relating to the organization of Colored Troops, An officer, will be assigned to the charge of the Bureau, with such number of clerks as may be designated by the Adjutant General.

II --   Three or more field officers will be detailed as Inspectors to supervise the organization of colored troops at such points as may be indicated by the War Department in the Northern and Western States.

III --   Boards will be convened at such posts as may be decided upon by the War Department to examine applicants for commissions to command colored troops, who, on Application to the Adjutant General, may receive authority to present themselves to the board for examination.

IV --   No persons shall be allowed to recruit for colored troops except specially authorized by the War Department; and no such authority will be given to persons who have not been examined and passed by a board; nor will such authority be given any one person to raise more than one regiment.

V -- The reports of Boards will specify the grade of commission for which each candidate is fit, and authority to recruit will be given in accordance. Commissions will be issued from the Adjutant General's Office when the prescribed number of men is ready for muster into service.

VI -- Colored troops may be accepted by companies, to be afterward consolidated in battalions and regiments by the Adjutant General. The regiments will be numbered seriatim, in the order in which they are raised, the numbers to be determined by the Adjutant General. They will be designated: "——Regiment of U. S. Colored Troops."

VII -- Recruiting stations and depots will be established by the Adjutant General as circumstances shall require, and officers will be detailed to muster and inspect the troops.

VIII -- The non-commissioned officers of colored troops may be selected and appointed from the best men of their number in the usual mode of appointing non-commissioned officers. Meritorious commissioned officers will be entitled to promotion to higher rank if they prove themselves equal to it.

IX -- All personal applications for appointments in colored regiments, or for information concerning them, must be made to the Chief of the Bureau; all written communications should be addressed to the Chief of the Bureau, to the care of the Adjutant General,

BY ORDER OF THE SECRETARY OF WAR
E. D. TOWNSEND, Assistant Adjutant General

civilwar.org/education/history/primarysources/war-department-general-order.html citing General Order No. 143, May 22, 1863; Orders and Circulars, 1797-1910; Records of the Adjutant General's Office, 1780's-1917; Record Group 94; National Archives.

The recruitment of African Americans for the United States Colored Troops (USCT) was under General Orders No. 135, issued November 14, 1863. This order authorized assistant provost marshals throughout Missouri to recruit slaves, contrabands, or free blacks into military service and to compensate loyal slave owners up to $300 for each slave they allowed to enlist."[221]

Just a few days prior, on November 10, 1863, General John M. Schofield issued Special Order 307, "an order that prohibited the selling of slaves from the State."[222]

However, for some months, "the negroes of loyal men in Franklin County [were] flocking to the town of Washington, on the line of the Pacific railroad, where some troops [were] stationed, and there they are protected, and are indulging in a life of idleness and dissipation."[223]

In all, 8,344 Africans served the USCT from Missouri.[224]

At this writing, it is unlikely that any of Richard and Lucinda Jackson's slaves served in the Civil War. Arthur Jackson was still a youth, and, therefore, never participated in the Civil War. Judging from the 1860 Federal census, there were two, possibly three black males in the Jackson household 'of age' by 1863. Was one of these young men Arthur's older, eligible siblings? Were any given leave by their Union-sympathizing master? Or, did they escape to do join the War effort?

Only one black man with the Jackson surname was *recruited* from Franklin County, Missouri.[225] One 18-year-old Andrew Jackson enlisted as a Private at Washington on June 5, 1863, and joined the 56th Regiment, United States Colored Troops Infantry, Company D.[226] No black servicemen were located from Franklin County who named Jackson as their slaveholder.[227]

The U.S. Federal government at this time assessed an income tax on certain businesses to help fund the Civil War. The only member of the Franklin County Jackson family to be assessed for this annual, Federal Internal Revenue tax, was Dr. John Wesley Jackson, in April 1863, when he paid $10 for a "Class B license" as a physician at Labadie, Franklin County, Missouri.[228] He was graduated from the St. Louis Medical College in the spring of 1863.[229]

The 1863 Franklin County tax rolls list only "J. W. Jackson" in Section 31, Township 44 North, Range 1 East. He paid $1 Poll tax; $1.16 State tax for his $50 assessment in other property.[230]

Since John Wesley Jackson was the only member of the Jackson family to be assessed both the local, state and Federal tax in 1863, he was obviously the only male of age in the family with resources of his own. This means the assessment was likely conducted *after* August when a significant event took place in the Franklin County Jackson household.

The family's patriarch, Richard L. Jackson, Sr., died at age 66 years and one month, on August 10, 1863. Within a couple of days, he was buried east of Gray Summit, Franklin County, Missouri, in the North Cemetery.[231]

Death of a Slaveholder

I try to imagine this time for the Jackson family, including my slave ancestor, Arthur Jackson, who was about seven years, five months old when his master died. Remember the scene in the movie, *Gone With the Wind*, when Scarlett O'Hara's mother lies-in-state and the future looked quite uncertain for the heroine? Though not quite as dramatic, I still picture Richard Jackson lying in state in his wood coffin, likely in a parlor, and Arthur and perhaps his parent(s) and sibling(s) viewing his body and wondering—fearing—their fate as slaves.

"In Missouri slave society, the death of the master was an uncertain time for the slaves and their families. Estates handled the disposition of slave property in a variety of ways: The estate often hired the slaves to generate income; if requested, the courts partitioned the slaves among the heirs, either in kind or through sale; the slaves stayed with the family; often slaves took this opportunity to run away; the heirs might dispute ownership or the will of the deceased; or, on rare occasions, some or all of the slaves received their freedom." Even if the latter, "too often the family nullified or ignored the will and maintained the slaves in bondage."[232]

"Widows were unable to alienate their slaves if there were

other heirs, and consequently hired them out as a means of income. The slaves of orphans and of estates in probate were annually hired out by the court, bond being necessary 'for the amount of hire.'"[233] "In addition to the cash paid by the hirer, he also furnished the slave with medical attention, food, and a customary amount of clothing. An old slave claims that the hired slave of western Missouri usually received two pairs of trousers, two shirts, and a hat the first summer, a coat and a pair of trousers in the winter, and two pairs of trousers the second summer."[234]

The least desirable action is that slaves might be sold at auction. "Their sale was the only means to divide equally the material value of, for example, four bondspersons among three heirs or the reverse."[235] A slave sale would also disperse and break-up African American family units that may have been formed. It might also lead to the unexpected and untimely suicide of a slave, or slave couple in a murder-suicide, when, rather than be "sold downriver," slaves would take their own lives.

When a white slave master died prior to the emancipation requirement, there is a possibility that their estate records, if they survive, often provide a detailed inventory and appraisal of everything (and everyone) they owned. Logically, then, one might expect a master's slaves to be named, stating how much they were worth, and likely their age.

To corroborate or elaborate on this, probate cases were published in newspapers, and if an auction were to be held to settle the estate, a comprehensive list all the slaves that were going to be sold at the public sale might be located. News articles following after a noteworthy sale might have provided additional details.[236]

Although Franklin County newspapers from that time period do not survive, the Four Rivers Genealogical Society, Washington, Missouri, have indexed Franklin County probate records, and the Washington Historical Society, Washington, Missouri, have collaborated with the Missouri State Archives to microfilm and conserve the originals.

Probate of Richard Ludlow Jackson, Sr.

A probate packet survives for Richard L. Jackson, Sr., though his Last Will and Testament *did not* enumerate specific property, real or personal. It was dated on February, 27, 1855, eight years prior to his death and before to the family emigration from Virginia to Missouri. His Will was included in a probate/estate filed after his death in 1863 with the Franklin County, Missouri, Probate Court at Union, Missouri.

Naming and leaving everything to his wife, Lucinda, executrix, she filed an inventory of the estate on November 30, 1863, to wit (**bolded items** appear to have been retained by Lucinda, or given to her children, rather than sold).

$30.00 cash on hand	1 corn sheller
$219.38 cash received for horse and tobacco	1 grind stone 3 scythe and cradles
5 beds, bedsteads and bedding	2 mowing scythes
2 dozen chairs; 1 prep; 2 tables	1 jacks screw
1 book case	Lot carpenters tools
1 lounge	2 wagons
2 looking glasses	3 axes
1 clock	3 double-trees
5 pair fire irons	6 single-trees
1 tin safe	3 sets double-wagon harnesses
2 lamps	4 stacks oats
3 two-horse plows; 5 single-horse plows	21 stacks wheat
4 shovel plows	600 bushels corn in bottom
1 harrow	8 barns tobacco
2 iron wedges	5 head horses
1 mattock	2 yoke oxen
6 hoes	6 cows
1 spade	3 steers
3 log chains	6 calves
1 wheat fan	25 head hogs
	11 slaves, old and young

Context clues therein reveal, in part, the lifestyle of this family. For instance, the family of six (the two eldest siblings already out of the household) slept on five beds; but, in how many bedrooms? What would eight barns of tobacco have looked like . . . planted and harvested by 11 slaves "young and old."

This line item is the *only mention* of Jackson's slaves in the entire probate/estate packet. Did "old and young" hint they were less productive and worth less? Richard and Lucinda had owned 12 slaves, three years prior in 1860.[237]

The first settlement of the estate was in December 1863, after the sale of some livestock and harvesting of crops:

Apples	$ 60.00
Oats	$ 50.00
Corn	$ 212.62
Tobacco	$1,517.49
Horse	$ 105.00
Oxen	$ 60.00
Subtotal	$2,005.11
Credits against the estate	-$1,619.24
Balance	$ 385.87[238]

1864 [Arthur turned 8 in March]:

Early in 1864, Dr. John Wesley Jackson entered the Union Army and was appointed surgeon of the 40th Regiment, Missouri Volunteers, and served in that capacity until the close of the War.[239]

A January 20, 1864, sale of the personal estate of Richard L. Jackson, Sr., realized $677.75. Inventory sold consisted of livestock and farm implements, most of which was sold to Jackson's three eldest sons: John Wesley Jackson, Thomas B. Jackson, and Richard Ludlow Jackson, Jr. Eight neighbors purchased minor lots.

It's fairly clear that the Jackson family's slaves were not sold. Rather, given the division of farm implementation, it might be surmised that at least some of Lucinda Jackson's 11 slaves were divided between her children, or possibly "hired out" to other farmers.

The slaves may have also been manumitted and offered the option to stay and continue living and farming with the Jackson family. "As early as Spring 1864, many Missouri planters began offering wages or the share-crop option to their slaves as an incentive for them to remain tending the crops. This had a noticeable impact as 1864 brought a drastic reduction in Colored Troop recruitment."[240]

Thomas B. Jackson, having purchased the majority of the farm equipment, assumed responsibility for a majority if not all of the Jackson family slaves of age and capable of performing manual labor. His brother, Richard L. Jackson, Jr., may also have had some slave assistance, at least until he moved to Holt County.[241]

To John W. Jackson
1 pair hatchers
4 planes
2 pair h[--?--]
1 corn huller

To Thomas B. Jackson
2 shovel plows
1 ball tongue plow
4 farming plows
1 double-tree
1 single-tree
2 hoes
1 scythe and cradle
1 mowing scythe
1 grubbing hoe
1 drawing knife
1 jack and 1 pore plain
4 planes
1 hand saw
1 square
1 adze
1 mallet and spade
1 grind stone
1 set harness
3 collars
1 black cow

1 white calf
1 red calf
1 gray mare
1 yellow colt
  (Milk & Cider)
1 sow; 7 pigs
1 sow; 7 pigs
1 large kettle
1 wagon

To Richard L. Jackson, Jr.

1 shovel plow
2 farming plows
1 double-tree
1 single-tree
2 sets plow gear
Bridles and collars
1 red cow
1 [--?--] horse

To William Tubbenny
1 shovel plow
1 sash
1 smoothing plane
1 hand saw
2 squares
1 jack screw
1 red calf

To J B Mitchell
1 scythe and cradle

To W. Falwell
1 log chain

To J. B. Reynolds
2 little saws
2 heifers

To John Groff
1 jack plane
1 carpenters plow

To A. M. Groff
1 yellow colt
  (Milk & Peaches)

To Dick Wood
2 augers

To L. L. Nunn
1 roon[--?--] cow

"The final full year of [Civil War] combat in Missouri mirrored the previous two twelve-month cycles. From January through August small skirmishes and guerilla activity unsettled the state.... While [Confederate] Generals Shelby and Price were pushing westward, Generals James Fagan and Marmaduke were struggling to fight a strong rearguard action against General Rosecran's Federals advancing from the east." After significant action on the western border with the Battle of Independence, Battle of the Blue River at Byram's Ford; and, Battle of Westport, ended in Southern retreat, "The Confederates limped back into Arkansas and Texas defeated and demoralized."[242]

Prior to the summer of 1864, Franklin County only lost four lives directly attributed to the Civil War.[243] Then, on September 30, Confederate General Sterling Price and his army of 16,000 entered Franklin County and remained for four days.

In the Jackson family's neighborhood of Gray Summit was located Camp Franklin, an important rendezvous of Union soldiers in 1864.[244] The Enrolled Missouri Militia (EMM) that had been raised in Franklin County aided in operations against Price in October, 1864.[245]

Thomas B. Jackson enlisted at Washington, Missouri, on October 1, 1864, as a private in Captain Gildehaus' Company M of the 54th Regiment of the EMM. The company was ordered into active service immediately.[246]

Price sent a Confederate force to Franklin (today, Pacific) who successfully burned the railroad bridges over the Meramec River and at Gray Summit. Colonel Gale in command of Union forces at Washington evacuated his 600 troops across the Missouri River in stern wheelers. Munitions were taken by boat to St. Charles to avoid being commandeered by Price. Many Washington citizens also sought refuge across the Missouri River on October 3, when Price's army burned railroad property and occupied Washington for half-a-day. His Confederate troops "confiscated livestock, food and any valuables they could find.... By October 5 the EMM had returned and Price's forces had left the county."[247]

In less than a week the amount of property destroyed, including horses and mules driven away, amounted to a conservative estimate of $500,000 (in 1864 dollars). Although never definitely ascertained, it was estimated that about 60 Franklin Countians died at the hands of Price's men.[248]

The following month, they were relieved from duty by Colonel Daniel Q. Gale on November 15.[249]

1865 [Arthur turned 9 in March]:

The Emancipation Proclamation was effective, January 1, 1863. President Abraham Lincoln, however, "did not have Commander-in-Chief authority over the four slave-holding states that had not declared a secession: Missouri, Kentucky, Maryland and Delaware."[250]

Slaves in Missouri were emancipated two years later on January 11, 1865, by an ordinance of immediate emancipation. This made Missouri the first slave state to emancipate its slaves before the adoption of the 13th Amendment to the U.S. Constitution in April 1865.[251]

Imagine this momentous six-month period and how it played out for the 11 slaves of Lucinda Jackson. The soonest enumeration that would include African Americans in Franklin County after emancipation would be in the 1868 Missouri State Census. Of course, many had dispersed by then.

Arthur Jackson was about 8 years, 10-months-old in January 1865, when slaves in Missouri were officially emancipated. Judging from the most accurate or realistic birth date, he turned 9-years-old on March 4, 1865.

There is a strong probability that he continued to live in a family unit with at least his mother, and possibly siblings (and/or half siblings) with their former mistress, Lucinda Jackson, and family.

Sometime in 1865, Dr. John Wesley Jackson, returned to his medical practice at Labadie and Washington, Missouri.[252]

Notes on Post Civil War Reconstruction

Once African American citizens—after twelve generations of enslavement—were emancipated, their freedom "did not occur instantaneously.... Rather, freedom unfolded over time and space and was informed as much as memories of the past as by expectations and visions for the future...only the formal institution of slavery died in 1865."[253]

"The Civil War drastically altered black life in America. Former slaves were thrust into a fundamentally new social, political, and economic situation."[254] Freedmen and women set out on their own, for the most part. They had little or no money; few possessions other than the clothes on their backs; and, no formal education.

In fact, a statute was passed in Missouri in 1847, "which provided that 'no person shall keep or teach any school for the instruction of any negroes or mulattoes, in reading or writing in this State' under a penalty of $500 or not more than six months' imprisonment or both."[255] Southern states had harsher, more long-standing laws of these kinds. The result was a vast population of Americans who were illiterate. Arthur Jackson was among them.

He never learned to read or write, judging from his responses to the U.S. Census enumerators between 1880-1930.[256]

Still, former slaves strived to establish independent lives and communities that included but also transcended those long-held ties of kinship. This resulted in massive movements and exoduses of black populations seeking workable and respectable places to call home.

"At war's end, slaves became free but essentially homeless and landless"[257] and some without family or friend.

"The first consideration was food and clothing, and it frequently happened by the time these were secured there was neither time nor money for schooling. And yet many of them...managed to equip themselves for the work of life, because they were prompted by a spirit of service to the race to make the necessary sacrifices."[258]

For the next decade, all Americans worked through the era known as Reconstruction (1866-1877). For African- Americans, they had a, "small window of opportunity to define the meaning of their new freedom, but always in the context of the political uncertainties that continued to prevail between the North and the South."[259] "At no time during this period did African Americans have any power to formulate or affect the decisions about their fate at the national level."[260] Then, the clock began turning back.

At the heart of the American dream is life, liberty and the pursuit of land. And, "had any serious consideration been given to freedmen and their desire for land, which they knew how to manage and cultivate, the lives of African American families would be entirely different today."[261] Rather, a system of labor contracts (many professed by the Freedmen's Bureau under the War Department) continued the mechanism of dependency whereby the most common way for an African American to make money after the Civil War was to sell one's labor. Affordable, tillable land was hard to come by, and harder yet for an African American to secure.

Many resorted to sharecropping and tenant farming. Many other "former slaves migrated to the cities. . . "on a wing and a prayer" . . . hoping for better lives for themselves and their families."[262]

Reparations? "The only compensation for slavery was paid to loyal slave owners in the border states of Maryland, Missouri and Kentucky as well as those who owned slaves in the District of Columbia."[263]

"Slavery died hard in Missouri, and the slave code mentality lived on for many years after the Civil War."[264]

Trying to think logically about these next few years in Arthur's lifeline, I asked myself, "What would a newly freed slave do first, second, next, and so on?"

They were first required to legally marry, as they had not been allowed previously. Throughout Missouri, there (hopefully) remain in County Recorder of Deeds offices, separate marriage books for African Americans starting in 1865. Some counties integrated "colored" marriages within existing registers, noting the racial differences. Franklin County's "Marriage Record, Book A, Colored, 1866-1875," includes four African Americans with the Jackson surname. There were none for the Pryor/Prior surname.[265]

Many slaves might have sought to reunite with lost kin separated by slave sales.[266] "Often former slaves traveled the South searching for their lost relatives."[267] But, in the case of this Jackson family, it appears that the slave family unit remained fairly nuclear (that is, in tact) while enslaved.

Arthur, at 9-years-old, likely continued to live with his natural mother until he reached young adulthood. It is also probable that they "stayed-on" as "retainers" with members of the Lucinda Jackson family in the early years of Reconstruction.

The next few years focus on the exact whereabouts of Lucinda and her children in order to place Arthur as well.

There remains a 7-year gap in Arthur's exact whereabouts between emancipation in 1865 and 1872, when his half sister was married; and, another gap from 1872 and 1880, when Arthur appeared in the U.S. Census with Richard L. Jackson, Jr., his young family, and Richard's mother, Lucinda Jackson.

Between September 1865 and January 1866, John W. Jackson purchased 74 acres of land from William L. and Nancy Jane Pursley and/or Charles W. and Adelin Blunt, in the **East ½ of the Northeast ¼ of Section 31, Township 44, Range 2 East**, Franklin County, Missouri. By 1878, John owned 95.13 acres in that quarter section, as pictured at the right from the Franklin County atlas printed in that year.[268]

The middle map shows John's widow, Virginia C. Jackson, owning 100-acres in the 1898 Atlas, which then also included 80 adjacent acres to the northwest in Section 29, and 80 acres to the east in Section 32.

The bottom map shows Joe Winnisdoerfer and W. Reppeto owning Mrs. Jackson's former acreage the three adjoining sections, as identified in the county's 1930 Plat Book.

This property is ¼ mile south and ½ mile east of Labadie, Missouri, city limits.

The 1961 Franklin County plat map shows T. G. McLaughlin [sic.] owning what had been assigned to Joe Winnisdoerfer in 1930.

Thomas MacLaughlin's wife, Virginia (Jackson) MacLaughlin, was the daughter of Dr. Jabez Jackson and granddaughter of John W. and Virginia (North) Jackson.

1866 [Arthur turned 10 in March]:

Dr. John Wesley Jackson again located in St. Louis; but, only for a year. He returned to Labadie, Missouri, in 1867.[269]

1867 [Arthur turned 11 in March]:

Lucinda filed the second settlement of her husband's estate on June 4, 1867:

Balance on settlement as of December 1865:	$385.87
Interest, 12 months	$34.73
Subtotal	$420.60
To witness of November 1863	-$1.00
Balance	$419.60[270]

Dr. John Wesley Jackson married on October 10, 1867, to Virginia Carter "Jennie" North, daughter of Flavius J. and Frances C. North, well-known settlers of Franklin County. Flavius was the son of Franklin County pioneer, James North, whose home remains a private residence to this day (2015).[271]

1868 [Arthur turned 12 in March]:

In January 1868, Thomas B. Jackson purchased 80 acres of land from J. Barton and Ruth Gamble in Section 14, Township 43, Range 1 East, Boles Township, Franklin County, Missouri.[272]

Dr. James Polk Jackson was graduated from the St. Louis Medical College in 1868 (his brother, John, graduated there in 1863), after having studied for one year in the collegiate department of the University of Michigan; this might explain his absence from his Franklin County family.[273]

Lucinda Jackson filed the third settlement of Richard L. Jackson's estate on June 8, 1868:

Balance on settlement as of December 1865:	$419.60
Interest, 18 months	$25.17
Subtotal	$444.77
Settlement cost	-$1.00
Balance	$443.77[274]

When the 1868 Missouri State Census was taken, both Lucinda Jackson and her son, Thomas B. Jackson, headed households elsewhere in Boles Township, Township 43, Range 1E.

John W. Jackson was not found to be listed. Several original pages of tabulations from the state mandated census of Franklin County have been determined to be missing and presumed lost. However, Township 44, Range 2E, where John owned property, is believed to have survived and is indexed.[275]

Other family members living with Lucinda and Thomas as heads of households were only identified by gender and age range. The author has provided a likely "match" for them [in brackets] in the table below.

One hypothesis for the added family members is that, perhaps, George W. and Virginia (Jackson) Thomas, and family, may have been living with Lucinda at this time.

The "colored" members of the household were very likely former African American servants who, at least for a time, continued to live with their former masters.

1868 Missouri State Census, Franklin, Co., Mo.
Lucinda Jackson and son, Thomas B. Jackson
and 10 'free colored' persons (former slaves)
Township 43, Range 1 East
(See also chart below "1868 and 1870 Age Projections African Americans")

ENUMERATION   LIKELY MATCH

L[ucinda] E[dwards] Jackson

ENUMERATION	LIKELY MATCH
2 white males up to 10 years	1. s/o George/Virginia Thomas
	2. Matthew Thomas [about 11]
2 white males 21 to 45 years	1. Richard L., Jr. [about 25]
	2. George Thomas [about 38]
1 white female 10 to 18 years	1. Anna Thomas [about 13]
2 white females 21 to 45 years	1. Lucy [about 28]
	2. Virginia Thomas [about 33]
1 white female over 45 years	1. Lucinda E. [about 58]
2 colored males 0 to 10 years	**[Arthur was 12]**
1 colored female 0 to 10 years	**[Arthur's half sister was apx. 13]**
1 colored female 21 to 45 years	**[Arthur's mother was apx. 27]**

T[homas] B. Jackson

ENUMERATION	LIKELY MATCH
3 white males 21 to 45 years	1. Thomas B. [b.ca. 1842]
	2. Male; same age bracket as Thomas
	3. Male; same age bracket as Thomas
no white females	
3 colored males 0 to 10 years	
2 colored males 21 to 45 years	
1 colored female 21 to 45 years	

1869 [Arthur turned 13 in March]:

By March 26, 1869, Dr. James P. Jackson established himself as the first physician to settle in Bigelow, Holt County, Missouri.[276] He also opened the first drug store.[277]

On September 9, 1869, Lucinda Jackson filed the fourth and **final settlement** in the estate of her husband:

Balance on settlement as of June 1868:	$ 443.77
Interest, 1 year, 3 months	$ 33.28
Cash on Inventory	$ 30.00
Interest, 5 years, 10 months	$ 10.50
Sale Bill	$ 677.75
Interest, 2 years, 8 months	$ 108.46
Subtotal	$1,303.76
Credits	-$ 830.31
Balance	$ 473.45[278]

The *Franklin County Observer* published the final settlement on November 19, 1869.[279] After six years, the estate of Richard L. Jackson, Sr., was finally settled on December 10, 1869.

Balance on settlement as of September	$ 473.74
Interest, 3 months	$ 7.10
Subtotal	$ 480.55
Credits	-$ 285.21
Balance	$ 195.34[280]

On December 20, 1869, James P. Jackson purchased 40 acres of land in Meramec Township, Franklin County, Missouri.[281]

1870 [Arthur turned 14 in March]:

1870 was the first year that African Americans, as free citizens, were enumerated individually by name, age, gender, race, and birthplace in the U.S. Census.[282] Prior to 1870, they were, as slaves, listed individually without a name; but, by approximate age,[283] gender and skin tone, or complexion (i.e., perceived race).

Furthermore, "many times in 1870, former slaves lived near, or with their former owners."[284]

Below are the approximate ages of the former African American slaves of Richard and Lucinda Jackson, as they *might they have been listed* in the 1868 Missouri State Census and/or the 1870 U.S. Census. One, possibly two elders disappeared from the roster between 1850 and 1860. Original 1850 'family unit' underlined:

1868 and 1870
Age Projections of African Americans,
Former Slaves,
of Richard L. and Lucinda Jackson, Sr.

Census Statistics 1850	1860			Age Projections 1868	1870
40 b m	X				
20 m f	X (could be 40-year-old below)				(Arthur's grandmother?)
	40 [b.ca. 1820]	black	female	48	50 (Arthur's grandmother?)
5 m f	19 [b.ca. 1841]	mulatto	female	27	29 (Arthur's mother?)
	16 [b.ca. 1844]	black	male	24	26
3 b m	14 [b.ca. 1846]	black	male	22	24 (Arthur's uncle?)
	13 [b.ca. 1847]	mulatto	male	21	23
	13 [b.ca. 1847]	black	female	21	23
2 b f	12 [b.ca. 1848]	black	female	20	22 (Arthur's aunt?)
	12 [b.ca. 1848]	black	male	20	22
	8 [b.ca. 1852]	mulatto	female	16	18 (Arthur's half sister)
	7 [b.ca. 1853]	black	male	15	17
	4 [b.ca. 1856]	mulatto	male	12	14 (Arthur Jackson)
	1 [b.ca. 1859]	black	female	8	10
				5 children under 10 born since 1860 (apx.)	

Franklin County U.S. Census Statistics

1860		1870
16,465	whites	27,925
1,601	slaves	
19	free 'colored'	2,173
18,085	TOTAL	30,098[285]

140

Lucinda's two youngest sons had moved across the state to the western edge of Missouri and were enumerated in the 1870 U.S. Census for Benton Township, Holt County, Missouri:

Name	Race	Gender	Age	Occupation	Birthplace
Jackson, Richard L. [Jr.]	White	Male	28	druggist	Virginia
Jackson, James P.	White	Male	26	physician	Virginia

Both were living in the dwelling of a female saloon keeper, Mrs. Olive Bridgeman. With them was another physician, Marcus Rhoades.

Richard L. Jackson, Jr., claimed to own $700 in real estate and $2,000 in personal property. A newspaper article published years later looked back to November 12, 1870, stating that "at that time, R. L. Jackson and P. Hoover each conducted hotels at Bigelow."[286]

His brother, James P. Jackson, owned $1,500 in real estate and $2,500 in personal property. Compared with neighbors' enumerations, the inflated figures *may* have some connection to their father's estate having been recently settled.

The 1870 U.S. Census would provide critical information about the Jackson and Thomas family members. Only Richard L. and James P. (above) have yet been found.

A 130-page-by-page search in Boles Township, Franklin County, Missouri, was also made for Arthur Jackson, Lucinda Jackson, or her children: Virginia "Jennie" (Jackson) Thomas; Dr. John Wesley Jackson; Lucy Christina Jackson; and, Thomas B. Jackson.

Also, since Dr. James P. Jackson had purchased 40 acres in Meramec Township in Franklin County, those pages were also searched sequentially.

In both attempts, these Jackson/Thomas family members were not found to be enumerated *in Franklin County, Missouri.*

141

1871 [Arthur turned 15 in March]:

For a time Dr. James P. Jackson was in partnership with Dr. Marcus M. Rhoades, in the firm, "Jackson and Rhoades," in Holt County, Missouri.[287]

In May 1871, Dr. Jackson was also documented as one of the incorporators of Bigelow, Holt County, Missouri.[288]

1872 [Arthur turned 16 in March]:

Arthur's half sister, an African American named Miss Mary "Mollie" Jackson Pryor/Prior, married Thomas Sharp in Falls City, Richardson County, Nebraska, on October 10, 1872.[289] Their marriage license claimed she was 18-years-old.[290] Thomas Sharp was born in 1837, in Louisville, Kentucky, and had served in the United States Colored Troops during the Civil War (Capt. James L. Sherman's Company G, 68th U.S. Colored Volunteer Infantry).[291] Their marriage license claimed he was 31-years-old in 1872.[292]

This is the first instance with a definite connection to Arthur since emancipation. For the next thirty years, Arthur and his half sister, Mary "Mollie" Jackson (Pryor/Prior) Sharp, would live in the tri-state area of Doniphan County, Kansas; Richardson County, Nebraska; and, Holt County, Missouri.

Richard Ludlow Jackson, Jr., married Laura E. Johnson on January 28, 1872, in Des Moines, Polk County, Iowa.

Brothers Dr. John Wesley Jackson and Dr. James Polk Jackson entered the College of Physicians and Surgeons in New York, New York, in 1872. John gave his residence as Labadie, Missouri. It is not known if Mrs. John Jackson resided in New York with her husband, remained at their home, or lived with her parents in Franklin County during his absence. James enrolled in the College of Physicians and Surgeons with a home residence of Bigelow, Franklin County, Missouri.[293]

George W. Thomas, divorced from his first wife, re-married at age 39 to Eliza C. Dangerfield, 24, in Kanawha County, West Virginia, November 20, 1872.[294] George's teenage children by his first wife, Virginia Catherine (Jackson) Thomas, appear to have continued to live with other relatives.

1873 [Arthur turned 17 in March]:

In February 1873, Dr. John Wesley Jackson and Dr. James Polk Jackson requested and early examination from the College of Physicians and Surgeons faculty. James, whose thesis was on Malignant Remittent Fever, noted he had urgent business in Missouri, and John, whose thesis was on Post-partum Hemorrhage, claimed to have been "indisposed." Both requests were granted, and the College trustees awarded their diplomas under "special circumstances," which in their case, appears to be that they had already earned MDs from Saint Louis Medical College.[295]

Following his graduation from the College of Physicians and Surgeons in New York, Dr. John Wesley Jackson was appointed chief surgeon of the Missouri Pacific Railroad, and established a railway hospital, the first in the United States, at Washington, Missouri.[296]

In July, Dr. James Polk Jackson, along with Charles S. Armstrong and Robert Gillis, purchased the drug store (and Post Office) of L. Sloan in Bigelow Township, Holt County, Missouri.[297] Jackson sold his interest in the business in 1875, and it is believed practiced medicine in and around Mound City, Missouri, until 1877.

Arthur's half sister, Miss Mary "Mollie" Jackson (Pryor/Prior) Sharp, had a child, Catherine A. "Kate" Sharp. Kate's death certificate, tombstone, and her father's veteran's pension file verify she was born July 21, 1873. When her mother died in 1902, Kate was living in Oregon, Holt County, Missouri. She died in 1941 and is buried with her family in Maple Grove Cemetery.[298]

On October 1, 1873, Virginia Catherine (Jackson) Thomas died and was buried in Baldwin Cemetery at Mound City, Holt County, Missouri.[299]

1874 [Arthur turned 18 in March]:

In April, Richard Ludlow Jackson, Jr., "retired from the Star Hotel at Bigelow," Holt County, Mo. Isaac B. Currier took charge of the hotel.[300]

Dr. and Mrs. John Wesley Jackson located in Washington, Franklin County, Missouri, in 1874, and were there at least through 1878 where they had, "on the banks of the Missouri a beautiful and cultured home."[301]

1875 [Arthur turned 19 in March]:

On February 1, 1875, Richard Ludlow Jackson, Jr., received from the Holt County Court $25 for the "support of a pauper."[302]

Later in the year, Richard and family, along with his 65-year-old mother, Lucinda Jackson; sister, Lucy Jackson; and, niece, Annie Thomas, were enumerated in the 1875 Kansas State Census in Doniphan County.[303] Jackson, listed as a "hotel keeper," worked for the hotel owner, Ohio native, R. W. Frome.

Arthur Jackson was not located in the 1875 Kansas State Census enumeration.

His half sister, Mary "Mollie" Jackson (Pryor/Prior) Sharp gave birth to a son, William Henry Sharp, on January 25, 1875, in Craig, Holt County, Missouri.[304] When his mother died in 1902, Henry was living in Forest City, Holt County, Missouri. Henry died in 1935 and is buried near his parents and siblings in Maple Grove Cemetery, Oregon, Holt County, Missouri.[305]

Also in Holt County, Missouri, James P. Jackson sold his drugstore (the first in Bigelow) to C. S. Armstrong in 1875.[306] These men would, in 1879, become brothers-in-law, when James' sister, Lucy Christina Jackson, married Charles Swanson Armstrong.

1876 [Arthur turned 20 in March]:

Dr. and Mrs. John Wesley Jackson, sons Jabez[307] and Walter;[308] and, John's sister, Lucy Jackson, were enumerated in the 1876 State Census in Franklin County, Missouri.[309] A black woman named Lucy Irwin was also in the household.

In Holt County, Missouri, the 1876 State Census[310] enumerated:

Name	Age	Page/Location
Jackson, Thomas B.	21-45	237/Township 61[311]
, Mary	21-45	
Jackson, Richard [Jr.]	21-45	232/Bigelow[312]
, Laura	21-45	
, Maud	under 10	

145

Neither Arthur Jackson nor Lucinda or James P. Jackson were located in the 1876 Franklin or Holt County State Census.[313]

1877 [Arthur turned 21 in March]:

Arthur's half sister, Mary "Mollie" Jackson (Pryor/Prior) Sharp, had a daughter, Hattie, born in Craig, Holt County, Missouri, on January 18, 1877; she died about April 1880.[314]

Dr. James P. Jackson, also in Holt County, had some news of his own:[315]

> —Dr. ████████ of Mound City, intends to remove to St. Louis about the first of September, and is now disposing of his property in Holt county. He has sold his residence to M. B. Moore, and the Central Hotel, in Mound City, to Daniel Stanley, of Hiawatha Kansas.

1878 [Arthur turned 22 in March]:

In 1878, Dr. James Polk Jackson assisted in the establishment at Washington, Missouri, the first hospital department of the Missouri Pacific Railroad. His brother, Dr. John Wesley Jackson, was the hospital's chief surgeon.[316] They continued at this location until 1884.

A historical atlas of Franklin County was published in 1878 that included biographies and detailed landholdings (John W. Jackson's farm was previously detailed in this work).

Land that Thomas B. Jackson had purchased in Boles Township—Section 14, Township 43, Range 1 East—in January 1868 was liquidated by the time the 1878 Atlas was created.

146

And, land in Meramec Township—Section 34, Township 41, Range 2 West—that James P. Jackson had purchased in December 1869 was already assigned to different owners by 1878.

1879 [Arthur turned 23 in March]:

Arthur's half sister, Mary "Mollie" Jackson (Pryor/Prior) Sharp, "became a member of the A. M. E. church at White Cloud," Doniphan County, Kansas, in 1879.[317]

In 1879, Dr. James P. Jackson established a hospital at Garnett, Kansas, for the Lexington Branch Railway, and the road between Paola and Wichita, and was in charge of it for two years.[318]

Lucinda's daughter, Lucy Christina Jackson, married Charles Swanson Armstrong in Franklin County on April 23, 1879. *Lucinda would definitely have been present on this important date; though she may not have lived there at that time.*

1880 [Arthur turned 24 in March]:

"Dr. J. W. Jackson, Washington, Mo., on May 25, 1880, lost a wrist band, gold plated, and offer suitable reward for its delivery at the central drugstore."[319]

Richard Ludlow Jackson, Jr., farmer, and family, along with his 68-year-old mother, Lucinda Jackson, were enumerated in the June 11, 1880, U.S. Census in Bigelow Township, Holt County, Missouri.

1880 Census, Bigelow Township, Holt Co., Mo.
Richard L., Jr., Laura, Lucinda, and Arthur Jackson and Matthew Thomas

Name	Race	Gender	Age	Relationship	Birthplace
Jackson, Richard L.	White	Male	35	head of household	Virginia
Jackson, Laura	White	Female	23	wife	Ohio
Jackson, **Edgar**	White	Male	1	son	Missouri
Jackson, Lucinda	White	Female	68	mother	Virginia
Jackson, Arthur	Black	Male	21	hired farm laborer	Virginia
Thomas, Matthew	White	Male	23	nephew	Virginia

147

This is the benchmark document that connected the author's great great grandfather, Arthur Jackson, to his slaveholding family, Mr. and Mrs. Richard Ludlow Jackson, Sr., and Lucinda Edwards (Deatley) Jackson.

Arthur reported being a 21-year-old black farm laborer, having been born in Virginia about 1859, and whose mother and father were Virginians.

This study presumes that Arthur's first appearance in 1860 as a 4-year-old slave of Richard L. and Lucinda Jackson places his birth date to 1856.[320] Therefore, he may more likely have been 24 in 1880. (See Appendix A for *Arthur Jackson's Age, Race, and Literacy in Historical Documents*.)

Another historical connection concluded only recently after connecting Arthur with his half sister, Mary "Mollie" Jackson (Pryor/Prior) Sharp, was that she and her young family lived in the household next to Arthur and "their white family:"

1880 Census, Bigelow Township, Holt Co., Mo.
Thomas and Mary "Mollie" Jackson (Pryor/Prior) Sharp

Name	Race	Gender	Age	Occupation	Birthplace
Sharp, Thomas	black	male	40	farm laborer	Kentucky
Sharp, Mary	black	female	25	wife	Virginia
Sharp, **Catherine A.**	black	female	6	daughter	Missouri
Sharp, **William H.**	black	male	5	son	Missouri

Interestingly, the patriarch of the Jackson family, Richard Ludlow Jackson Sr., was a descendant of **William** H. and **Catherine** (Ludlow) Jackson. The naming convention used by

Thomas and Mary Sharp for their first two children may be a coincidence. But, perhaps, Mary "Mollie" Jackson (Pryor/Prior) Sharp's mother (i.e. Arthur Jackson's mother) *may* have descended from a slave of William and Catherine (Ludlow) Jackson, in Fredericksburg, Spotsylvania County, Virginia. Thomas Sharp's parents, by the way, were Samuel and Mary (Owen) Sharp.

As before stated, if Mary "Mollie" was born May 1, 1855, and Arthur was born March 11, 1856 (apparently by two different fathers: one possibly named Pryor/Prior, and one named Jackson), this would mean that at least these two slave children migrated as infants from Kanawha County, Virginia, to Franklin County, Missouri, in 1859 with the Richard L. and Lucinda Jackson family. Arthur and Mary "Mollie's" mother, perhaps still nursing, also migrated to Franklin County, Missouri.

1881 [Arthur turned 25 in March]:

Arthur's half sister, Mary "Mollie" Jackson (Pryor/Prior) Sharp, had a son, James Arthur Sharp, born in Craig, Holt County, Missouri, on February 11, 1881. When his mother died in 1902, James was living in Forest City, Holt County, Missouri; he is buried near his parents and siblings in Maple Grove Cemetery, Oregon, Holt County, Missouri.[321]

In 1881, Dr. John Wesley Jackson established his official headquarters at Sedalia, pictured below, where his work continued.[322]

1882 [Arthur turned 26 in March]:

Dr. John W. Jackson was listed as an officer of the Medical Department of the University of Kansas City in 1882. He became its President in 1886 and served until his death in 1890.[323]

Dr. James Polk Jackson located in Kansas City by 1882, to become professor of surgery in the Medical Department of the University of Kansas City from 1882 to 1889 when he became Dean, and continued this position for its successor, the University Medical College, until 1896.[324]

University Medical College and Hospital
Corner of 19th Street and Campbell, Kansas City, Missouri
Postcard courtesy Kansas City Public Library

1883 [Arthur turned 27 in March]:

Between 1880 and 1883, Arthur may likely have continued to live with Richard Ludlow Jackson, Jr., and family. Sometime in 1883, Richard Jackson and family migrated to Camp Crook, Dakota Territory (later Harding County, South Dakota).[325]

150

"In 1883 a number of Iowa Native Americans moved to Indian Territory preferring to live in the older community village way of life…. However, despite their efforts to block allotment, their lands were divided anyway. Today the Iowa Reservation in Nebraska and Kansas is approximately 2,100 acres (8.5 km^2) in size, and has more than 150 residents."[326]

The Iowa Reservation of the Iowa Tribe of Kansas and Nebraska straddles the borders of each of the counties where Arthur and his family would later reside: southeast Richardson County, Nebraska, northwestern Doniphan County, Kansas, and northern Brown County, Kansas. Tribal headquarters are west of White Cloud, Kansas."[327]

1884 [Arthur turned 28 in March]:

Arthur Jackson is recorded in the family Bible as having married Melissa E. Anderson in Holt County, Missouri, on October 25, 1884. No marriage record has been located. If they were considered an inter-racial couple they would not have been legally allowed to marry.

In 1884, Dr. John Wesley Jackson transferred his headquarters as surgeon for the Missouri Pacific Railroad, to Kansas City, Missouri.[328] His son, Jabez Jackson, at age 15, with a class of 17 graduated under Professor Holloway at Sedalia, Missouri, in June. In September, Jabez entered Washington University in St. Louis, "to take a classical course" in medicine.[329]

Jabez North Jackson

1885 [Arthur turned 29 in March]:

Arthur was not located in the Kansas State Census. One Arthur Jackson appeared as a waiter in the 1885 State Census for Omaha, Douglas County, Nebraska. A wife was not recorded; this may or may not be the subject of this biographical sketch.

In 1885, Dr. John Wesley Jackson resigned his position with the Missouri Pacific Railroad and accepted the position of chief surgeon of the Wabash Railroad system.[330]

1886 [Arthur turned 30 in March]:

Dr. John W. Jackson built a fine home on the northeast corner of 15th and Broadway in downtown Kansas City. Dr. Jackson died in the home in 1890; but, the Jackson family remained in this home until 1906-1907 when they moved elsewhere in the city. They continued to rent the home, and by June 1932, Dr. Jabez North Jackson leased the land to the Atlantic, Pacific and Gulf Oil Company for, "a large filling and motor car service station."[331]

Today (2015), this corner has been obliterated by the west-bout 70 Highway off-ramp that runs beneath Bartle Hall Convention Center.

1887 [Arthur turned 31 in March]:

Arthur was mentioned in the "White Cloud" column of the *Weekly Kansas Chief* newspaper, previously transcribed in this biography. At that time, he and his first wife, Melissa, lived on the Giles A. Briggs farm. Melissa was stricken with paralysis, and Arthur was *"working upon the "dump" at Mission Creek"* for an unnamed railroad.

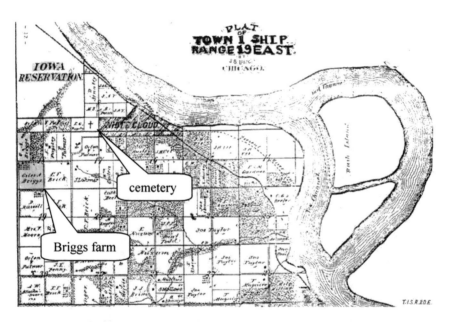

Giles A. Briggs farm where Arthur and Melissa Jackson lived is in the Southwest ¼ of Section 18, just south of the Iowa Reservation. Melissa may have been buried in the cemetery denoted with a Christian cross "†" just west of White Cloud. Giles Briggs (1816-1898) and Eliza (O'Banion) Briggs (1824-1898) are in the Olive Branch Cemetery. Doniphan County, Kansas, Atlas, 1878, by J. S. Birch, Chicago. Detailed here is Township 1 South, Range 19 East.

1888 [Arthur turned 32 in March]:

Arthur's first wife, Melissa E. (Anderson) Jackson, died on April 3, 1888, in White Cloud, Doniphan County, Kansas.

The family Bible shows that Arthur married Melissa's sister, Ida May Anderson, on September 18, 1888. As before, a marriage record has never been located. If they were considered to be an interracial couple, then they would have been forbidden to legally marry. The author's grandfather, Roy Jackson, always said that, *"Grandma wore a thick, gold wedding band as if to say, 'See, we're married.'"*

1889 [Arthur turned 33 in March]:

Arthur and Ida's first child was stillborn in White Cloud, Doniphan County, Kansas. They named her Mary E. Jackson, presumably named after Arthur's sister (maybe his mother, too?).

Meanwhile, Jabez North Jackson graduated with a Bachelor of Arts from Central College in Fayette, Howard County, Missouri. That fall he took up the study of medicine and attended University Medical College in Kansas City, Missouri.

1890 [Arthur turned 34 in March]:

Arthur was listed on the White Cloud, Doniphan County, Kansas, tax rolls.

Jabez North Jackson received a Master of Arts from Central College in Fayette, Missouri. And, he graduated with a prize of surgical instruments from the University Medical College.

Jabez's father, Dr. John Wesley Jackson, "while performing a charitable surgical operation was inoculated with blood poisoning and became ill" in January, 1890. The chief surgeon of the Wabash Railroad, and president of the North American Surgeons Association, died in Kansas City, Mo., March 13, 1890.[332]

John Wesley Jackson was revered among his colleagues in the health and medical field, and several Kansas city newspapers in the days between his death and burial printed tributes to him. He is buried in Elmwood Cemetery in Kansas City. (See Appendix B)

1891 [Arthur turned 35 in March]:

Arthur and Ida's second child, Edgar Walter Jackson, was born on September 1, 1891, in White Cloud, Doniphan County, Kansas.[333] On September 28, the *Weekly Kansas Chief,* published at Troy, Doniphan County, Kansas, included Arthur's name among the members of the White Cloud Republican Club.[334]

1892 [Arthur turned 36 in March]:

William Andrew Thomas, son of Virginia Catherine (Jackson) Thomas, of White Cloud, died in Kansas City, February 11, 1892, and was buried there in Elmwood Cemetery.[335]

1893

1894

1895 [Arthur turned 39 in March]:

Arthur and family were enumerated in the Doniphan County, Kansas, State Census. Arthur was identified as "black." In the next household are three grandchildren of Virginia Catherine (Jackson) Thomas, who were living with their mother, Cordelia "Delia" (Rowland) Thomas, who had re-married to Samuel V. Lear after their father, William Andrew Thomas, died in 1892.[336] Arthur continued to live near the Thomas-Lear family until 1902 to 1905.

1896 [Arthur turned 40 in March]:

Arthur and Ida's third child, Jabez Jackson, who throughout his life would go by "Davies, Javies, Javis, Jarvis, and Jack" Jackson, was born April 7, 1896, in White Cloud, Doniphan County, Kansas.[337]

1897 [Arthur turned 41 in March]:

Lucinda lived with her son, James Polk Jackson, on East 8th Street, in Kansas City, Jackson County, Missouri.[338]

1898 [Arthur turned 42 in March]:

Jabez North Jackson served in the Spanish-American War.[339]

**Dr. Jabez North Jackson
in military uniform and
regalia, courtesy
Sally Harris Wolfe**

1899 [Arthur turned 43 in March]:

Arthur and Ida's fourth child, Hazel Mae Jackson, was born May 21, 1899, in White Cloud, Doniphan County, Kansas.

Dr. Jabez Jackson was identified as a member of the Jackson County Medical Society (today, Metropolitan Medical Society). In the composite below, courtesy the Jackson County Historical Society Archives, J. N. Jackson is on the far right, fourth down.

1900 [Arthur turned 44 in March]:

Arthur and Ida Jackson and family appeared in the White Cloud, Doniphan County, Kansas, Census, on June 13, 1900. Arthur and Ida are both listed as "black," although Ida's race attribution is clearly a mistake; she is consistently listed as white with the exception of this one enumeration.

As in 1895, living near Arthur and Ida were Samuel V. and Cordelia "Delia" (Rowland) Thomas-Lear family, with her children from her previous marriage to William Andrew Thomas, grandchildren of Virginia Catherine (Jackson) Thomas.[340]

The matriarch of the Jackson family, Lucinda Jackson, was staying with her daughter, Lucy, in June 1900 when the U.S. Census taker visited the Armstrong home in Benton Township, Holt County, Missouri:

Name	Birth date	Birthplace
Armstrong, Charles	Dec. 1834	Pennsylvania
Armstrong, Lucy	Dec. 1839	Maryland
Jackson, Lucinda	Feb 1811	Virginia

Later that year, the Jackson family arranged to have their patriarch exhumed from his grave in Gray Summit, Franklin County, Missouri, where he had been laid to rest in 1863. Richard Ludlow Jackson, Sr., was transported to Elmwood Cemetery in Kansas City and reinterred on October 10, 1900.

Lucinda continued to live with her sons in Kansas City. Her association with her well-respected offspring ranked her among the elite in Kansas City society.

And, Lucinda was a "real daughter;" that is, a daughter of a Revolutionary War patriot, James Deatley (born in 1750 Richmond County, Virginia, and died in 1843 in Westmoreland County, Virginia). Lucinda joined the Elizabeth Benton Chapter of the National Society, Daughters of the American Revolution.[341]

Lucinda attended Troost Avenue Methodist Church.[342]

I wonder if Lucinda ever had a desire, or an opportunity, to meet-up again with any of her former "servants," including my great great grandfather, Arthur Jackson.[343]

She did reach-out in 1901 to reconnect with friends and relatives in her native state of Virginia:

> *The post master at our Court House a few days ago received a letter from Mrs. Lucinda E. Jackson, of Kansas City, also making inquiries as to her relatives in this county* [Spotsylvania] *and in Westmoreland. She moved to Missouri many years ago, is 91 years old and in good health. The letter of three pages is well and legibly written with her own band and without the use of glasses. She was Miss DeAtley, an aunt of Capt. James T. DeAtley, formerly of Fredericksburg.[344]*

Lucinda's grandson, Dr. Jabez North Jackson, became Secretary of the University Medical College in Kansas City in 1900, which he held for two years.[345]

1901 [Arthur turned 45 in March]:

Arthur and Ida's fifth child, Dollie Frances Jackson, was born December 8, 1901, in White Cloud, Doniphan County, Kansas.

Dr. James Polk Jackson died in Kansas City, Missouri.[346]

Dr. Jabez North Jackson, pictured at the right, graduated from the University Medical College in Kansas City in 1901. He also won a prize of medical instruments.[347]

1902 [Arthur turned 46 in March]:

In February 1902, Arthur Jackson's half sister, Mary "Mollie" Jackson (Pryor/Prior) Sharp, died in Forest City, Holt County, Missouri:

> ***Miss Mollie Pryor was born in Virginia, May 1, 1855,*** *and died at her home in Forest City, Mo., February 16, 1902, in the 47th year of her age. She was united in marriage at Falls City, Neb., October 10, 1875 [sic.], to Thomas Sharp. Four children were born to them, three of who, Mrs. Kate Hayes, of Oregon, and two sons, Henry and James, of Forest City, together with a husband, and* ***one brother, Arthur Jackson, of White Cloud, Kas., survive.*** *She became a member of the A. M. E. church at White Cloud, Kas., in 1879, and has lived a true, consistent Christian life to the time of her death. She had suffered long from cancer, and prayed that she might leave world of sorrow and suffering, and begged her relatives and friends to so live that they might meet her in Heaven. The remains were brought to Oregon and laid to rest in the cemetery here. The members of the bereaved family feel truly grateful to those friends for their help and sympathy in their hours of affliction and sorrow.[348]*

[Thomas Sharp, pictured at the right, died in 1928. Though it may never be known if Arthur was apprised of Thomas' death, it is safe to say that *if* the two families had kept even minimally in touch in the years following Mollie's death, that that relationship ceased in 1928. Thomas and Mollie's daughter, Mrs. William (Kate Sharp) Hayes, died in St. Joseph, Mo., in 1941. Kate's death certificate, completed by an adopted daughter, Allie (Hayes) Autry, listed "Mary Pryor," as Kate's mother.]

Between 1902 and 1905, Arthur and Ida Jackson and family moved from White Cloud, Doniphan County, Kansas, to Irving Township, Brown County, Kansas.

1903

1904

1905 [Arthur turned 49 in March]:

Arthur and Ida Jackson and family appeared in the Irving Township, Brown County, Kansas, State Census. Arthur and the children were listed as "mulatto;" Ida was "white."

Arthur and Ida's sixth child, Reginald Brewster Jackson, was born May 19, 1905, most likely at Hiawatha, Brown County, Kansas. Uncle Reg always insisted he was born in Rulo, Richardson County, Nebraska. His 1936 application for a Social Security number and World War II discharge papers both show Rulo.

1906 [Arthur turned 50 in March]:

At the time of her death at age 95 in November 1906, Lucinda Edwards (Deatley) Jackson was visiting her daughter in Mound City, Holt County, Missouri.

In attendance at her funeral and/or graveside services in Holt and Jackson Counties— beyond her immediate family and fellow DAR members— was most likely her former "servant," Arthur Jackson, and possibly other *extended* relatives from Mollie's family.

Dies at Ripe Old Age

Mrs. Lucinda Deatley Jackson peacefully breathed her last at 3:15 a.m. November 30th at the home of her daughter, Mrs. C. S. Armstrong. She was permitted to reach the unusual age of 95 years and 10 months, having been blessed with good health together with a happy, buoyant disposition.

She was born in February 1811, in Westmoreland County, Virginia, the vicinity of the birthplace of Gen. Washington and Gen. Robert E. Lee. She was married to Dr. R. L. Jackson, of Fredericksburg, Va., in 1828. To this union were born seven children, two of whom survive, Mrs. C. S. Armstrong of this city, and Mr. R. L. Jackson, of North Dakota. She leaves nine grandchildren, three great grandchildren, and one great great grandchild.

She united with the M. E. Church South in 1830 and lived a consistent member to the time of her death.

Her last conscious moments were spent in singing hymns and in repeating scripture.

Her funeral service was held at the home of Mr. and Mrs. Armstrong, by Rev. Gillies, of the Methodist church.

She was taken to Kansas City and funeral services were again were conducted by Rev. Henry Nelson Bullard, assisted by the pastor of the Troost Avenue Methodist Church.—Mound City News.[349]

Lucinda is buried next to her husband, Richard Ludlow Jackson, Sr., in the Jackson plot at Elmwood Cemetery, Kansas City, Missouri.

1908 [Arthur turned 52 in March]:

Arthur and Ida's seventh and last child, Oliver Wadsworth Jackson, was born October 3, 1908, in Hiawatha, Brown County, Kansas.

1909

1910 [Arthur turned 54 in March]:

Arthur and Ida Jackson and family were enumerated in the Irving Township, Brown County, Kansas, U.S. Census. Arthur was identified as a "mulatto." While Ida was "white," the children were also "mulatto."

1911

1912

1913 [Arthur turned 57 in March]:

After nearly 30 years living in Doniphan and Brown Counties in Kansas, Arthur and Ida Jackson and family moved to Kansas City, Jackson County, Missouri. Their first stop was in Harlem, Clay County, Missouri, an enclave on the north shore of the Missouri River just across from downtown Kansas City.[350]

There, they may have made connections with, or may have even migrated to Kansas City at the suggestion of Dr. Jabez North Jackson. Dr. Jackson might also have assisted his family's former servant in gaining advice on housing, education, and employment. Their prospects for either may have been limited, depending on whether the Arthur Jackson family would be perceived as a black, biracial, or white family.

Dr. Sherry Schirmer, Charles Coulter, and Dr. Gary Kremer each have researched and written extensively on Kansas City's African American cultural landscape.[351] "In 1890 there were 13,700 African Americans who called Kansas City home."[352] By

1910, Kansas City's black population had increased to 23,566, with a significant community that developed east of the Troost thoroughfare.[353] "The growth of Kansas City's black population was part of a larger story of African American migration from southern to Midwestern and northern states, and from rural to urban areas of Missouri."[354] And, as Kremer writes, "White Kansas Citians, much as their urban cousins across the state in St. Louis, responded to this influx of African Americans by restricting them from living in white residential neighborhoods."[355]

As you will see, Arthur Jackson and family appeared to have at least skirted the racial dividing lines that existed in Kansas City at that time, and ended up 'passing for white' . . . and eventually 'becoming white.'

1914 [Arthur turned 58 in March]:

The Jacksons lived at 319 East 47th Street, Kansas City, Mo., when Ida Jackson first enrolled son, Reginald "Reg", into E. C. White School (site of the Kansas City Public Library's Plaza Branch today, 2015). Reg—previously identified as "mulatto" on census returns when living in Kansas—was recorded by the Kansas City School District as being "white." His Caucasian mother personally registering her son likely played a factor. And, one may never know if, or what role, Dr. Jabez Jackson may have had in interactions such as these with his 'cousins.'

Ironically, in this year when the Jacksons were settling into their new life in "the big city," Dr. Harrison Anthony Trexler in 1914 published his doctoral thesis, *Slavery in Missouri*, the first, thorough study of the subject, expounding on W. O. Blake's *History of Slavery* and the Slave Trade published in 1860.

It is also in this moment in time when Arthur Jackson's historically biracial family began to integrate—or pass for—a Caucasian family . . . with one exception. Likely, Arthur, as a black man, faced prejudice and discrimination in his daily life.

"Racial obstacles facing African Americans in Kansas City have been frequently documented. Black customers were not allowed to try on clothes in most downtown stores. Seating in most

of the major theaters downtown was on a segregated basis.....
Although they were not subjected to segregated seating in public
transportation, African American patrons were frequently abused
by drivers and white passengers alike."[356] Other areas where
segregation existed in Kansas City at this time include:

* *Education/schools.* Black and white students were not
  allowed to be educated in the same classroom, or school.
  Black teachers were not allowed to teach white students.

* *Church/religion.* While definitely segregated, Arthur and
  Ida were not known to have attended any church.

* *Recreation/amusement.* From juke joints to parks and
  movie houses and theaters, blacks and whites typically had
  segregated facilities. For instance, on January 15, 1952, a
  young attorney and future Supreme Court Justice,
  Thurgood Marshall, represented the Kansas City plaintiffs
  suing to integrate the all white Swope Park swimming pool.
  Prior to that, if a black child entered an all-white, public
  swimming pool, the child would be whisked away and the
  entire pool drained and re-filled.[357]

* *Medical/health.* It was through
  the initiative and effort of Dr.
  Jabez North Jackson, a
  grandson of Arthur's former
  slaveholders, Richard Ludlow
  and Lucinda Edwards (Deatley)
  Jackson, Sr., "that a staff of
  Negro physicians to carry on
  work among members of their
  own race was created. Now, as
  a result of his efforts, the
  Negroes of Kansas City have
  their own modern hospital
  facilities and personnel."[358]

**Dr. Jabez North
Jackson, courtesy
Sally Harris Wolfe**

* *Housing/residential settlement.* Before the Civil Rights and Equal Housing acts of the 1960s, blacks in Kansas City were confined to certain, selected pockets with invisible, but clearly understood neighborhood boundaries.

For decades—generations—blacks in Kansas City had lived in older and less desirable locations, and oftentimes in inferior housing stock. "The challenge to find decent, livable housing was the most daunting [challenge] African Americans faced in Kansas City in the 1920s."[359] Frequently, "restrictive covenants" denied "Negroes" (and Jews) from purchasing property in many inner city areas, and most suburban neighborhoods. *If* Arthur was identified as black at this time, he and his family may have only been allowed to live in selected areas in Kansas City. However, it is possible that either his white wife, Ida, their older "white" children, or even Dr. Jabez Jackson might have been involved in arranging their living quarters;

* *Employment.* Author Charles Coulter wrote, "The city possessed a thriving black professional class, and black workers held semiskilled positions a smattering of industries (primarily the packing houses and related industries)."[360]

Coulter, continued, "Kansas City's African American communities contained a significant population of janitors and domestic workers...who remained at the bottom of the job ladder."[361] But, African American workers were not allowed to join major unions, which was the "main obstacle to black employment in some categories of work.... The list of organized occupations that...excluded African Americans was long."[362] Coulter's book, *Take Up the Black Man's Burden,* is a detailed and thorough study of all of the aforementioned issues as they existed in Kansas City from 1865-1939.

319 East 47th Street (between McGee and Oak Streets) where the Arthur Jackson family lived in a rented house the first four years after their arrival in Kansas City, no longer stands.[363] In fact, none of the Kansas City houses or apartment buildings where they lived between 1914-1931 have survived.

William Rockhill Nelson, founder of the *Kansas City Star* newspaper, and his family lived in an impressive home on 20-acres, *Oak Hall*, catty-corner to northeast of the lot where the Jacksons resided between 1914 and 1918. Nelson died in 1914 at the age of 74. When the last Nelson heir died in 1927, Nelson's Will provided for *Oak Hall* to be razed for a museum of art. Through Nelson and Mary Atkins families' bequests, the Nelson-Atkins Museum of Art was constructed.[364] Groundbreaking for the art museum was June 16, 1930. Arthur lived blocks away and likely saw the museum's early phases.

Foundations of Kansas City's famous Country Club Plaza shopping district two blocks west of 319 East 47th began in 1907—seven years before the Jacksons settled in the area— and "opened in 1923

to immediate success."[365] The stretch where 319 East 47th once stood was changed to "Brush Creek Boulevard," and is today (2015) called "Emmanuel Cleaver II Boulevard." Three condominium/apartment buildings (like "Whitehall" pictured above) dominate the block at this location between McGee and Oak Streets.[366]

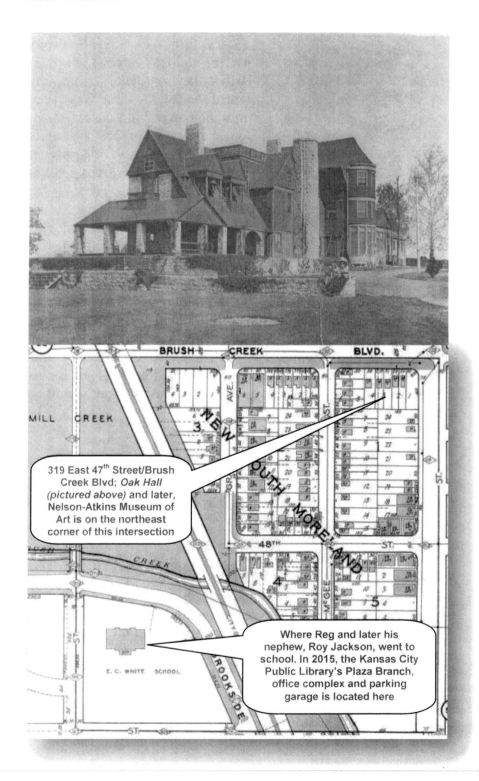

319 East 47th Street/Brush Creek Blvd; *Oak Hall (pictured above)* and later, Nelson-Atkins Museum of Art is on the northeast corner of this intersection

Where Reg and later his nephew, Roy Jackson, went to school. In 2015, the Kansas City Public Library's Plaza Branch, office complex and parking garage is located here

1915 [Arthur turned 59 in March]:

The Jacksons lived at 319 East 47th Street, Kansas City, Mo., when the Kansas City city directory census data was collected. It is the first directory in which Arthur is listed. He was a contractor.

1916 [Arthur turned 60 in March]:

The Jacksons lived at 319 East 47th Street, with the same reported data as above.

1917 [Arthur turned 61 in March]:

The Jacksons lived at 319 East 47th Street, Kansas City, Mo., when the Kansas City city directory census data was collected. Arthur was still a contractor. Their two eldest sons, Edgar and Jabez, registered for the draft, their official World War I records documenting the young men as "white." Between 1917 and 1918, East 47th Street was renamed to Brush Creek Boulevard at this location (see the 1925 Atlas on the facing page).

Virginia Carter (North) Jackson, widow of Dr. John W. Jackson, died in Kansas City and was buried in Elmwood Cemetery. Arthur and his family likely attended the funeral.

1918 [Arthur turned 62 in March]:

The Jacksons likely did not move; but, were listed at 317 Brush Creek Boulevard (formerly East 47th Street), Kansas City, Mo., when the Kansas City city directory census data was collected. Arthur was then listed as a yardman.

Arthur's grandson, Roy Weldon Jackson, was born on August 13, 1918, to his son, Jabez "Davies/Javies/Javis/Jarvis/Jack" Jackson and his wife, Grace (Clifford) Jackson.

By September 2, 1918, however, Arthur and Ida Jackson had moved to 4724 Summit, when their son, Reg, was enrolled to attend E. F. Swinney School, located on West 47th Street, between Holly and West Prospect Place (Jarboe).

Today (2015) a modern parking structure and a ca. 1920s Tudor-style apartment house is located where the Jacksons lived at 4724 Summit, between September 1918 to 1919

1919 [Arthur turned 63 in March]:

The Jacksons lived at 4724 Summit, Kansas City, Mo., when the Kansas City city directory census data was collected.[367] Arthur was then listed as a contractor. This rented house, since razed, was on the west side of the Country Club Plaza.

On January 29, 1919, more than 8,000 residents convened at the Kansas City Convention Hall for the tricentennial of the first reported landing of people of African descent on American soil 300 years prior. "The celebration was loosely timed to coincide with the anniversary of the Emancipation Proclamation."[368]

Arthur may have *wanted* to attend; but, he most likely did not. Certainly Ida would not have been in favor of this so-called act of solidarity by her black husband, a fact that they were obviously attempting by this time to distance or remove themselves.

While "the twenty-one years between the First and Second World Wars, particularly the decade 1919-1929, were important ones for Kansas City's black residents,[369]" the Arthur Jackson family was passing for a white family, skirting the invisible, yet

170

highly observed segregated neighborhoods of Kansas City.

Consistently, since the 1880s, census takers visiting the Jackson household had identified Arthur as "mulatto" or "black;" his wife, Ida, as "white;" and, the children, "mulatto."

This shifted consistently when, in 1920, Arthur was first and for the next 13 years identified as "white."

1920 [Arthur turned 64 in March]:

The Jacksons lived at 4705 West Prospect Place (Jarboe), Kansas City, Mo., when the Kansas City city directory and census data was collected. Arthur was then listed as a contractor.[370]

When the U.S. Census was taken on January 14, Arthur was listed as a white landscape gardener.

By this time at age 64, Arthur established himself as a landscape gardener, a profession that he—and eventually his children and young grandson, Roy—would be mutually employed until Arthur's death in 1931 at nearly 75-years-of-age. Roy recalled:

Dad [Jabez] and two of my Uncles worked with Grandpa at landscape gardening ... Uncle Ed and Uncle Ollie drove the truck. I often worked with them too, and I remember customers complaining that they were working me so hard and at such a young age. I was from 10 to 12 years old then. I remember they had a large barrel with a pump hooked to a hose and my job was to manually pump the contraption to keep the pressure up on the hose so that the men could spray whatever it was they were spraying up into the trees. I got $1 a day when I worked with them.

The Jacksons did yard work for wealthy families along Kansas City's illustrious Ward Parkway and surrounding well-to-do neighborhoods. It is conceivable that they were also employed by Dr. Jabez North Jackson, the grandson of Arthur's former master.

1921 [Arthur turned 65 in March]:

The Jacksons continued to live at 4705 West Prospect Place (Jarboe), Kansas City, Mo., when the Kansas City city directory census data was collected.[371] Arthur was then listed as a landscape gardener.

Prospect Place had been Jarboe Street in that area earlier, and later-on it was changed back to Jarboe. This address, too, skirts the Kansas City Country Club Plaza's western boundary.

1922 [Arthur turned 66 in March]:

1607 Oak

The Jacksons lived downtown at 1607 Oak, Kansas City, Mo., when the Kansas City city directory census data was collected. There was no occupation listed for Arthur. Today (2015) this once residential area is a commercial district, and the Jackson's old address would now face the massive, modern, glass and metal, $200 million Kansas City Star printing and distribution plant.

When their son, Oliver "Ollie," was enrolled to attend E. F. Swinney School on June 1, 1922, the family was living at 2829 Cherry.

They were still in the Union Hill neighborhood on September 4, when Ollie was transferred to Longfellow School, which remains standing today (2015): it would have been either next door to the Jackson's house, or a couple of houses south.

2829 Cherry, Kansas City, Missouri, today (2015) part of the parking lot for Longfellow School

Longfellow Elementary, 2830 Holmes, Kansas City, Missouri

By November 7, however, the Jacksons moved to 2937 Cherry. Ollie on that date was transferred to Lathrop elementary school. He may have had developmental or behavioral issues needing more structure, or specialized training. Lathrop Mechanical Trades School, pictured below, at 1214 Central in downtown Kansas City, had been an industrial school since 1913.[372]

1923 [Arthur turned 67 in March]:

The Jacksons remained in the Union Hill neighborhood when they moved to 131 East 31st Street, as revealed when the Kansas City city directory census data was collected. Arthur was then listed as a gardener.[373]

Arthur's grandson, Roy, said the house was right where the landmark red. KCTV-5 broadcast tower at 125-129 East 31st Street has loomed 1,042-feet over that area of Kansas City since its construction was completed in 1956. It is the second largest free-standing tower in the United States.[374]

1924 [Arthur turned 68 in March]:

The Jacksons lived at 304 East 34th Street, Kansas City, Mo., when the Kansas City city directory census data was collected. Arthur was then listed as a landscape gardener.

Today (2015) this property is 2-3 lots east of 34th and Gillham Road/Plaza, adjacent to the south of the mammoth Costco parking lot, and immediately to the east of the Foreign Language Academy soccer fields.[375]

The Jackson's 1924-1927 home (or apartment) at 304 East 34th Street was next door to the west of this now, lone-standing apartment building at 34th and Gillham Road/Plaza. The KCTV broadcast tower has been visible in the distance since 1956.

1925 [Arthur turned 69 in March]:

The Jacksons remained at 304 East 34th Street, Kansas City, Mo., when the Kansas City city directory census data was collected. Arthur was then listed as a landscape gardener.

1926 [Arthur turned 70 in March]:

The Jacksons remained at 304 East 34th Street, Kansas City, Mo., when the Kansas City city directory census data was collected. Arthur was then listed as a landscape gardener.

1927 [Arthur turned 71 in March]:

The Jacksons continued to live at 304 East 34th Street, Kansas City, Mo., when the Kansas City city directory census data was collected. Arthur was then listed as a landscape gardener.

1928 [Arthur turned 72 in March]:

The Jacksons moved, again, closer to the Country Club Plaza, to 508 West 46th Street., Kansas City, Mo., when the Kansas City city directory census data was collected. Arthur was then listed as a landscape gardener.

Today (2015), this and adjoining lots once dotted with modest dwellings, is now a parking lot between Washington and Pennsylvania that serves surrounding apartment buildings north of the Country Club Plaza.[376]

Arthur's brother-in-law, Thomas Sharp, died in St. Joseph.[377]

1929 [Arthur turned 73 in March]:

The Jackson's moved directly north about three-and-a-half full city blocks, to the north of the African American neighborhood, Steptoe.

They lived in a house between Washington and Wornall   at 414 Boone (later changed to West 42nd Terrace), Kansas City, Mo., when the Kansas City city directory census data was collected. Arthur was then listed as a landscape gardener.[378]

The Steptoe neighborhood is described in detail elsewhere in this biography, as it was the 'stomping grounds' of Arthur's grandson, Roy Weldon Jackson, the author's grandfather. Roy, who had been shifted between relatives as a young boy, recalled:

"In the summer of 1929, at age 11, I returned to my Grandparents' who were then living at 414 Boone (now called 42nd Terrace), although my father and his second wife, Florence, lived a couple doors up the street at 418.

"I was enjoying attending Allen Elementary (located at 42nd and Waddel, 706 West 42nd St. to be exact). Believe it or not, at that young age, I got job as a bicycle delivery boy for Crown Drug Store on the northwest corner of Westport Road and Broadway in the Westport neighborhood of Kansas City. I worked hard and earned my own spending money. It was at this time that I tried smoking cigarettes. Grandma caught me one day, and she said, "If you're going to smoke, you can smoke in front of me." She must have known something after having raised four rambunctious boys; it just wasn't the same not having to sneak about. All in all, life seemed to be squaring up for me."

1930 [Arthur turned 74 in March]:

On April 2, 1930, Arthur and Ida Jackson and grandson, Roy, while living at 414 Boone (later changed to West 42nd Terrace) were enumerated in the U.S. Census. They were all enumerated as "white."

On August 16, 1930, Arthur and Ida's son, Edgar Walter Jackson, committed suicide by shooting himself with a rifle in his brother's car, while Jabez was in a pool hall at 5th and Cherry.[379] The reason for this tragic loss was never mentioned or remembered by survivors who were questioned by the author some 50 years later. Nothing was known to have been recorded, and its effect on the family, particularly on Ed's parents, Arthur and Ida Jackson, are unknown. The next few months were surely filled with sadness and mixed emotions with regard to the untimely loss of their son.

1931:

Arthur Jackson died on February 5, 1931, one month shy of turning 75-years-old on March 4. Arthur's grandson, Roy, said he,

"clearly remembered having looked out the window to see his grandfather sitting on the porch at just the moment that Arthur's head tilted to one side and rested gently on the post rail. Thinking his old Grandfather had dozed-off, he didn't know what had happened until a little while later when Grandma Ida went to check on him. It was in the dead of winter. She discovered that Arthur had died quietly and peacefully while sitting there. Arthur's death certificate says his cause of death at 7:45 a.m. was chronic myocarditis with general arteriosclerosis as a contributory factor."

Arthur was buried in a newly opened suburban cemetery, Floral Hills, southeast of the then Kansas City limits. Today, Floral Hills is incorporated into Kansas City proper, and its east/front entrance is parallel to Blue Ridge Boulevard, which separates Kansas City and Raytown, Missouri.

Had Arthur been presumed to be black in 1931, the family would not have been allowed to bury him in this cemetery; but, rather, in a segregated cemetery for "Negroes." However, for at least the last 11 years of his life, Arthur had been perceived and documented to be "white." The 1920 and 1930 Censuses and his death certificate identified him as "white."

"By and large, the experience of slavery was one that our ancestors were anxious to leave in the past."[380] But, "the history and memory of slavery and emancipation endured in the bodies and lived experiences of both former slaves and the generations of black Americans born in slavery's wake."[381] What Arthur may have revealed about his past to others, including his children, will never be known. Whatever truths they did know, Arthur's family definitely denied their progenitor's race and ethnicity . . . the truth . . . that Arthur Jackson had been born a slave.

BORN A SLAVE

Postscript

ARTHUR JACKSON

Born March 4, 1856
Charleston, Kanawha Co., Virginia (West Virginia)

Died February 5, 1931
Kansas City, Jackson Co., Missouri

My great great grandparents, Arthur Jackson and Ida May (Anderson) Jackson—who died 16 years after Arthur in 1948—rest in peace in Floral Hills Cemetery in Kansas City. They never lived to see marriage equality for interracial couples, like themselves. They never lived to see the civil and equal rights movements remove prejudicial barriers and propel our nation forward. They never lived to see an American citizen with African descent become President of the United States. And, they never lived to see the day when each American—regardless of any inward or outward difference in character, belief or orientation—is viewed and treated in all areas of daily life with fairness and true equality.

Equal Housing and Block Busting

In 1964, Arthur's grandson, Roy W. Jackson, and his wife, Nancy B. (Rogers) Jackson, were the first owners of a new, model home in Raytown, Missouri . . . not far from Floral Hills.

They spent months searching for a newer, larger home for their family of three teenage children. Roy and Nancy said they spent many nights after he got off work at Sheffield steel mill to go look for houses. Finally, they had decided to build a new home near 73rd and Hedges (also in Raytown). But, when Roy found structural flaws in the concrete foundation, he cancelled the contract.

One night soon thereafter, Roy came home and told Nancy they needed to go right away to look at a home that had come available in Raytown. Nancy said she was frying chicken in a cast iron skillet, and she just turned off the gas and they went to visit the 'model home' in a new housing development at 78th and Woodson. This was a home the builder used to tour prospective homebuyers through; and, it was the one that Roy and Nancy secured and lived in for upwards of 40 years.

Here is the ironic twist which the author is not proud to admit; but, it is a historical fact. My Grandparents were among the "white flight" that typified the emigration of whites into new, suburban, Kansas City neighborhoods after desegregation…and particularly after the Equal Housing Act of 1964. They were the first white family to move from their block (59th and Walrond) in southeast Kansas City after African Americans were suddenly "allowed" to move into neighborhoods that had previously been "restricted" from 100 years of systematic segregation that had been ever-present since the Civil War.

I became aware of a practice of the real estate industry called "block busting." That concept is so far removed from my experience that it was hard for me to get my head around. I asked Grandpa about this a few years ago, prompted by a black woman who had come into the Jackson County Historical Society Archives—where I had served as archivist since 2000—to research the history of her home. She lived near Grandpa's old neighborhood. Grandpa said that their prime motivation in moving was for a larger home for their family. They were living in a small, two bedroom house on Walrond.

Still, Grandpa admitted that he and Grandma didn't want to be the first whites to sell to blacks. It was not socially acceptable among close-knit neighbors in this era right after the Equal Housing Act.

They made an agreement with their new home builder that he would buy their old house from them when they moved to the new one in Raytown. The builder, essentially, was an intermediary. He, then, would be the one to sell to the first black family to live in that neighborhood...my Grandparent's former home.

I looked up these transactions at the Jackson County Recorder of Deeds, and it happened just as Grandpa said. My Grandparents bought their home at 78th Street and Woodson in Raytown on October 12, 1964 (Lot 35 in a subdivision called Woodvue), from Gerald L. and Mary K. Schwartz, who, in turn, bought the double lot from my Grandparents on Walrond in Kansas City (Lots 12 and 25 from the subdivision, Beaufort Resurvey Lots 26, 27, 28, and 30).[382] Schwartz, then, sold my grandparent's former house to an African American couple, LeRoy and Alberta F. Harris, who had moved from 3403 South Benton.[383]

The paradoxical pill our family must swallow is that Roy—unwittingly *a grandson of a former African American slave*—fell into the socially acceptable practice of discrimination that, in part, defines his generation. Times have changed, though individuals in neighborhoods and communities continue today to try and overcome seeming differences for more harmonious integration and assimilation.

A Final, Sacred, Resting Place

After I graduated from college in 1993, began working, and lived in a couple of apartments, I finally became a new homeowner like my Grandparents. For 15 years between 1999 and 2014 I lived in a beautiful home on Gregory Circle, less than a quarter mile from Floral Hills cemetery where Arthur and Ida Jackson, and other relatives, are buried.

Several years ago my Grandpa Roy Jackson purchased an empty plot next to his Grandpa Arthur Jackson, for my intended, eventual resting place. I'm proud that I will one-day rest in eternity next to my great great grandfather, Arthur Jackson, who was born a slave.

African Genes

Years ago when his niece, Mary (Johnson) Bentley, asked about the Jackson family's history, her Uncle Reg Jackson told her, *"You don't want to know. You'd be embarrassed."* He was definitely referring to the fact that we have African blood in our genes.

I believe this truth about our family's unique history has resonance with others who have equally intriguing family stories that should be researched, documented, and shared. Hopefully, this work proficiently highlights our family's heritage in context of the on-going saga of Kansas City history . . . and American history.

My two brothers and I are the only three, direct, male descendants of Arthur and Ida Jackson.

In December 2010, I ordered a Y-Chromosome DNA test through Ancestry.com. This tests a man's deep patrilineal, or male-line ancestry, using the DNA on his Y chromosome (Y-DNA) through Y-STR testing. This is useful because the Y-chromosome passes down almost unchanged from father to son. That is, the non-recombining and sex-determining regions of the Y-chromosome do not change.

With all that I'd learned in historical documents about my great great grandfather, Arthur Jackson, I had an impression in my mind that the test results would come back with a big map of Africa.

Guess what? It did!

Ancestry.com determined that the migration pathways of our direct, ancient paternal ancestors, "the Language People (haplogroup E1b1a; E-M2 in shorthand)," point directly to Africa: *"Your ancestors may have lived in west and Sub-Saharan Africa, particularly **Cameroon** and **Benin**."* [384]

"Advancements in DNA analyses, along with African shipping records, have revealed ...[only]... a relatively small number of African groups supplied the lion's share of the ancestral African population."[385] "Most of today's African American population can trace their ancestry back to one of just 46 ethnic groups."[386] Arthur's ancestors may have been from one of

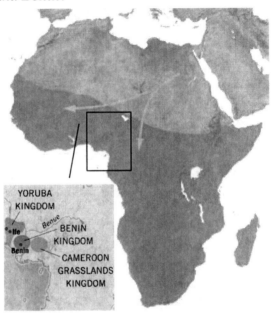

only 14 modern-day ethnic groups specifically connected with historically-adjacent Cameroon/Biafra Grasslands and Benin Kingdoms:

Ethnic Group	Location Today
Bamun	Cameroon
Bamileke	Cameroon
Duala	Cameroon
Fulbe/Fulani/Peulh/Fula	Cameroon, et al.
Ibibio	Cameroon, et al.
Tikar	Cameroon
Bariba	Benin
Ewe, et al.	Benin
Fon	Benin
Mahi	Benin
Yoruba	Benin, et al.[387]

Arthur's paternal ancestral pedigree ties directly and uninterrupted to Africa without any European (or, Caucasian) influences.

If, then, Arthur was in any way "mulatto," the European influences would have come from his maternal ancestry. Was Arthur's mother mulatto (meaning that she may have had a white father and a slave mother)? In 1860 when Arthur was about 4-years-old, there were two female slaves in the Richard and Lucinda Jackson, Sr., family of child-bearing age:

40 [b.ca. 1820]   black   female
19 [b.ca. 1841]   mulatto female

If the 19-year-old mulatto female was Arthur's mother, she would have been 15 when she gave birth. The 40-year-old black female would have been about 36. Either is a possibility.

And, in the case of the mulatto designation, any European influence is yet another mystery for the ages . . . and another edition of *Born a Slave*.

Another participant in the Ancestry.com DNA program, Golden Charles Owen "Joe" Jackson, "has a very close match" to my DNA, from within 1-7 generations. All 43 locations, or markers that were tested matched exactly. In the scheme of thousands of years of human ancestry, our "very close match" is VERY close. We are 'long lost cousins' to be sure.

Unfortunately, for the first and revised editions of this publication, specific information about our common ancestor(s) is just beyond our present-day knowledge. This means that while we know the common location of our earliest known ancestors in America, we do not *yet* know their individual names or circumstances.

Joe Jackson claims that his earliest known Jackson ancestor, *"is listed on early census as being from both VA and MD. I believe it's really Charles Co., MD, and that's on the edge of both states."* You might recall that Richard L. and Lucinda Edwards (Deatley) Jackson, Sr., lived with their young family in Charles County, Maryland, just over the line from Lucinda's ancestral

Westmoreland County, Virginia, between 1828 and 1842. Richard's parents, William and Catherine (Ludlow) Jackson, were also nearby in Spotsylvania County, Virginia. In that locality and in that time frame of less than 15 years, Joe's ancestors and mine—Arthur's progenitors—mixed, mingled . . . and dispersed.

Joe Jackson has two Jackson lines that intermarried and migrated to Kentucky as early as 1820. A future edition of this work will detail James E. Deatley's descendants . . . some of whom also migrated to Kentucky . . . with their slaves.

Time will tell if we are able to find our common progenitor(s).

Golden Charles Owen "Joe" Jackson's Earliest Known Ancestors

[Charles Co.?] Maryland line:

1-[Job ?] JACKSON
b: Maryland
d: before 8 Apr 1820
+ [Mary "Polly" ?]
b: Maryland
d: after 8 Apr 1820   Kentucky
...2-George JACKSON
...2-**Thomas JACKSON**
    b: ca. 1797   Kentucky
    d: before 1870   Kentucky

Virginia line:

1-Samuel JACKSON
    b: ca. 1765   Virginia/Maryland
    d: before 1870   Kentucky
    + [--?--]
    b: [--?--]
    d: between 1820–1830 Kentucky

...2-Elizabeth "Betsy" JACKSON
    b: before 1810   Kentucky
    d: before 1860   Kentucky

+8 Apr 1820 Bardstown, Nelson, Kentucky

3-**Samuel JACKSON** (b: ca 1823 – d: bf 1880)
    + Teresa Louisa JACKSON (b: before 1828 – d: after 1880)
      19 Dec 1844 Bardstown, Nelson, Kentucky

...**4-Thomas Elza "Elzie" JACKSON** (b: 2 Sep 1871 – d: 28 Jun1933)
+1) Ann STUMP/F (b: before 1900 – d: [--?--])
...5-Elzie JACKSON, Jr. (b: 13 May 1893 – d: [--?--])
...5-Arthur L. JACKSON (b: May 1896 – d: [--?--])
...5-Howard Robert JACKSON , Sr. (b: 6 Mar 1897 – d: 3 Oct 1974)
+2) Sarah Ann "Sallie" SHEPHERD (b: April 1883 – d: 27 Jun 1933)
...5-Loretta JACKSON (b: 11 Mar 1902 – d: [--?--])
...5-Sallie JACKSON (b: 28 Dec 1902 – d: [--?--])
...5-Chester Owen JACKSON (b: 24 Jan 1904 – d: 15 Aug 1976)
...5-Charles Earl JACKSON (b: 25 Jan 1906- d: [--?--])
...5-**William Pearl "Willie" JACKSON Sr.** (b: 25 Jan 1906–d: 23 Feb 1969)
+ Genevieve Ruby SCHROEDER (b: 1914 – d: 1979)
.........6-**Golden Charles Owen "Joe" JACKSON** (b: 1935-)
    + Billye D.
.........6-John Ronald Franklin "Buddy" JACKSON
.........6-Paul Kenneth "Jackie" JACKSON
...5-Carrie Lee JACKSON (b: 12 Oct 1908 – d: [--?--])
...5-Mabel Schrilla JACKSON (b: 9 Jan 1911- d: [--?--])
...5-Golden JACKSON (b: 5 Aug 1913 – d: [--?--])
...5-Ethel Mae JACKSON (b: 18 Oct 1915 – d: [--?--])
...5-Mildred Elizabeth JACKSON (b: 3 May 1919 – d: [--?--])
...5-Ruby JACKSON (b: 6 May 1922 – d: [--?--])
...5-Judea JACKSON (b: 27 Mar 1925 – d: [--?--])

This family—while having a nearly exact DNA match to Arthur's deep, paternal African ancestry—was set free by their white slaveholders in/around Charles County, Maryland, according to Joe Jackson. They were listed in the U.S. Census as 'freedmen' in 1790. While the males transferred African DNA directly to their male offspring, this particular family was considered 'white' by around 1793 when they migrated to Kentucky. In all likelihood, there were several early 'Jackson' males who descended from a common progenitor, and were sold to different slaveholders. Some slaveholders apparently set slaves free, others did not. Therefore, at least some of Arthur's male progenitors (and direct male ancestors) remained enslaved for one- to three-more-generations.

Appendix A

Arthur Jackson
Age, Race and Literacy
in Historical Records

Year	Age	Actual 1856	Race	Read/ Write?	Reported Age Residence
1856					Charleston, Kanawha, W/VA
1859		3			Boles, Franklin, MO
1860	4	4	mulatto		Boles, Franklin, MO
1870		14			
1880	21	24	black	NO	Bigelow, Holt, MO
1885	27	29	mulatto		Omaha, Douglas, NE
1890	27	34	N/A		White Cloud, Doniphan, KS
1895	34	39	colored		White Cloud, Doniphan, KS
1899	35	43	Afro-		White Cloud, Doniphan, KS
1900	41	44	black	NO	White Cloud, Doniphan, KS
1901			Afro-		White Cloud, Doniphan, KS
1905	47	49	mulatto		Irving, Brown, KS
1910	55	54	mulatto	YES	Irving, Brown, KS
1920	59	64	white	YES	Kansas City, Jackson, MO
1930	64	74	white	NO	Kansas City, Jackson, MO
1931	70	75	white		Kansas City, Jackson, MO

BORN A SLAVE

Appendix B

Jacksons Buried in Kansas City

Elmwood Cemetery

Name	Born	Died	Block:Date [relationship]
Annie P. (Thomas) Isbell	6 Oct 1856	22 Mar 1900	J: 24 Mar 1900 [w/o L. W. Isbell]
Charles Swanson Armstrong	31 Dec 1834	17 Mar 1918	K (Vault): 19 Mar 1918 [h/o Lucy (Jackson)]
Dollie	baby		K (Vault): 7 Nov. 1892 [d/o James P.]
Edna Earle	1876	24 Sep 1899	K (Vault): 27 Sep 1899 [d/o James P.]
Elizabeth "Lizzie" (Roberts)	1855	1884	K: 1884 [w/o James P.]
Ezra William Ober	30 Oct 1905	26 Apr 1980	[s/o Virginia (Isbell) Ober]
Florence Hinkle (Storey)	24 Jul. 1883	17 Oct 1967	C: 20 Oct 1967 [Jabez's second wife]
Gertrude M. (Grogan)	30 May 1861	26 Nov 1948	29 Nov 1948 [w/o James P.]
Jabez North (Dr.)	6 Oct. 1868	18 Mar 1935	C: 19 Mar. 1935 [s/o John Wesley]
James P. (Dr.)	16 Apr 1845	22 Nov 1901	K (Vault): 24 Nov 1901 [s/o RL & Lucinda]
Jane (Harwood) Ober	13 Jul 1901	18 Jan 1991	[w/o Ezra William Ober]
John Wesley	6 Nov. 1834	13 Mar 1890	C: 16 Mar 1890 [s/o RL & Lucinda]
Lucinda Edwards (Deatley)	11 Feb 1811	19 Nov 1906	K (Vault): 11 Dec. 1906 [matriarch]
Lucy (Jackson) Armstrong	24 Dec 1838	20 Nov 1922	J: 22 Nov 1922 [d/o RL & Lucinda]
Mgt Eliz (Jackson) Schaefer Harris	7 Oct 1906	10 Dec 1958	[d/o Jabez N.]
Richard Ludlow, Sr.	9 Jul 1797	10 Aug. 1863	K (Vault): 10 Oct 1900 [patriarch; re-interred]
Virginia "Jennie" Carter (North)	16 Jul. 1842	2 Dec 1917	C: 4 Dec. 1917 [w/o John Wesley]
Virginia Adele (Isbell) Ober	7 Aug 1882	11 Nov 1962	J: 15 Nov 1962 [d/o Annie & LW Isbell]
Virlea (Wayland)	23 Nov. 1877	5 Mar 1921	C: 7 Mar. 1921 [Jabez's first wife]
Walter Emmett (Dr.)	24 Oct. 1870	24 Oct 1934	C: 26 Oct 1934 [s/o John Wesley]
William Andrew Thomas	10 Oct. 1860	11 Feb 1892	J: 11 Feb 1892 [gs/o RL & Lucinda]

Floral Hills Cemetery

Name	Birth	Death	Marker
Arthur	4 Mar 1856	5 Feb 1931	15: 7 Feb 1931 [patriarch]
David Wayne	14 Feb 1969	living	15: [g g gs/o Arthur & Ida]
Dollie Frances (Jackson) Johnson 8 Dec 1901		15 Feb 1959	15: 17 Feb 1959 [d/o Arthur & Ida]
Dorothy Frances (Johnson) Rittermeyer 31 Aug 1927		13 Aug 2011	15: [gd/o Arthur & Ida]
Hazel Mae (Jackson) Levine 21 May 1899		30 Aug 1985	15: 3 Sep 1985 [d/o Arthur & Ida]
Ida May (Anderson)	5 May 1869	15 Sep 1948	15: 17 Sep 1948 [matriarch]
John Rittermeyer			15: [h/o Dorothy (Johnson)]
Louis Levine			15: [h/o Hazel Mae (Jackson)]
Nancy Beatrice (Rogers) 6 Jun 1922		12 Mar 2002	15: [h/o Roy]
Reginald Brewster	19 May 1905	27 Aug 1982	33: 30 Aug 1982 [s/o Arthur & Ida]
Reginald Wayne	1 Aug 1949	10 Dec 2010	15: 14 Dec 2010 [g gs/o Arthur & Ida]
Roy Weldon		living	15: [gs/of Arthur & Ida]
Virginia Lee		living	15: [g gd/o Arthur & Ida]
William Weldon Johnson 16 Dec 1894		11 Jul 1970	15: 14 Jul 1970 [h/o Dollie Frances]

Green Lawn Cemetery

Name	Birth	Death	Marker
Jabez "Davies/Davis/Javis/Jarvis" 7 Apr 1895		22 Jun 1952	23 Jun 1952 [s/o Arthur & Ida]

Mt. Washington Cemetery

Name	Birth	Death	Marker
Edgar Walter	1 Sep 1891	16 Aug 1930	18 Aug 1930 [s/o Arthur & Ida]
Thomas Greenwood MacLaughlin 27 Jan 1896		23 Sep 1990	26 Sep 1990 [h/o Virginia]
Virginia (Jackson) MacLaughlin 17 Jan 1902		18 Jan 1969	21 Jan 1969 [d/o Jabez]

Cremation

Name	Birth	Death	Marker
Oliver Wordsworth	3 Oct 1908	31 Oct 1965	2 Nov 1965 [s/o Arthur & Ida]

d/o=daughter of   **gd=granddaughter**   **g gd=great granddaughter**
s/o=son of   **gs=grandson**   **g gs=great grandson**
h/o=husband of   **w/o=wife of**

---

[1] The author coins and defines the term, histiogeneography™ as a comprehensive, documented, biographical study of one's life, or chronological timeline, in historical context, comprising genetic, genealogical, geographical and cultural landscapes.

[2] Jackson, David W. *Direct Your Letters to San Jose: The California Gold Rush Letters and Diary of James and David Lee Campbell, 1849-1852.* (Kansas City, Mo.: The Orderly Pack Rat, 2000), xiii.

[3] Postma, Johannes. *The Atlantic Slave Trade.* (Westport, Ct.: Greenwool Press, 2003), xiii.

[4] Sylvester, Theodore L. and Sonia Benson, eds. *Slavery Throughout History: An Almanac.* (Detroit, Mi.: UXL, an imprint of the Gale Group, 2000), 229.

[5] Antislavery.org and Freetheslaves.net (retrieved 1 Feb 2015).

[6] Andrews, William W., ed. *From Fugitive Slave to Free Man: The Autobiographies of William Wells Brown.* (Columbia, Mo.: University of Missouri Press, 2003), 1.

[7] Rodriguez, Junius P., ed. Slavery in the United States: A Social, Political and Historical Encyclopedia. Volume 1. (Santa Barbara, Ca.: ABC-CLIO, 2007), 150.

[8] Foster, Robin. "Untangling the genealogy of the former slaveholder and enslaved." http://www.examiner.com/list/untangling-the-genealogy-of-the-former-slave-holder-and-enslaved (visited 6 Nov 2013).

[9] His name was Sengbe Pieh / Joseph Cinqué, played by Djimon Hounsou. According to Wikipedia.com, *"Amistad* is a 1997 historical drama film directed by Steven Spielberg based on the notable uprising in 1839 by newly abducted Mende tribesmen who took control of the ship *La Amistad* off the coast of Cuba, and the international legal battle that followed their capture by a U.S. revenue cutter. It became a United States Supreme Court case of 1841."

[10] Edgar Walter Jackson, according to his 1930 death certificate, "shot self through head."

Jabez "Jarvis" Jackson was an alcoholic and lived a hard life, as attested by his son. His Missouri Death Certificate, however, certificate merely states 'bronchopneumonia' as his cause of death in 1952.

Oliver Wadsworth "Ollie" Jackson was said to have been hit on the back of the head with a shovel in a brawl. He was admitted to Larned State Hospital, Larned, Kansas, March 19, 1948 [his mother died September 15, 1948], and discharged January 26, 1965, while on convalescent leave which began November 7, 1963. He died October 31, 1965, in Wichita, Sedgwick County, Kansas, and his body was donated to science with the K.U. Medical Center.

Dollie Frances (Jackson) Johnson's 1959 post-Valentine's Day suicide was recorded on her death certificate as, "death by hanging; found hanging in

193

basement; left note." Dollie's niece, Betty Jackson, recalled that her aunt had a history of depression or mental illness; but, that she was 'coy' about it so that it was never obvious. More than once when an ambulance would be called to the Johnson home, Dollie would limp out to the ambulance as if to appear physically unwell, rather than mentally unstable. On the night that Dollie's body was discovered in the basement of her home, Betty remembered her young cousins were brought over to her house and the kids were sequestered in an adjoining room while Dollie's husband, Bill Johnson, Ted and Mary (Johnson) Bentley (and possibly John and Dorothy (Johnson) Rittermeyer) quietly conversed with Betty's parents, Roy and Nancy Jackson.

[11] Jackson, David W. *Kansas City Chronicles: An Up-to-Date History.* (Charleston, Sc.: The History Press, 2010), 78-81.

[12] Arthur's penchant for music may have been learned from his childhood days as a slave. "Making music was one of the few freedoms [slaves] could enjoy, and they used their songs to turn misery and sorrow into art. Work songs, shout songs, sorrow songs, and jubilees are among the names African Americans gave to these oral compositions. In the tradition of their ancestors, the slaves would make up the story they wanted to tell, putting into words whatever thoughts came to mind, and pass it along in song.... For the slaves, the field shouts or hollers and other forms of the songs [and jogs and shuffles] that developed were means of communicating with one another. (Nolen, 17-18, 24).

[13] Roy Jackson's pupil records, Kansas City School District Records. Edward Prices' Addition was in the southeast ¼ of Section 19, Township 49, Range 33.

[14] Arthur's 1931 Missouri Death Certificate has March 4, 1860, as his birth date. His grave marker has 1857. This histiogeneography™ asserts 1856 as his most accurate birth year. No official birth record was ever created. And, Arthur died prior to the origination of Social Security numbers (in late 1936 and early 1937), at which time he would have had to file a delayed birth certificate to properly document his birth. See Appendix A for a study of Arthur's reported and projected age over his lifetime.

[15] "To fully grasp the distinction of mulatto-identified people as opposed to those who were black-identified, a differentiation of objective must be established. Whites objectified race when it came to person of color, and they used various classifications of "race" to bar certain individuals of certain rights, while also allowing limited access to specific rights for others. The identification, 'black,' was...based on lineage, particularly matriliny—especially during the slavery era of the United States. The designation of 'mulatto,' was based not on lineage, but rather on physical appearance—for some who fit the technical definition of the original sense of the word, that is, the first-generation offspring of a white person and a black-identified person, were, in some cases (especially during slavery) , identified solely as Blacks, but, in other cases, afforded the privilege of passing as Whites. Phenotype was the key in designating an individual as 'mulatto,' for a majority of the descendants

of black-white mixes fell somewhere in the distinction of possessing appearances that suggested both 'white' and 'black' ancestry…. Persons who were listed as 'mulatto' on one census would be listed as 'black' or, even more drastically, 'white' on other censuses. Again, the perception of the enumerator and his or her intent was key in these racial designations given to persons of color during this time." McClain, Carlton Dubois. *Mulattoes in the Postbellum South and Beyond: The Invisible Legacy of an Afro-European People, Custom, and Class in Americas' Binary and Three-Tier Societies.* (n.p.: Carlton Dubois McClain, 2014), 23, 41.

[16] The author found a Dennis Botts living near the Jacksons in White Cloud for a number of years, and has research on this Botts family who are NOT related to Arthur in any way. There is also research gathered on several Dennis Jacksons in the tri-state area in question; no links have yet been ascertained.

[17] Nine Dennis Jacksons appear to have been Civil War pensioners. "United States Civil War and Later Pension Index, 1861-1917," index, *FamilySearch* (https://familysearch.org/pal:/MM9.1.1/N4T7-ZZG : accessed 21 Sep 2014), Dennis Jackson, various dates from 1885-1928; citing "Organization Index to Pension Files of Veterans Who Served Between 1861 and 1900," *Fold3.com*; NARA microfilm publication T289.

[18] Copy of this letter shared by Mrs. Bentley in the possession of the author.

[19] 1885 Nebraska State Census. This Arthur Jackson was a 27-year-old mulatto working with others in what appeared to be a hotel in the city's 3rd Ward. The house number in 1885 was 106 South 10th Street. It cannot be confirmed if this is "our" Arthur Jackson, or not. If so, where was his 'wife?'

[20] "In the United States, anti-miscegenation laws (also known as miscegenation laws) were state laws passed by individual states to prohibit miscegenation, nowadays more commonly referred to as interracial marriage and interracial sex." http://en.wikipedia.org/wiki/Anti-miscegenation_laws_in_the_United_States (retrieved 25 Jan 2013).

[21] http://listverse.com/2011/01/25/10-fascinating-interracial-marriages-in-history/ (retrieved 25 Jan 2013).

[22] This seems like a remarkable story, especially since there is no remote evidence that Arthur was in any way related to or connected with any Native American Nation. James White Cloud (May 15, 1840 - July 16, 1940) Chief of the Iowa Native American Indian Nation, was the son of Chief Mahaska the Younger (aka. Frances White Cloud) (1810-1852) and Mary Roubidoux, who was the son of Mahaska/Chief White Cloud (1784-1834). James White Cloud was married four times, his second, third and fourth marriage ending in divorce. He served as a scout for the 14th Cavalry during the Civil War. His first wife, whom he had married on February 28, 1867, died in 1914, and she is buried with James in Tesson Cemetery near the northeast corner of Brown County. On 22 July 1885, James White Cloud was identified as "second chief" to the Iowa Indians residing in Nebraska and Kansas when he and a majority of other tribal

members voted "No" to the proposition of selling their land. (see Congressional Record, Vol. 2336, Ex. Doc. No. 70, "Message from the President of the United States transmitting a letter from the Secretary of the Interior relative to the sale of the Sac and Fox and Iowa Indian Reservations," p. 7-9.). The author has not yet found evidence to support the land grant, big house and/or head rights issue.

[23] Missouri State Legislature. *Missouri Session Laws*, 1840-1841, 39; National Historical Publishing Co. *History of Atchison and Holt Counties, Missouri*. (St. Joseph, Mo.: National Historical Publishing Co., 1882), 100.

[24] *Holt County Sentinel*, 23 Feb. 1877 and 30 Sep. 1892.

[25] After two children died in August and September 1852, Jackson likely headed to California the following spring when winter broke and vegetation along the trails would support a journey.

[26] Findagrave.com; History Publishing Co. *History of Holt County, Missouri*. (St. Joseph, Mo.: History Publishing Co., 1917), 224; *History of Holt and Atchison Counties*, 130; *St. Joseph Gazette*, 5 Sep 1923, 9. Andrew P. Jackson patented on 1 Apr 1846, the SW4 of Section 5 in Township 59, Range 37; on 20 May 1851, he patented the SW4 of Section 17, Township 60, Range 38; and, on 1 Jan 1852, he patented the E2 NW4 of Section 5 and the E2 NW4 of Section 8, Township 61, Range 38, according to the U.S. Department of the Interior, Bureau of Land Management, General Land Office Records online database. See also 1877 *Illustrated Historical Atlas of Holt County*, Missouri, 23, 43.

[27] E-mail from Jim MacLaughlin to the author, 27 Sept. 2011. The Smithsonian website that he referred to is an online "Memory Book" hosted by the Smithsonian Institution's National Museum of African American History and Culture.

[28] Mr. MacLaughlin suggested getting together with the author to "compare notes;" but, he never extended an invitation. The author located a daughter of Mr. MacLaughlin's through online Family History Project data available in March 2010 at elmwoodcem-kc.org. Among an exchange of e-mails between March 2010 and September 2011, she wrote that she was quite busy; and, also that she didn't think that her father was all that interested. In December 2014, the author, while researching online for this histiogeneography,[TM] was saddened to find Mr. MacLaughlin's obituary from the month before…and then a tribute to him on a daughter-in-law's blog.

[29]The author's "new best friend" mentioned the possibility of him one day visiting and touring the author through this Franklin County, Missouri, property.

[30] Dr. Dorothy Witherspoon in her lecture and book by the same title, *Researching Slave Ancestry.*

[31] http://www.vahistorical.org/research/genealogy.htm (retrieved 2 August 2012). This lesson is reiterated by Kathleen Brandt, internationally-known and respected genealogist.

[32] Woodtor, Dee Parmer, Ph.D. *Finding A Place Called Home: A Guide to African American Genealogy and Historical Identity*. (New York: Random

House, 1999), 218.

[33] "Negro Nomenclature." *Kansas City* (Mo.) *Star*, 5 Oct 1905, p. 5, editorial.
[34] Kathleen Brandt presentation, "Leaping Over Brickwalls: Using African American Research," delivered at a Black History Month program, "Falling in Love With Your Ancestors," co-sponsored by the Midwest Afro-American Genealogy Interest Coalition (M.A.G.I.C.) and the Midwest Genealogy Center, delivered on 28 Feb. 2015.
[35] "Washington: The 'Blackest Name' in America," http://www.huffingtonpost.com/2011/02/21/washington-blackest-name-america_n_825884.html (retrieved 20 Sept. 2014).
[36] Howell, Donna Wyant. *I Was a Slave: True Life Stories Dictated by Former American Slaves in the 1930's. Book 5: The Lives of Slave Children.* Voice of Will Daily. (Washington, D.C.: American Legacy Books, 2004), 13.
[37] See Diane Mutti Burke's research and writings in *On Slavery's Border*.
[38] Andrews, 179. Brown provides the lyrics to a few plantation songs.
[39] Howell, Book 5. Voice of Hilliard Yellerday, 13. The system of slave breeding/procreation is also discussed by John Simkin in his encyclopedia, *Slavery in the United States*, and is the topic of a motion picture, "The Escapening," due to be released in movie theaters in March 2016. See also, Smithers, Gregory D. *Slave Breeding: Sex, Violence, and Memory in African American History.* (Gainesville, Fl.: Univ. of Florida, 2012), and, Foster, Thomas A. "The Sexual Abuse of Black Men under American Slavery." *Journal of the History of Sexuality* (2011) 20:3, 445-64.
[40] Trexler, Harrison Anthony, Ph.B. *Slavery in Missouri, 1804-1865.* Johns Hopkins University Studies in Historical and Political Science, Series 32, No. 2. (Baltimore, Md.: Johns Hopkins Press, 1914), 88.

Harrison Anthony Trexler was born on 6 December 1883, in Freeport, Illinois, the son of Filbert and Lelia (Perkins) Trexler.

He was graduated in 1906 with a Bachelor's degree in Philosophy from Hastings College, Hastings, Nebraska; in 1909 with a postgraduate degree from the University of Chicago; and, in 1914 with a Ph.D. in History from Johns Hopkins University, Baltimore, Maryland, which published his thesis, "Slavery in Missouri, 1804-1865."

Trexler married Nell Bullard (1885-1970) on 12 July 1916. They were the parents of two sons: James Hugh Trexler, Sr.; and, David William Trexler, who was born 22 Apr 1920; married Dorothy G. in 1921; became a Lieutenant in the United States Navy during World War II; died 13 Jul 1987; and, is buried in the Fairview Cemetery, La Junta, Otero, Co.).

Trexler, in 1907, became Professor of History at Hardin College, Mexico, Missouri. In 1910, he was Acting Professor of History and Political Science at Allegheny College, Meadville, Pennsylvania. In 1913, he became Assistant Professor of History and Political Science at the University of Montana in

Missoula. By 1919, Trexler taught became Professor of Political Science at Whitman College, Walla Walla, Washington. He served as Professor of History and Political Science at Birmingham Southern College, Birmingham, Alabama, by 1923. He also taught at Johns Hopkins in the summers of 1924 and 1925. And, in 1929, he was appointed Professor of History at the Southern Methodist University, Dallas, Texas, a position he held until his retirement in 1950.

Of his many memberships were the American Historical Association, Mississippi Valley Historical Association, Southern Historical Association, Missouri Historical Society, and Beta Theta Pi.

A bibliography of his published work includes:

- Silver Production and the Montana Campaign of 1896 (1908);
- Slavery in Missouri, 1804-1865, Johns Hopkins University (1914);
- The Value and the Sale of the Missouri Slave, *Missouri Historical Review*, 179-198 (1914);
- Flour and Wheat in the Montana Gold Camps, 1862-1870: A Chapter in Pioneer Experiences and a Brief Discussion of the Economy of Montana in the Mining Days (1918);
- The First Confederate Capital (Birmingham Southern College Bulletin (1928);
- The Confederate Navy Department and the fall of New Orleans, Southern Methodist University (1933);
- The Confederate Ironclad "Virginia" ("Merrimac"), *University of Chicago Press* (1938);
- The Davis Administration and the Richmond Press, 1861-1865, reprinted from the *Journal of Southern History* (1950);

Trexler died on 19 Mar. 1974, in Dallas, Texas, at age 90-years-old. He and his wife, Nell, are buried there in the Sparkman Hillcrest Memorial Park Cemetery.

Trexler's grandchildren include: James Hugh Trexler, Jr., and Sam Trexler.

[41] Trexler, 88, citing the law (Statutes, 1865, Ch. 113, Secs. 12-16). The children previously born to such parties were thereby legitimatized.

[42] Trexler, 88.

[43] Howell, Book 5. Voice of Ben Chambers, 12.

[44] Goodheart is also author of *1861: Civil War Awakening*. "Washington: The 'Blackest Name' in America," http://www.huffingtonpost.com/2011/02/21/washington-blackest-name-america_n_825884.html (retrieved 20 Sept. 2014).

[45] "Negro Nomenclature." *Kansas City* (Mo.) *Star*, 5 Oct 1905, p. 5, editorial.

[46] Trexler, 91, quoting Robert B. Price of Columbia, Mo., in 1914.

[47] Trexler, 91, quoting Col. J. L. Robards of Hannibal, Mo., in 1914.

[48] "Negro Nomenclature." *Kansas City* (Mo.) *Star*, 5 Oct 1905, p. 5, editorial.

[49] Danforth, Nelson. Slave Narrative--Missouri. Transcripts compiled from the WPA Writer's Projects, 1936-1938. George P. Rawick Papers, Series 5. State Historical Society of Missouri, St. Louis Research Center. http://law.wustl.edu/staff/taylor/SLAVES/danforth.htm (retrieved 30 Aug 2012).

[50] "Washington: The 'Blackest Name' in America," http://www.huffingtonpost.com/2011/02/21/washington-blackest-name-

america_n_825884.html (retrieved 20 Sept. 2014).

[51] http://www.vahistorical.org/research/genealogy.htm (retrieved 2 August 2012)

[52] "Slave Surnames: Where Are They From?" http://msualumni.wordpress.com/2009/06/25/slave-surnames-where-are-they-from/ (retrieved 28 Aug 2012).

[53] "Slave Surnames: Where Are They From?" http://msualumni.wordpress.com/2009/06/25/slave-surnames-where-are-they-from/ (retrieved 28 Aug 2012).

[54] In 1990 Jackson was 13th. http://hailtoyou.wordpress.com/2010/ 11/24/the-blackest-surnames-in-the-usa/; and, http://en.wikisource.org/wiki/1990_Census_Name_Files_ dist.all.last_(1-100) (retrieved 20 Sept. 2014).

[55] Woodtor, 178.

[56] "Dr. John W. Jackson." 1878 *Atlas, Franklin County, Missouri*, 37. When the War of 1812 started, Jackson would have been 15-years-old. His military file has not yet been located; there were several Richard Jacksons who served that conflict from Virginia. It also does not appear that he, nor his wife, applied for a War of 1812 pension. See: Butler Stuart Lee, *Guide to Virginia Militia Units in the War of 1812* (Athens, Ga.: Iberian Publishing Co., 1988), 211-214. He also did *not* receive a military bounty land warrant in Missouri (which were only issued for lands in Carroll, Chariton, Cooper, Howard, and Saline Counties/Districts) after an Act of Congress, 6 May 1812. Dunaway, Maxine. *Missouri Military Land Warrants: War of 1812.* (Maxine Dunaway, 1985). Until the passage of an act approved 27 July 1842, the warrants could not be used for land outside those counties/districts and were not assignable.

[57] "Dies at Ripe Old Age," Holt County Sentinel, 7 Dec 1906, 1.

[58] His birth date and place of Fredericksburg, Virginia, is recorded in the Daughters of the American Revolution membership application of a great granddaughter of Lucinda's, Carole Messer Oberlitner, Hermosa, South Dakota, National No. 666200. Another source, the 1878 *Atlas of Franklin County, Missouri*, stated that Richard Ludlow Jackson was born in Spotsylvania County, Virginia, where his parents had settled upon immigrating to America.

[59] "Dr. John W. Jackson." 1878 *Atlas, Franklin County, Missouri*, 37.

[60] "Slave Owners Spotsylvania County, 1783 (Continued)," *The Virginia Magazine of History and Biography* (Jan. 1897): 4:3: 294.

[61] Crozier, William Armstrong, ed. *Spotsylvania County Records, 1721-1800: Being Transcriptions from the Original Files at the County Court House ...* (Baltimore, Md.: Southern Book Co., 1955), 65, 67, 78, 83. William Jackson likely died post 1800; he is not indexed between 1722-1800 in this book. Nor does he appear to have owned land in Spotsylvania County in the same time period.

[62] Their Fathers were Soldiers: Reminisces of the Revolutionary Period by Two True Daughters. *Kansas City* (Mo.) *Star*, 31 Jan 1898, p. 9.

[63] Trebay, Guy. "Virginia's Lost History: Exploring the Lost History of Virginia's Northern Neck," *New York Times*, 25 Nov 2012, Travel section, 1, 7.

[64] 1830 Census, Westmoreland County, Virginia.

[65] 1850 Census, Kanawha County, Virginia, says "Maryland."

[66] The 1850 Census, Kanawha County, Virginia, says "Maryland." The 1860 Census, Franklin County, Missouri, says "Maryland." The 1878 Atlas of Franklin County, Missouri, says that he was born in Westmoreland County, Virginia, "on the farm of his grandfather, Col. James T. Deatley, known as Fairview, an estate adjoining that of Lawrence Washington, brother of Gen. George Washington." His 1890 obituary says, "Clark County, Maryland."

[67] Postma, Johannes. *The Atlantic Slave Trade*. (Westport, Ct.: Greenwool Press, 2003), xxi.

[68] "On January 1, 1808, the importation of slaves into the United States was formally, and finally, abolished. The act, though significant, had limits. An illegal slave trade did continue, though in smaller numbers than had been true of the legal trade. The law also did nothing to stop the sale of those already held in slavery. For the next several decades, as many a million enslaved African Americans were sold within the United States." http://blog.oup.com/2012/01/slave-trade/ (retrieved 15 Jan 2015).

[69] The 1850 Census, Kanawha County, Virginia, says "Maryland." The 1860 Census, Franklin County, Missouri, says "Virginia." The 1900 Census, Holt County, Missouri, says "Maryland."

[70] The 1850 Census, Kanawha County, Virginia, says "Maryland." The 1860 Census, Franklin County, Missouri, says "Virginia." The 1875 *Illustrated Historical Atlas of Holt County, Missouri*, lists "Spotsylvania Co., Va.," 30. The 1900 Census, Woods County, Oklahoma, says, "Virginia," and also listed "Mar 1840" as his birth month and year. Findagrave.com for Byron-Amoria Cemetery in Amorita, Alfalfa County, Oklahoma, provides his exact birth and death dates.

[71] I have found no explanation for the teenage, white female, unless she may have been a niece of the couple.

[72] The 1878 Atlas, Franklin County, Missouri, biography for John Wesley Jackson says his family moved to Kanawha County in 1844. Richard Ludlow Jackson, Jr., obituary, states he was born in 1842 in "Charlestown, West Virginia."

[73] The 1850 Census, Kanawha County, Virginia, records the child's birthplace as "Virginia." The 1860 Census, Franklin County, Missouri, says "Virginia." Richard's obituary says "Charlestown, West Virginia." But, Charlestown is in Jefferson County where the Jacksons never lived; it should have read Charleston, Kanawha County. To complicate the emigration timeline, the 1878 Atlas for Franklin County, Missouri, includes a biography for John Wesley Jackson that says they moved to Kanawha County in 1844 (which would make Richard, Jr., having been born in Charles County, Maryland).

[74] Stinson, Helen S. *A Handbook for Genealogical Research in West Virginia. County: Kanawha*. (n.p., n.d.). And, thanks to Fred Thomas for clarification per e-mail correspondence with the author on 26 Oct 2015.

[75] Sylvester, Theodore L. and Sonia Benson, eds. *Slavery Throughout History: An Almanac*. (Detroit, Mi.: UXL, an imprint of the Gale Group, 2000), 227-228.

[76] Postma, Johannes. *The Atlantic Slave Trade*. (Westport, Ct.: Greenwool Press, 2003), xxi.

[77] Sylvester, Theodore L. and Sonia Benson, eds. *Slavery Throughout History: An Almanac*. (Detroit, Mi.: UXL, an imprint of the Gale Group, 2000), 227-228.

[78] Biography of the Honorable Henry J. (Jefferson) Samuels, Archives & History Library, The Cultural Center, 1900 Kanawha Blvd., E. Charleston, W.Va. 25305-0300. Transcribed from handwriting by Harry E. Pontius. http://www.wvencyclopedia.org/articles/456 (retrieved 5 April 2013).

[79] http://www.wvculture.org/history/slavery.html

[80] http://www.wvculture.org/history/slavery.html

[81] Dunaway, Wilma A. *Slavery in the American Mountain South*. (Cambridge Univ. Press, 2003), 130-131.

[82] http://www.wvculture.org/history/slavery.html

[83] Phil M. Conley, editor-in-chief. *The West Virginia Encyclopedia*, 372-373; James Morton Callahan. *The Semi-Centennial History of West Virginia*. And, Ambler, Charles Henry. *A History of West Virginia*, Prentice-Hall, 1933, pp. 109, 230-233.

[84] http://www.rootsweb.ancestry.com/~wvkanawh/Early/abtkan.html

[85] Deatley was born in Richmond County, Virginia. During the Revolution he served at least one year, and was believed by his daughter, Lucinda, to have been at Yorktown. "Their Fathers were Soldiers: Reminisces of the Revolutionary Period by Two True Daughters." *Kansas City* (Mo.) *Star*, 31 Jan 1898, 9. Also, James Deatley pension application, DAR applications; "History and Genealogy, Westmoreland County, Virginia: James E. DeAtley (Deatly)" posted at: http://www.rivahresearch.com/westmorelandcty/vitals/resources/familyand http://www.rivahresearch.com/westmorelandcty/vitals/resources/cemetery/locusthillcemetery.html (retrieved 16 June 2012). Thelma Louise DeAtley, daughter of Edward and Eleanor Agnes (Jones) DeAtley, who died in 1985, was buried in the same cemetery; her obituary gave the location as *Poplar Hill*; courtesy Francesca Henle Taylor, Genealogy Volunteer, Westmoreland County, Virginia; http://news.google.com/newspapers?id=xW1WAAAAIBAJ&sjid=FuQDAAAA IBAJ&pg=6472%2C2048823 (retrieved 28 Apr 2013).

[86] "Law" was the name that appears in DeAtley's estate papers. One source says Washington's nephew ("Their Fathers were Soldiers: Reminiscences of the Revolutionary Period by Two True Daughters." *Kansas City* (Mo.) *Star*, 31 Jan 1898, p. 9). The 1878 *Atlas of Franklin County, Missouri*, p. 37, names

Lawrence as Washington's brother. [George Washington's eldest half-brother was named Lawrence, who died in 1752]. Lawrence Augustine Washington (11 Apr 1774-15 Feb. 1824) was a nephew of George Washington (a son of Samuel Washington and his fourth wife, Anne Steptoe. They also had a son, Lawrence Augustine Washington, Jr. (26 Feb 1791-1875).]

Lawrence Augustine Washington, Sr., had an estate known as "Campbellton," which was owned by Colonel Robert James Washington, in 1912. Wright, T. R. B. *Westmoreland County, Virginia : Parts I and II : A Short Chapter and Bright Day in its History* (Richmond, Va.: Whittet & Shepperson, printers, 1912), 152. Also, Eubank, H. Ragland. *The Authentic Guide Book of Historic Northern Neck Virginia.* (1934).

It also happens that James E. DeAtley's Will on file in the Westminster Courthouse was co-executed by a son, George E. DeAtley, and Lawrence Washington. This would have been Lawrence Augustine Washington, Jr. (1791-1875), grand nephew of George Washington, who lived on an estate named, "New Blenheim."

Regardless of the relationship, it's safe to say that "Fairview" adjoined an estate once belonging to *one* Lawrence Washington.

[87] Trebay, Travel section, 7.

[88] Courtesy Francesca Henle Taylor Genealogy Volunteer, Westmoreland County, Virginia, who located and copied DeAtley's estate file located in Book 19, Fiduciaries and Accounts, Westmoreland County, Virginia, page 372.

[89] *Free Lance Star*, 29 Mar. 1929, courtesy Francesca Henle Taylor Genealogy Volunteer, Westmoreland County, Virginia; http://news.google.com/newspapers?id=09dNAAAAIBAJ&sjid=x4oDAAAAIB AJ&dq=deatley%20oak%20grove&pg=7340%2C2971342 (retrieved 28 Apr. 2013).

[90] http://www.rivahresearch.com/westmorelandcty/vitals/resources/ families/DeatleyJames.html, courtesy Francesca Henle Taylor, Genealogy Volunteer, Westmoreland County, Virginia.

[91] Courtesy Francesca Henle Taylor Genealogy Volunteer, Westmoreland County, Virginia, who located and copied DeAtley's estate file located in Book 19, Fiduciaries and Accounts, Westmoreland County, Virginia, pages 372, 376, and 392.

[92] http://www.vahistorical.org/research/genealogy.htm (retrieved (2 August 2012)

[93] The only possibility that James was born in Stafford County would be if Lucinda had, for whatever reason, been traveling at the time she delivered. 1850 Census, Kanawha County, Virginia, says "Virginia." The 1860 Census, Franklin County, Missouri, says "Virginia."

[94] According to the 1850 U.S. Census. Note that a mulatto child was definitely a fair skinned African American, who may or may not have had Caucasian ancestry. The distinction between black and mulatto was likely very much a

subjective distinction made by the census enumerator.

[95] Kanawha County, (West) Virginia, Deed Book P, page 301.

[96] Kanawha County Circuit Court file 1848-19, includes a narrative, notes, capias warrant (bench warrant), and record of bail. This data is from typewritten "Index cards to court records, Kanawha County, West Virginia: 1754-1933," and microfilmed by the Family History Center (LDS film 249656) from originals at the West Virginia University Library, Morgantown, West Virginia. This index is to the loose papers, also at the West Virginia University Library.

[97] Burke, Diane Mutti. *On Slavery's Border: Missouri's Small Slaveholding Households, 1815-1865.* (Athens, Ga.: University of Georgia Press, 2010), 111-112.

[98] Trexler, 28.

[99] Lucinda inherited slaves from her father's estate. The eldest female may well be Hannah, who was given to her by her father before he died. The three young children were born after James Deatley's Will was drafted in 1841, and my likely be Hannah's "increase." The child underlined, as will be discussed later, may well be Arthur Jackson's mother.

[100] 1850 U.S. Census, Kanawha County, Virginia. Population Schedules of Free Persons and Slave Schedules abstracted for Richard L. Jackson.

[101] Federal Non-Population Census Schedules, 1850-1880 http://www.archives.gov/research/census/nonpopulation/reference-report-1850-1880.pdf (retrieved 27 Aug 2012).

[102] 1850 U.S. Census, Kanawha County, Virginia. Agricultural Schedules. The value of his farming implements and machinery was $200; livestock totaled $524; and value of animals slaughtered was $70. Ann Thomas, the mother of George Thomas who married Richard and Lucinda's daughter, Virginia Catherine, was also enumerated near the Jacksons, as was a James Thomas. None of these people were found in the 1860 Agricultural schedules.

Locating the microfilmed Agricultural Schedules for Kanawha was a challenge; but, a microform copy was eventually discovered at the University of North Carolina at Chapel Hill. And, as it turns out, the 1850 and 1860 Kanawha County, Virginia, Agricultural and Manufacturing Census Records are microfilmed and arranged among West Virginia materials. The author is indebted to Claire Kluskens at the National Archives, and Beth L. Rowe, Regional Documents Librarian and Head of Documents and Microforms Section for their diligence and kindness.

According to Kluskens, the microform (and the original schedules) are also at the West Virginia Department of Archives and History. In the 1920s, before the National Archives was created in 1934, the U.S. Census Bureau offered the 19th century non-population census schedules to the states, and many of them took them, including West Virginia. In the 1960s the National Archives attempted to reclaim them (either on microform, or the originals). The National Archives were unsuccessful in procuring either microform or the originals from West

Virginia.

[103] http://www.rootsweb.ancestry.com/~wvkanawh/census/1850stat.html (retrieved 18 August 2012).

[104] http://www.rootsweb.ancestry.com/~wvkanawh/census/1860stat.html (retrieved 18 August 2012).

[105] Kanawha County Court file 1850-11, includes a narrative, summon, 12 subpoenas, account, 2 writs, 3 bonds, petition, verdict, jury instructions, exceptions, notes on case, transcript and notice.

[106] Kanawha County, (West) Virginia, Deed Book Q, page 660.

[107] Kanawha County Circuit Court file 1851-27, includes a narrative, summons, note, 2 Fifa, bond and notice.

[108] Kanawha County Circuit Court file 1851-33, includes a narrative, 2 accounts, 4 affidavits, 4 subpoenas, and summons.

[109] Kanawha County Circuit Court file 1851-33, includes a narrative, 2 summons, note, bond, notice, and 2 Fifa.

[110] Kanawha County Circuit Court file 1851-35, includes a narrative, note, 3 summons, and Fifa.

[111] Kanawha County Circuit Court file 1852-15, includes summons, affidavit, and suggestion.

[112] Kanawha County County Court file 1852-17, includes Fifa.

[113] Kanawha County County Court file 1852-18, includes 2 summons, order, and bond.

[114] Kanawha County Circuit Court file 1852-21, includes a narrative, note and summons.

[115] Kanawha County Circuit Court file 1852-73, includes Fifa.

[116] Kanawha County Circuit Court file 1852-73, includes Fifa.

[117] Kanawha County Recorder of Deeds records. The license was issued on 31 October; they were married by James M. Brown. 1850 and 1860 Censuses. Also, e-mail correspondence between the author and Thomas family descendants.

[118] Kanawha County Court file 1853-3, includes Capias.

[119] Kanawha County Court file 1853-3, includes summons.

[120] Kanawha County Court file 1853-23, includes bond, notice ($289).

[121] Kanawha County Circuit file 1853-30, includes 2 notices, judgment, bond, and 2 Fifas.

[122] Kanawha County, (West) Virginia, Deed Book S, page 329.

[123] Kanawha County Circuit file 1854-28, includes Fifa.

[124] Kanawha County Circuit file 1855-26, includes a narrative and summons.

[125] Kanawha County Circuit file 1855-39, includes a narrative, 2 accounts, 2 bonds, due bill, capias warrants, Fifa, and 19 statements.

[126] The case Kanawha County Court case file 1856-28 included a narrative, summon, note, bond and notice.

[127] Kanawha County Court file 1856-28, includes a narrative, summon, note, bond, and notice.

[128] Kanawha County Court file 1856-26, includes F. C. bond, notice and Fifa.
[129] Kanawha County Court file 1856-26, includes F. C. bond, notice and Fifa.
[130] Kanawha County Court file 1856-27, includes F. C. bond, notice and Fifa.
[131] Kanawha County Court file 1856-28, includes F. C. bond, notice and Fifa.
[132] Kanawha County Court file 1856-29, includes a narrative, 2 summons, note and Scifa.
[133] Kanawha County Court file 1856-31, includes F. C. bond, notice and Fifa.
[134] Kanawha County Court file 1856-31, includes a narrative, summons, 25 subpoenas, 2 accounts, notice, and deposition.
[135] Kanawha County Circuit Court file 1856-35, includes a narrative, summons, and note.
[136] Kanawha County Circuit Court file 1856-36, includes Fifa.
[137] Kanawha County Circuit Court file 1856-37, includes a narrative, summary, note and 2 Fifas.
[138] Kanawha County Circuit Court file 1856-38, includes 2 Fifas.
[139] Kanawha County Court file 1856-59, includes F. O. C. Bond, and notice.
[140] Kanawha County Recorder of Deeds, Register of Births.
[141] Kanawha County Court file 1857-35, includes a summon.
[142] Kanawha County Court file 1857-35, includes a F. C. Bond and notice.
[143] Kanawha County Court file 1857-37, includes a F.C. bond, notice, and a Fifa (a judgment or lien against a Defendant's property).
[144] Kanawha County Court file 1857-38, includes a F.C. Bond, Fifa, and notice.
[145] Kanawha County Court file 1857-38, includes a F.C. bond, notice, and Fifa.
[146] Kanawha County Court file 1857-39, includes a F.C. bond, notice, and Fifa.
[147] Kanawha County Court file 1857-71, includes a narrative, note, summon, F.C. bond, and notice.
[148] Kanawha County Court file 1857-71, includes a narrative, summon, note, F.C. bond, and notice.
[149] Kanawha County Circuit Court file 1857-78, includes a F.C. bond, and 2 Fifas.
[150] Kanawha County Circuit Court file 1857-89, includes a narrative, summon, 3 subpoenas, 2 notes, plea, 2 Fifas, assignment, notice and F.C. bond.
[151] "Law! Law! Law!," *Kanawha Valley Star*, 2 Mar 1858, 2.
[152] Kanawha County Circuit Court file 1858-9, includes 2 Fifas, F.C. bond, and notice.
[153] Kanawha County Court file 1858-30, including summons.
[154] Kanawha County Circuit Court file 1858-38, includes narrative, account, publications, summon, and affidavit.
[155] Kanawha County Court file 1858-54, includes a summons, accounting and cover.
[156] Conrad, Howard Louis, ed. "James P. Jackson." *Encyclopedia of the History of Missouri*. Volume 3. (Southern History Co., 1901), p. 398-403. James' biography states "The father brought his family to Missouri in 1849," which

clearly should be 1859. The 1878 Atlas of Franklin County, Missouri, p. 37, records both 1858 and 1859 in the same biography for Dr. John Wesley Jackson.
[157] "Death of Dr. J. P. Jackson," *Kansas City* (Mo.) *Star*, 22 Nov 1901.
[158] Conrad, Howard Louis, ed. "James P. Jackson." *Encyclopedia of the History of Missouri*. Volume 3. (Southern History Co., 1901), p. 398-403.
[159] If, by chance, this was the reason the Jacksons may have relocated to Missouri, little would they have known that, "in 1857 the people of Franklin County complained of their slaves escaping by [rail]." Trexler, 178.
[160] Switala, William J., *Underground Railroad in Delaware, Maryland, and West Virginia*, Stackpole Books, 2004 pgs. 120-123
118http://en.wikipedia.org/wiki/History_of_slavery_in_West_Virginia#cite_ref-34
[161] *Born in Slavery: Slave Narratives from the Federal Writers' Project, 1936-1938*. Ohio Narratives, Volume XII. Anna Smith, 85.
[162] "Slaves In Missouri In 1860: There Were 114,000 in the State, One County Only Had No Slaves." *Howard County* (Mo.) *Advertiser*, 9 Jan 1903. http://www.usgennet.org/usa/mo/topic/afro-amer/slavesinmo.html (retrieved 2 August 2012)
[163] Trexler, 44.
[164] Leigh, E. M.D. *Bird's-Eye Views of Slavery in Missouri*. (St. Louis, Mo.: Keith & Woods, C. C. Bailey, James M. Crawford, C. Witter, 1862). Also, "Slaves In Missouri In 1860: There Were 114,000 in the State, One County Only Had No Slaves," *Howard County* (Mo.) *Advertiser*, 9 Jan 1903. http://www.usgennet.org/usa/mo/topic/afro-amer/slavesinmo.html (retrieved 2 August 2012). Also, Kiel, Herman Gottlieb. *Centennial Biographical Dictionary of Franklin County, Missouri*. Reprinted; originally published in 1925. (Washington, Mo.: Washington Historical Society), 231.
[165] Claggett, Steve. "Civil War in Franklin County." *Four Rivers Genealogical Society* (August 2014): 28: 3: 6.
[166] Greene, Lorenzo J., Antonio F. Holland and Gary Kremer. "The Role of the Negro in Missouri History, 1719-1970." *Official Manual, State of Missouri, 1973-1974.* http://law.wustl.edu/staff/taylor/manual/manual.htm (retrieved 2 August 2012)
[167] Trexler, 11-12, citing the Seventh Federal Census, p. 654-655, and the Eighth Federal Census, Population, p. 280-283.
[168] Claggett, 6.
[169] Greene, Dr. Lorenzo J., Antonio F. Holland, and Gary Kremer. "The Role of the Negro in Missouri History, 1719-1970." *Official Manual*, State of Missouri, 1973-1974. http://law.wustl.edu/staff/taylor/manual/manual.htm (retrieved 2 August 2012). These statistics were previously published in 1914 in Trexler, p. 39. For this study, however, the price of slaves is inconsequential since there is no evidence that the Jacksons ever sold slaves. And, the ones that they acquired may have been through inheritance with increase.

[170] Trexler, 45. "Letters from old residents and slaveholders in all parts of the State deny that in Missouri, at least, slave breeding was ever engaged in as the antislavery people so often charged. The better classes at any rate frowned upon the practice."
[171] Glanker, Bill. "From Slavery to Freedom: The Slaves of Valentine Hunter." *The Missouri State Archives: Where History Begins.* (Jefferson City, Mo.: Robin Carnahan, Secretary of State in partnership with the Friends of the Missouri State Archives, 2012). (Summer): 6-7.
[172] Trexler, 13-18.
[173] Trexler, 27.
[174] Trexler, 13-18.
[175] Trexler, 27. Mr. George F. Shaw of Independence, Missouri, formerly of Franklin County, said that there were few overseers in the latter county, as general farming was the rule.
[176] Trexler, 90.
[177] Dr. Lorenzo J. Greene, Antonio F. Holland and Gary Kremer. "The Role of the Negro in Missouri History, 1719-1970. Official Manual, State of Missouri, 1973-1974. http://law.wustl.edu/staff/taylor/manual/manual.htm (retrieved 2 August 2012)
[178] Trexler, 26-27. Law of July 4, 1825 (Revised Laws, 1825, vol. i, p. 310, sec. 90).
[179] In 1860 Missouri ranked seventh in tobacco culture, producing 25,086,196 lbs. (Eighth Federal Census, Agriculture, pp. xliv, 88-94). Tobacco was raised to a greater or less degree throughout the eastern and central regions. Many farmers raised tobacco, not as a staple, but as they did corn or wheat. Trexler, 26.
[180] It is here where Arthur Jackson as a youth gained some experience at raising hogs, which he would attempt in his young adulthood.
[181] 1860 U.S. Census, Franklin County, Missouri. Agricultural Schedules. The value of his farming implements and machinery was $200; livestock totaled $1,230; and value of animals slaughtered was $185.
[182] 1860 U.S. Census, Franklin County, Missouri. Population Schedules of Free Persons; Slave Schedules; and Agricultural Schedules abstracted for Richard L. Jackson.
[183] 1860 U.S. Census, Franklin County, Missouri. Population Schedules of Free Persons; Slave Schedules; and Agricultural Schedules abstracted for Richard L. Jackson.
[184] 1860 Franklin County tax rolls, as researched by Sue Lampe, volunteer researcher, Four Rivers Genealogical Society, Washington, Franklin County, Missouri. Richard L. Jackson's son, John Wesley Jackson, paid $.38 for Poll tax and $.88 State tax for an assessment of $250 in personal property; he owning no real property at this date.
[185] Personal correspondence between the author and Four Rivers Genealogical

Society, represented by Sue Lampe, 18 July 2012, who undertook a deed search from 1850 through 1865, and also tax records in 1860, 1862 and 1863.

[186] The author has compiled significant data about the Jacksons as grantors and grantees in Franklin County deeds. This study continues as this biography goes to press, and may be incorporated in a future edition.

[187] 1860 U.S. Census, Slave Schedules, Boles Township, Franklin County, Missouri, Page 275, lines 12-15.

[188] There is one Ann Thomas, age 64, in the 1870 U.S. Census for Spring Vale, Dranesville Township, Fairfax County, Virginia (Page 29/271). Thomas family descendants show Thomas Matthew Thomas was born in 1791 and died in 1840 in Buckingham County, Virginia; and, Ann S. (Ward) Thomas was born in 1804, and died in 1871 in Ohio. E-mail correspondence with the author.

[189] 1850 U. S. Census, population schedule, Kanawha County, Virginia, page 39, lines 20-23; 1850 U. S. Census, slave schedules, Kanawha County, Virginia, page 10, lines 14-32. The ages of the slaves is ordered here chronologically; on the census, they 'may' be listed in family groups.

[190] The comparison here attempts to match each slave from 1850 to 1860, understanding that ages of slaves in Census returns cannot be relied upon religiously…and that a fair number of slaves were acquired and disposed of within a decade.

[191] This is the best match should Arthur's father have been in the Thomas household--and would have very likely carried the Thomas surname. This slave would have been 18 in 1856 when Arthur was born. He would have been about 32 in 1870. There are two, free, black men with the Thomas surname in the 1870 U.S. Census for Charleston Township, Kanawha County, West Virginia:

Jerry Thomas, age 35, born in Maryland; and,
John Thomas, 37, Virginia.

Jerry Thomas was also in the 1880 U.S. Census for Malden, Kanawha County, West Virginia (ED53 P8). He was listed as age 50, born in Maryland, with his wife, Mary, 41; and children: Sallie, 20; Henry S., 14; Samuel, 11; James, 8; Margaret, 4; Horatio A., b. July 1879.

Jerry Thomas was surely a former slave of the Ann Thomas family. Ann's son (George's brother) was named Jerry.

A third man, John Thomas, 40, Virginia, was in Louden Township of Kanawha County. Of course, Arthur's father could have migrated with the Jackson and Thomas families as they moved west. And, he may have been from a completely different plantation yet unknown.

[192] Claggett. 6.

[193] Claggett, 6.

208

[194] Goodspeed. *History of Franklin, Jefferson, Washington, Crawford, and Gasconade Counties, Missouri.* (Goodspeed, 1888), p. 243-247, 260.
[195] Goodspeed. *History of Franklin, Jefferson, Washington, Crawford, and Gasconade Counties, Missouri.* (Goodspeed, 1888), p. 243-247, 260.
[196] "The Civil War in Missouri." 1861. http://www.mocivilwar.org/history/1861.html (retrieved 30 Aug 2012).
[197] Goodspeed. *History of Franklin, Jefferson, Washington, Crawford, and Gasconade Counties, Missouri.* (Goodspeed, 1888), p. 243-247, 260.
[198] Sims, Edgar Barr. *Making a State: Formation of West Virginia.* (Charleston: E.B. Sims, 1956).
[199] "General Orders No. 135 (U.S. War Department)." (2014) In *Ohio Civil War Central*, Retrieved September 14, 2014, from Ohio Civil War Central: http://www.ohiocivilwarcentral.com/entry.php?rec=1192.
[200] Woodtor, 216.
[201] Howell, Book 5. Voice of Sallie Paul, 12.
[202] Howell, Book 5. Voice of Martin Ruffin, 36.
[203] Howell, Book 5. Voice of Simon Gillman, 37.
[204] Nolen, Rose M. *Hoecakes, Hambone, and All That Jazz.* Missouri Heritage Reader series. (Columbia, Mo.: University of Missouri Press, 2003), 13. This book offers an easy-to-read, comprehensive life of a typical Missouri slave.
[205] Greene, Lorenzo J., Gary R. Kremer, and Antonio F. Holland. *Missouri's Black Heritage.* Revised. (Columbia, Mo.: University of Missouri Press, 1993), 33. A detailed picture of daily life is explored in the essay, "From Sunup to Sundown: The Life of the Slave," 25-41.
[206] Born in Slavery: Slave Narratives from the Federal Writers' Project, 1936-1938. Ohio Narratives, Volume XII. Nan Stewart, p. 86. Also, Rawick, George P., ed. *The American Slave: A Composite Autobiography.* Westport, CT: Greenwood Publishing, 1972, 19 vols. (Vol. 16 (b) p. 86-91; Nan Stewart.
[207] Rawick, George P., ed. *The American slave: A Composite Autobiography, Supplement II.* Westport, CT: Greenwood Publishing, 1979, 10 vols. (4):1096-1108;Slave (4)(a):295-7; Eli Davison.
[208] Rawick, George P., ed. *The American slave: A Composite Autobiography, Supplement II.* Westport, CT: Greenwood Publishing, 1979, 10 vols. (5): 1553-70; Lizzie Grant. Also, http://freepages.genealogy.rootsweb.ancestry.com/~ewyatt/_borders/Texas%20Slave%20Narratives/Texas%20G/Grant,%20Lizzie.html (retrieved 18 August 2012).
[209] Trexler, 93.
[210] "The Civil War in Missouri." 1862. http://www.mocivilwar.org/history/1862.html (retrieved 30 Aug 2012).
[211] Goodspeed. *History of Franklin, Jefferson, Washington, Crawford, and Gasconade Counties, Missouri.* (Goodspeed, 1888), p. 243-247, 260.
[212] "The Civil War in Missouri." 1862.

http://www.mocivilwar.org/history/1862.html (retrieved 30 Aug 2012).

[213] The author is inclined to believe that the Range was *actually* **2 East**, given that all future and current Boles Township landholdings of the Jackson family are within the same section and township number; but, **Range 2 E**, rather than 1 E, as provided by research conducted by Four Rivers Genealogical Society.

[214] 1862 Franklin County tax rolls, as researched by Four Rivers Genealogical Society, represented by Sue Lampe, Washington, Franklin County, Missouri. The tax books have not dates of payment or assessment; on some of the original tax books, Lampe reports, "we are lucky to have a year given." "J. W. Jackson" is listed on the tax rolls at that same location on the rolls, but with no taxes assessed. This 'might' mean that John Wesley Jackson was away in the military during the Civil War. Personal correspondence between the author and Lampe, 18 July 2012.

[215] "The Civil War in Missouri." 1863.
http://www.mocivilwar.org/history/1863.html (retrieved 30 Aug 2012).

[216] The 1850 U.S. Census shows John Wesley Jackson and Thomas B. Jackson having been born in Maryland. The 1860 Census shows John Wesley Jackson born in Maryland, and Thomas B. and Richard, Jr., in Virginia. National Archives and Records Administrations (NARA); Washington, D.C. *Consolidated Lists of Civil War Draft Registration Records (Provost Marshal General's Bureau; Consolidated Enrollment Lists, 1863-1865).* Record Group: 110, Records of the Provost Marshal General's Bureau (Civil War).

[217] "The Saint Louis Medical College was originally organized in 1841 as the Medical Department of Saint Louis University. Almost immediately after its founding, and despite the medical department's nonsectarian board, public pressure...demanded that the department sever ties with the Roman Catholic university. Succumbing to this pressure, it became an independent institution under the name Saint Louis Medical College in 1855. The college affiliated with Washington University in 1891." http://www.digitalcommons.wustl.edu (retrieved 11 Feb 2015).

[218] As guerrilla warfare and recruiting increased, and as the state had been stripped of nearly all but the volunteer Missouri State Militia Cavalry regiments, General Schofield declared a compulsory militia enrollment on 22 July 1862. The new Enrolled Missouri Militia (EMM) could be called up in time of emergency to garrison key points in their locale or even to disrupt guerrilla encampments nearby. Many were not provided with uniforms and soon after their formation would wear white hatbands as a form of identification. http://en.wikipedia.org/wiki/Enrolled_Missouri_Militia (retrieved 11 November 2012).

[219] Woodtor, 151. Also, "100 Milestone Documents," http://www.ourdocuments.gov/doc.php?flash=true&doc=35. "The War Department issued General Order 143 on May 22, 1863, creating the United States Colored Troops. By the end of the Civil War, roughly 179,000 black men

(10 percent of the Union Army) served as soldiers in the U.S. Army, and another 19,000 served in the Navy."
[220] Woodtor, 152, as quoted by Benjamin Quarles in *The Negro in the Civil War.*
[221] http://www.sos.mo.gov/archives/provost/ (retrieved 4 Dec 2012). Also, http://www.usgennet.org/usa/mo/county/stlouis/ct.htm (retrieved 14 Sept 2014). And, http://www.archives.gov/research/african-americans/freedmens-bureau/missouri.pdf (retrieved 27 Jan 2015). "Originally the slave owner's consent was required before a slave could enlist. Order No. 135 of Nov. 1863 changed this, allowing enlistment without consent. If the owner did consented they were given some compensation. In addition, the order abolished the highly effective recruitment patrols. There was some dispute that these patrols were forcing some slaves against their will. Certainly they were opposed by most slave owners. Unfortunately the change required slaves willing to enlist, to travel to the recruitment stations, sometimes many miles away."

The original records are part of the National Archives and Records Administration, Record Group 105, Records of the Bureau of Refugees, Freedmen, and Abandoned Lands (Freedmen's Bureau), and comprise several series such as:

Field Office Records
Series M1908, *Records of the Field Offices for the State of Missouri, Bureau of Refugees, Freedmen, and Abandoned Lands, 1865–1872.* 24 rolls.

Other Records

M803, *Records of the Education Division of the Bureau of Refugees, Freedmen, and Abandoned Lands, 1865–1871.* 35 rolls.

M1875, *Marriage Records of the Office of the Commissioner, Washington Headquarters of the Bureau of Refugees, Freedmen, and Abandoned Lands, 1861–1869.* 5 rolls.

M1894, *Descriptive Recruitment Lists of Volunteers for the United States Colored Troops for the State of Missouri, 1863–1865.* 6 rolls.

M1895-06, *Washington Recruiting Station, December 1863-March 1864.*

[222] "A month later he modified it allowing the sale of any slave unfit for military service." "U.S. Colored Troops and the Plight of the Refugee Slave" (http://www.usgennet.org/usa/mo/county/stlouis/ct.htm (retrieved 14 Sept 2014).
[223] *Daily Missouri Republican* (St. Louis, Missouri), 28 Mar. 1863, p. 1, c. 1.

[224] http://en.wikipedia.org/wiki/United_States_Colored_Troops (retrieved 27 Jan 2015).

[225] National Archives and Records Administration, Record Group 105, Records of the Bureau of Refugees, Freedmen, and Abandoned Lands (Freedmen's Bureau), *Recruitment List of Volunteers for the United States Colored Troops for the State of Missouri.* M1894-06. http://www.sos.mo.gov/images/Archives/Provost/F1897.5.pdf (retrieved 4 Dec 2012).

Also, the Secretary of State of Missouri's "Missouri Digital Heritage" offers a database of soldiers' records that covers the War of 1812 through World War I, as abstracted from Record Group: "Office of the Adjutant General," Series: "Record of Service Card, Civil War, 1861-1865," Box: 43, Reel: s00873.

The author's search encompassed all soldiers with the Jackson surname who served in the United States Colored Troops (particularly the 18th, 56th, 60th, 62nd, 65th, 67th, 68th, Infantry Regiments and 3rd Artillery Regiment), numbering some 140 individuals. Some enlistment cards did not provide an enlistment place.

[226] Secretary of State of Missouri's "Missouri Digital Heritage" database of soldiers' records that covers the War of 1812 through World War I, as abstracted from Record Group: "Office of the Adjutant General," Series: "Record of Service Card, Civil War, 1861-1865," Box: 43, Reel: s00873. Andrew Jackson was mustered in on August 12, 1863, at St. Louis.

[227] National Archives and Records Administration, Record Group 105, Records of the Bureau of Refugees, Freedmen, and Abandoned Lands (Freedmen's Bureau), *Recruitment List of Volunteers for the United States Colored Troops for the State of Missouri.* M1894-06. http://www.sos.mo.gov/images/Archives/Provost/F1897.5.pdf (retrieved 4 Dec 2012).

Also, the Secretary of State of Missouri's "Missouri Digital Heritage" offers a database of soldiers' records that covers the War of 1812 through World War I, as abstracted from Record Group: "Office of the Adjutant General," Series: "Record of Service Card, Civil War, 1861-1865," Box: 43, Reel: s00873.

The author's search encompassed all soldiers with the Jackson surname who served in the United States Colored Troops (particularly the 18th, 56th, 60th, 62nd, 65th, 67th, 68th, Infantry Regiments and 3rd Artillery Regiment), numbering some 140 individuals. Some enlistment cards did not provide an enlistment place.

[228] Internal Revenue Assessment Lists for the State of Missouri, 1862-1866. National Archives and Records Administration, Record Group M776. Division

8, District 2, Franklin County, Missouri, April 1863.

[229] "Dr. John W. Jackson." 1878 Atlas, Franklin County, Missouri, 37.

[230] Likely Range 2 East. 1863 Franklin County tax rolls, as researched by Sue Lampe, volunteer researcher, Four Rivers Genealogical Society, Washington, Franklin County, Missouri. The tax books have no dates of payment or assessment; on some of the original tax books, Lampe reports, *"we are lucky to have a year given."*

[231] Most likely, Jackson was interred in the North Cemetery, which is located between Old Highway 100 (Historic Route 66) and Park Lamar Drive, in Section 7, about a mile southwest of the town Gray Summit. His eldest son, John Wesley Jackson married Virginia "Jennie" Carter North, a daughter of an early Franklin County pioneer, Flavius Josephus North. And, the North Cemetery is very near Gray Summit (Section 8, Township 43 North, Range 2 East). The cemetery is listed in the 1898 Atlas of Franklin County, Mo., then on the property of S. F. North, Section 7, Township 43, Range 2 E, page 11. In 1900, as will be seen, Richard L. Jackson, Sr., was exhumed and re-interred in Elmwood Cemetery in Kansas City, Jackson County, Missouri.

[232] Glanker, Bill. "From Slavery to Freedom: The Slaves of Valentine Hunter." *The Missouri State Archives: Where History Begins.* (Jefferson City, Mo.: Robin Carnahan, Secretary of State in partnership with the Friends of the Missouri State Archives, 2012). (Summer): 6-7.

[233] *Missouri Session Laws*, 1828, ch. i, sec. 1; Trexler, 29.

[234] Statement of "Uncle" Peter Clay of Liberty. He adds that the slave was clever enough to go to his new employer in his worst rags in order to get the full quota of clothing. Trexler, 29.

[235] Frazier, Harriet C. *Slavery and Crime in Missouri, 1773-1865.* (Jefferson, N.C.: McFarland and company, Inc., Publishers, 2001), 111.

[236] No newspapers for Franklin County, Missouri, survive from 1863.

[237] Unfortunately, no identifying information about the slaves was recorded. Franklin County Probate Court, August 1863 Term. Estate of Richard L. Jackson, deceased August 10, 1863. Missouri State Archives microfilm roll number C40570. Richard is *not* listed in a separate microfilming of Wills, roll C2418. After microfilming, the original probate case files were released for preservation to the Washington Historical Society in Washington, Missouri.

[238] Franklin County Probate Court, August 1863 Term. Estate of Richard L. Jackson, deceased August 10, 1863. Missouri State Archives microfilm roll number C40570.

[239] "Dr. J. W. Jackson Dead." Kansas City (Mo.) Star, 13 Mar 1890. This event was said to have occurred in 1863 according to: Conrad, Howard Louis. "John W. Jackson." *Encyclopedia of the History of Missouri.* Volume 3. (The Southern History Company, 1901), 398-403.

[240] "U.S. Colored Troops and the Plight of the Refugee Slave," http://www.usgennet.org/usa/mo/county/stlouis/ct.htm (retrieved 14 Sept. 2014).

[241] Franklin County Probate Court, August 1863 Term. Estate of Richard L. Jackson, deceased August 10, 1863. Missouri State Archives microfilm roll number C40570.

[242] "The Civil War in Missouri." 1864. http://www.mocivilwar.org/history/1864.html (retrieved 30 Aug 2012).

[243] Claggett, 7.

[244] Gray Summit had formerly been called Port William when William North was postmaster from 23 Jan 1838 to 23 May 1844. Kiel, Herman Gottlieb. *Centennial Biographical Dictionary of Franklin County, Missouri.* Reprinted; originally published in 1925. (Washington, Mo.: Washington Historical Society), 202, 219.

[245] http://home.usmo.com/~momollus/FranCoCW/54EMM.htm (retrieved 11 Nov 2012). Kenneth E. Weant, Civil War Records: Missouri Enrolled Militia Infantry Regiments. Volume 7. (Arlington, Tx.: K. E. Weant, ca. 2010), 111-145.

[246] Thomas B. Jackson's military involvement was listed by Kiel, Herman Gottlieb. *Centennial Biographical Dictionary of Franklin County, Missouri.* Reprinted; originally published in 1925. (Washington, Mo.: Washington Historical Society), 122. The enlistment or muster roll for Thomas Jackson shows 34 days of service. Sources indicate that both the 54th and 55th Regiments were organized in Franklin County. See, *Annual Report of the Adjutant General of Missouri for 1864* (Jefferson City, Mo.: W.A. Curry, Public Printer, 1865), p. 310.

[247] Claggett, 7.

[248] Goodspeed. *History of Franklin, Jefferson, Washington, Crawford, and Gasconade Counties, Missouri.* (Goodspeed, 1888), p. 243-247, 260. Also, Claggett, 7.

[249] Thomas B. Jackson's military involvement was listed by Kiel, Herman Gottlieb. *Centennial Biographical Dictionary of Franklin County, Missouri.* Reprinted; originally published in 1925. (Washington, Mo.: Washington Historical Society), 122. The enlistment or muster roll for Thomas Jackson shows 34 days of service. Sources indicate that both the 54th and 55th Regiments were organized in Franklin County. See, *Annual Report of the Adjutant General of Missouri for 1864* (Jefferson City, Mo.: W.A. Curry, Public Printer, 1865), p. 310.

[250] Emancipation Proclamation. http://en.wikipedia.org/wiki/Emancipation_Proclamation (retrieved 30 Aug 2012).

[251] Trexler, 239-240.

[252] Conrad, Howard Louis. "John W. Jackson." *Encyclopedia of the History of Missouri.* Volume 3. (The Southern History Company, 1901), 398-403. Also, "Dr. John W. Jackson."1878 Atlas, Franklin County, Missouri, 37.

[253] Willis, Deborah, and Barbara Krauthamer. *Envisioning Emancipation: Black*

Americans and the End of Slavery. (Philadelphia, Pa.: Temple University Press, 2013), 23, 129-130.

[254] Greene, 88.

[255] Trexler, 83, citing *Missouri Session Laws*, 1846, p. 103, secs. I, 5.

[256] See Appendix, "Arthur Jackson Age, Race and Literacy in Historical Documents." Though there were a couple of census years where he responded positively to his ability, it's highly unlikely that he could read or write.

[257] Woodtor, 173.

[258] Caldwell, A. B., ed. "William Jackson" [no relation to the family of this study]. History of the American Negro. West Virginia Edition. Volume VII. (Atlanta, Ga.: A. B. Caldwell Publishing Co., 1923); http://www.wvculture.org/history/histamne/jacksonw.html (retrieved 16 Mar 2013).

[259] Woodtor, 173.

[260] Woodtor, 174.

[261] Woodtor, 180.

[262] Coggswell, Gladys Caines. Stories from the Heart: Missouri's African American Heritage. Missouri Heritage Reader series. (Columbia, Mo.: University of Missouri Press, 2009), 54-55.

[263] Woodtor, 174.

[264] Greene, 91.

[265] Abner Jackson (of Washington) and Frances Oliver were married by Moses Dickson, AME Church, 10 Sep 1868 (recorded 18 Jan 1869), p. 34.
Andrew Jackson and Nancy Davidson, 14 Dec 1876/24 Jan 1868, p. 32.
James Jackson and Elizabeth Roberts, 28 Jun 1867/9 Nov 1867, p. 29.
Joseph Jackson (age 27) and Adelia Good (24), 4 mar 1866/10 Jan 1867, his children: Joseph, James and Luke, p. 25. Missouri State Archives microfilm number C2388.

[266] According to Woodtor, "most African American newspapers well into the twentieth century carried personal ads in which former slaves were still looking for anyone who had knowledge of the whereabouts of their lost kin," 190.

[267] Greene, 89.

[268] John also purchased 40 acres in Southeast ¼ of the Southeast ¼ of Section 30 from Spencer J. Coleman in December 1871; but, he sold it to David North in December 1873.

There were several recordings in various books between the three parties involving the East ½ of the Northeast ¼ of Section 31, Township 44, Range 2E, including: a Warranty Deed from the Pursley's to Jackson dated 14 Sep 1865, Book X, p. 609; a Deed of Trust from Jackson to Pursley, 15 Sep 1865, Book A, p. 35; a Warranty Deed from Jackson to Blunt, 27 Jan 1866, Book Y, p. 147; a Warranty Deed from Blunt to Jackson, 27 Jan 1866, Book Z, p. 327; and, a Warranty Deed from Blunt to Jackson, 10 Oct 1866, Book Z, p. 328.

Other incidental recordings for lots and modest parcels of land acquired and disposed throughout Franklin County by John W. Jackson and his brothers, Thomas B. and James P., were also noted and are maintained in the author's personal research papers.

John W. Jackson's land passed to his widow in 1890, and most of that listed in his probate case file and on the 1898 Atlas had been sold by the time the 1930 Plat Book was published. *However, John W. and Virginia C. Jackson descendants own some of their ancestor's Franklin County land to this day* (2015). A more thorough study of the Franklin County Recorder of Deeds records is required for a complete account of the Jackson's Franklin County postbellum landholdings.

[269] "Dr. John W. Jackson."1878 Atlas, Franklin County, Missouri, 37.

[270] Franklin County Probate Court, August 1863 Term. Estate of Richard L. Jackson, deceased August 10, 1863. Missouri State Archives microfilm roll number C40570.

[271] "Dr. John W. Jackson."*1878 Atlas, Franklin County, Missouri*, 37. Also, National Register of Historic Places, Nomination-Application (1983): "In addition to farming, James North established a tannery, built the first water mill in the county, and practiced medicine. Following their arrival in Franklin County about 1817, the North family earned a prominent position in the county gentry, who supplied most of the early leaders and established a social and political influence which persisted for many years. James and Flavius North held state and county offices of public trust throughout their lives. Over generations, the family contributed to the progress of the county as physicians, lawyers, farmers, and teachers." http://dnr.mo.gov/shpo/nps-nr/84002534.pdf (retrieved 2 Feb 2015).

[272] The recordings included a Deed of Trust from Thomas to Charles Reinhard on 4 Jan 1868, Book B, p. 53; a Deed of Trust and Mortgage from Thomas to Charles Jones, Book 2, p. 105; and a Deed of Trust in 1874, Book 10, p. 441. Thomas disposed of the land sometime after 1874 and by 1878 (pending a more thorough study of the Franklin County Recorder of Deeds records).

[273] Conrad, Howard Louis. "James P. Jackson." *Encyclopedia of the History of Missouri*. Volume 3. (The Southern History Company, 1901), 398-403.

[274] Franklin County Probate Court, August 1863 Term. Estate of Richard L. Jackson, deceased August 10, 1863. Missouri State Archives microfilm roll number C40570.

[275] The census took over a year to complete beginning in January 1868 and ending in early 1869. Claggett, Steven F. *1868 Census, Franklin County, Missouri (Surviving Records)*. (Washington, Mo.: Four Rivers Genealogical Society, September 2007), Preface and Introduction. The original census scheduled are preserved by the Washington Historical Society. They *1876*

Missouri State Census, Franklin County, is also available on Missouri State Archives microfilm roll number C33796.

[276] *Holt County Sentinel,* 26 Mar 1869; *History of Holt and Atchison Counties,* 196. Conrad, "James P. Jackson," 398-403.

[277] *History of Holt and Atchison Counties,* 196.

[278] Franklin County Probate Court, August 1863 Term. Estate of Richard L. Jackson, deceased August 10, 1863. Missouri State Archives microfilm roll number C40570.

[279] Although the newspaper mentioned is no longer extant, even on microfilm, the settlement notice had been abstracted in a handwritten note found in a newspaper clipping file at the Four Rivers Genealogical Society.

[280] Franklin County Probate Court, August 1863 Term. Estate of Richard L. Jackson, deceased August 10, 1863. Missouri State Archives microfilm roll number C40570.

[281] The west 1/2 of the west 1/2 of the northeast 1/4. When he disposed of this property has not yet been researched and discovered. As will be seen in 1870, James P. Jackson is recorded as having opened the first drug store in Bigelow Township, Holt County, Missouri.

[282] The instructions to Assistant Marshals regarding "Personal Description" was as follows: *"Color. It ust be assumed that, when nothing is written in this column, "White," is to be understood. The column is always to be filled. Be particularly careful in reporting the class "Mulatto." The word here is generic and includes quadroons, octoroons, and all persons having any perceptible trace of African blood. Important scientific results depend upon the correct determination of this class in Schedules 1 & 2."*

[283] The instructions to Assistant Marshals in 1850 for Schedule 2-Slave Inhabitants was: *"If the age cannot be ascertained, insert a number which shall be the nearest approximate to it."*

[284] Wilson-Kleekamp, Traci L. *How Do I Put All the Information Together?* African American Genealogy: Part 5 of 5 Part Series. Missouri State Archives online presentations. http://www.sos.mo.gov/archives/presentations/default.asp?ap=aagene5 (retrieved 11 Nov 2012).

[285] Kiel, Herman Gottlieb. *Centennial Biographical Dictionary of Franklin County, Missouri.* Reprinted; originally published in 1925. (Washington, Mo.: Washington Historical Society), 231.

[286] "November 12, 1870," *Holt County Sentinel,* 15 Nov 1907.

[287] *Holt County Sentinel,* 24 Mar 1871.

[288] *Holt County Sentinel,* 26 May 1871, 3.

[289] "Sharp," *Holt County Sentinel,* 16 Feb. 1902, p. 1, c. 2. Also, Thomas Sharp's veteran's pension application file.

[290] If Mollie's birth date of May 1, 1855 (from her obituary) is correct, then she was actually 17 years, 5 months, 9 days old.

[291] Abraham "Abe" Sharp either sold Thomas Sharp, or, "sent him for safe keeping" to John Harvey Patterson in Howard County, Missouri, in 1862, "for fear I would go over into Kansas and become free." He enlisted at age 27 at Glasgow, Missouri, March 17, 1864, and was discharged February 6, 1866. In the fall 1867, he went to White Cloud, Doniphan Co., Kansas. He returned to his "old master's place" called Sharp's Grove, three miles north of Craig, Holt Co., Mo., in the fall of 1870, where he lived until his wife died in 1902 (except one year in 1879 when he returned to White Cloud). He as pensioned retroactively from February 6, 1866 at $2/month; at $4/month from June 2, 1886; at $10 from January 7, 1891; $12 from May 24, 1906; $15 from April 2, 1910; $21.50 from May 24, 1912; $27 from March 17, 1915. Thomas Sharp military file and pension file (Application No. 38987; Certificate No. 470291), National Archives and Records Administration (NARA), as found in *General Index to pension Files, 1861-1934;* Missouri Death certificate of his son, James A. Sharp; findagrave.com; and, "Negro Ex-Slave Dead," *St. Joseph News Press*, 18 Mar 1928. Thomas Sharp does not appear on the January 1, 1883, *List of Pensioners* for Holt County, Missouri that was compiled by the U.S. Pension Bureau.

[292] This would place his birth in 1841. His pension application lists 1836, 1837 and 1840 as his birth year on various affidavits; March 4, March 17, May 3, May 4 alternatively.

[293] McGillan, Jennifer. Research into 1872-1873 graduation catalogs, trustees minutes and faculty minutes by Jennifer McGillan, Archivist, Archives & Special Collections Augustus C. Long Health Sciences Library Columbia University Medical Center, 701 West 168th Street, New York, NY 10032 (transmitted to the author via e-mail 15 May 2013).

[294] West Virginia Division of Culture and History, Kanawha County, West Virginia, online marriage index, 1789, 1792 - 1797, 1800, 1802 - 1929, 1936, 1940-1967; http://www.wvculture.org/vrr/va_mcsearch.aspx (retrieved 7 May 2015). A descendant, Robert Thomas, located Eliza in the U.S. Census, age 13, living with her parents in North District, Pittsylvania County, Virginia; and, in the 1870 Census she is a domestic servant, age 22, living with one Hoffman family in Union, Kanawha County, West Virginia. M. Huffman testified to Eliza's age on her marriage license. E-mail correspondence between Thomas and the author.

[295] McGillan. Fred Thomas speculated: "...maybe they found out she [their sister, Virginia (Jackson) Thomass] was very sick and wanted to get back to her in Holt county and find out what was wrong with her and possibly help her. Urgent business and concern for a loved one can make one indisposed," per e-mail correspondence between Thomas and the author, 19 Nov 2015.

[296] His graduation year was cited as 1872 in Conrad, Howard Louis. "John W. Jackson." *Encyclopedia of the History of Missouri*. Volume 3. (The Southern History Company, 1901), 398-403. However, the biography for him in the 1878 Atlas, Franklin County, Missouri, likely more accurately pinpointed the

appointment in 1873.

[297] "Field Notes from Bigelow Township," *Holt County Sentinel*, 18 July 1873, p. 3. In the 7 March edition of the paper, James P. Jackson ran an ad for the sale of stock, an 82-acre farm on the road from Bigelow to Mound City, and three "good houses and lots in Bigelow, and 175-acres of number one bottom land," that he was offering for sale.

[298] Missouri Death Certificate, findagrave.com; Thomas Sharp pension file.

[299] With thanks to Fred Thomas for visiting the cemetery and literally digging around Virginia's tombstone, which had sunk into the ground to obscure her death date.

[300] *Holt County Sentinel*, 17 Apr 1874, 3.

[301] "Dr. John W. Jackson." 1878 Atlas, Franklin County, Missouri, 37. Also, 1874 and 1878 medical directories, as found Kiel files, Washington, Missouri Historical Society, courtesy Judy Schmidt, compiler.

[302] *Holt County Sentinel*, 17 Mar 1875.

[303] Richard and Laura's 1-year-old son, Henry, does not appear in the 1880 Census. It is presumed that Henry died between 1875-1880. Another son, Edgar, 1-year-old, appears five years later in the 1880 Census.

[304] 1880 Census, Bigelow Township, Holt County, Missouri; Missouri Death Certificate, findagrave.com; Thomas Sharp pension file.

[305] Death certificates and find a grave entries.

[306] *History of Holt and Atchison Counties,* 196. Also, *Holt County Sentinel*, 2 Apr 1875, announced James P. Jackson was going to locate at Mound City.

[307] The name "Jabez" had been used in Virginia Carter North's family. It so happens that Arthur Jackson in 1896 also named his second son Jabez, likely after Dr. John and Mrs. Virginia Jackson's son, Jabez North Jackson. As noted elsewhere in this study, Arthur's wife had claimed at one time that Arthur (born 1858) and Dr. Jabez North Jackson (born 1868) were ½ brothers.

[308] Arthur in 1891 named his first son, Edgar Walter, likely after Dr. John and Mrs. Virginia Jackson's son, Walter Emmett Jackson. This further solidifies Arthur's familial tidings to the 'white' Jackson family.

[309] *1876 Missouri State Census, Franklin County*. Missouri State Archives microfilm roll number C7661. John also appeared in the *1875 Franklin County Personal Tax Book, Boles Township*. Missouri State Archives microfilm roll number C34457. A search was made on the same roll of the *1876 Franklin County Land Tax Book* (for assessments of 1 August 18875); but, John's name was not located. It is possible his name was overlooked since most names assessed were crossed-through, presumably to indicate their taxes had been paid, and difficult to decipher.

[310] *1876 Missouri State Census, Holt County*. Missouri State Archives microfilm roll number C2762.

[311] He is also listed in the 1877 *Illustrated Historical Atlas of Holt County, Missouri*, in Section 18, Township 61, Range 39, with his Post Office at

Bigelow, 30.

[312] With 2 horses. He is also listed in the 1877 *Illustrated Historical Atlas of Holt County, Missouri*, in Mound City, 27.

[313] The census returns are difficult to read, so they could have been missed. Dr. James P. Jackson appears to have sold his practice by 5 May 1876, according to a "Take Notice" ad in the *Holt County Sentinel*. Jackson was listed among others in the Holt County Medical Society that met on June 26 at Craig, Missouri, *Holt County Sentinel*, 30 June 1876; and, on July 25 at Mound City, *Holt County Sentinel*, 4 Aug 1876.

[314] Thomas Sharp veteran's pension application.

[315] *Holt County Sentinel*, 3 Aug 1877.

[316] Conrad, Howard Louis. "James P. Jackson." *Encyclopedia of the History of Missouri*. Volume 3. (The Southern History Company, 1901), 398-403.

[317] "Sharp," *Holt County Sentinel*, 16 Feb. 1902, p. 1, c. 2.

[318] Conrad, Howard Louis. "James P. Jackson." *Encyclopedia of the History of Missouri*. Volume 3. (The Southern History Company, 1901), 398-403.

[319] German newspaper, Washington, Mo., 27 May 1880.

[320] Arthur's death certificate also lists 1856. Most all instances recording his birth *between* the 1860 Census and his 1931 Death Certificate document his age quite erratically.

[321] Missouri Death Certificate, findagrave.com; Thomas Sharp pension file.

[322] Conrad, Howard Louis. "John W. Jackson." *Encyclopedia of the History of Missouri*. Volume 3. (The Southern History Company, 1901), 398-403.

[323] Tharp, James A. Colleges of Medicine, Dentistry and Pharmacy, Kansas City, Missouri: Names of 3400 Graduates, 1871-1905. (Kansas City, Mo.: The Orderly Pack Rat, 2013), 101-105, 113-134.

[324] *History of Holt and Atchison Counties*, 196. Also, Conrad, Howard Louis. "James P. Jackson." *Encyclopedia of the History of Missouri*. Volume 3. (The Southern History Company, 1901), 398-403. Tharp, James A. Colleges of Medicine, Dentistry and Pharmacy, Kansas City, Missouri: Names of 3400 Graduates, 1871-1905. (Kansas City, Mo.: The Orderly Pack Rat, 2013), 101-105, 113-134.

[325] According to Richard L. Jackson's obituary.

[326] http://en.wikipedia.org/wiki/Iowa_people (retrieved 9 Jan 2015).

[327] http://en.wikipedia.org/wiki/Ioway_Reservation (retrieved 9 Jan 2015).

[328] Conrad, Howard Louis. "John W. Jackson." *Encyclopedia of the History of Missouri*. Volume 3. (The Southern History Company, 1901), 398-403.

[329] "Mound City," *Holt County Sentinel*, 12 Sept. 1884, p.4. This news reported while Jabez was visiting his aunt and uncle, Mr. and Mrs. Charles Armstrong.

[330] Conrad, Howard Louis. "John W. Jackson." *Encyclopedia of the History of Missouri*. Volume 3. (The Southern History Company, 1901), 398-403.

[331] "Leases Boyhood Homesite," *Kansas City* (Mo.) *Star*, 12 Jun 1932.

[332] *Franklin County Observer*, 24 Jan and 14 Mar 1890; "Dr. J. W. Jackson

Dead," *Kansas City* (Mo.) *Star*, 13 Mar 1890; "Death of Dr. J. W. Jackson," *Kansas City* (Mo.) *Daily Journal*, 14 Mar 1890; "A Great Physician," *Kansas City* (Mo.) *Times*, 14 Mar 1890; "Lying in State," *Kansas City* (Mo.) *Star*, 15 and Mar 1890; "Dr. J. W. Jackson's Funeral," *Kansas City* (Mo.) *Daily Journal*, 17 Mar 1890; and, [Filing of his Last Will], *Kansas City* (Mo.) *Daily Journal*, 25 Mar 1890.

[333] As noted elsewhere, the names Edgar and Walter were names common to the 'white' Jackson family. Quite likely, Edgar Walter Jackson was named after William Andrew and Cordelia "Delia" Thomas's son, Ernest Edgar, who had been born 18 Nov 1885 in White Cloud.

[334] This and a similar listing in the 11 Nov 1892, edition of the same newspaper are the only two indications of Arthur's political leanings.

[335] Lot 73, Block J. For a complete list of Jacksons buried here, see Appendix B.

[336] William Andrew Thomas was the youngest son of George W. and Virginia Catherine (Jackson) Thomas. William Thomas married Cordelia Rowland and they had three children. See also findagrave.com for Cordelia Lear.

[337] As noted elsewhere, the name Jabez was a name common to the 'white' Jackson family.

[338] "Their Fathers were Soldiers: Reminisces of the Revolutionary Period by Two True Daughters," *Kansas City* (Mo.) *Star*, 31 Jan 1898, p. 9.

[339] He was a surgeon with the rank of Major in the 3rd Regiment, Missouri Volunteer Infantry, enlisting 23 Oct. 1898.

[340] See also findagrave.com for Cordelia Lear. One daughter, Anna "Annie" (Thomas) Isbell, died 22 Mar 1900 in Springfield, Green County, Missouri. Her remains were transported for burial in Elmwood Cemetery on 24 Mar.

[341] *Lineage Book,* National Society Daughters of the American Revolution, Volume LVII, 1906, p. 152. Application No. 14354 of Mrs. Virginia Adele Ober, 56440. She was born in Parsons, Kansas, and the wife of Ezra William Ober.

Daughter of Lewis William Isbell and Annie P. Thomas, his wife.

Granddaughter of George W. Thomas and Virginia C. Jackson, his wife.

Gr-granddaughter of Richard L. Jackson and Lucinda Edwards Deatley, his wife.

Gr-gr-granddaughter of James Deatley and Lucy Edwards, his wife.

James Deatley (1750-1844) enlisted, 1777, and served under different commands until the surrender of Cornwallis. He was born in Richmond County and was a pensioner when he died in Westmoreland County.

DAR assigns James Deatley as Ancestor No. A031183; his National Archives Pension File is S10139.

Another great granddaughter of Lucinda's, Carole (Messer) Oberlitner, Hermosa, South Dakota, also became a DAR member in 1982 when in Rapid City, South Dakota, National No. 666200. Her DAR membership application cited another descendant, Sandra (Deatley) Greenhalph, National No. 522346, who may be a descendant of James Deatley through a sibling of Lucinda's.

Descendants of another of James Deatley's children, Henry L. Deatley, have also become DAR members. One, Marcia Kay (Nelson) Shavlik's National No. 862103 application refers to three other application numbers: 558825, 842753, and 764027 (Gayle Clark Ingleheart Wynsome).

[342] 26th and Troost Avenue, Kansas City, Missouri.

[343] One example of such a meeting during this time period was publicized in the *Kansas City* (Mo.) *Star*, 6 Dec 1901, "Visits her Former Slave:"

"Whatever has been written in fiction or story about the bond of affection that exists between mistress and slave, none has a more substantial foundation that that which has brought together Mrs. Emma Florence Cockrell Follin, of Bowling Green, Ky, and her former slave, Mrs. Alice Harris of 612 Cottage Lane, Kansas City. Mrs. Follin came to Kansas City last night and is now visiting for a day the negro woman whom she has not seen for nearly forty years. Whatever some may think of the lack of propriety of such an act one has only to see Mrs. Follin in the Negro home to realize that what she is doing is right, because it is she who is doing it. She is a gentle woman in speech and action, coming from one of the best Missouri families and having as her cousin, Francis M. Cockrell, United States senator from this state.

"When the war broke out Mrs. Follin was then Emma Florence Cockrell, Daughter of T. N. Cockrell, of Glasgow, Mo. The Cockrells were slave owners. On their place were from twenty-five to thirty negroes. Just before the war "Miss Florence," as all the negroes called her and as they still call her, was 8 years old. At this time a girl-baby was born in one of the negro cabins. The child was named Alice and she was given to Miss Florence. Until she was 5 years old the negro child was almost constantly with her girl mistress.

"The rebellion finished, Alice was taken by her father and mother to Leavenworth, Kas, where she grew to womanhood and was married. She came to Kansas City in 1883. In the meantime the Cockrell family had separated, Miss Florence marrying Mr. Follin and removing to Kentucky. Ever since, however, the negro woman has had a vague remembrance of her young mistress and as she grew older the longing became stronger to once more see her. On February 22, this year, she wrote a communication to the Star explaining the facts and asking for Miss Cockrell's address, should anyone know it. She received several

answers, two being from Texas. All told the circumstances of Miss Cockrell's marriage and her address in Kentucky. A correspondence followed. A few days ago Mrs. Follin came to Glasgow to visit and wrote that she would come on to Kansas City last night to spend Saturday night and Sunday with Alice. It was there a reporter for the Star found her last night.

"She is a woman about 50 years old and speaks with an accent characteristic Of native Missourians and Kentuckians. The house in which she was stopping was scrupulously clean and neat. "It has been my desire for years," said Mrs. Follin, "to see some of the slaves from the old place, and especially Alice, but I presumed I should go down to my grave without having my wish gratified. So you see how glad it made me when I discovered where she was. We were always together, she being my particular property.

"There were no white children near, and even if there had been I doubt it I should have chosen them for playmates over Alice. There was no distinction of color. I remember once I was swinging her and she called out "Higher Miss Florence,". I obeyed and down she came, unconscious. Gracious, there were two frightened mothers--hers and mine. Another time we were playing in the attic and Alice crawled into an empty trunk. The lid fell and locked her in. I shall never forget how I wrestled with that lock and the joy I felt when I managed to open it. That time Alice was nearly smothered. "I believe", continued Mrs. Follin, "That there is a celebrated poem called "Genevra," which relates to a similar experience of a bride, although the ending was far more gloomy. It's strange I never thought of the coincidence before." She chatted thus for some time with an occasional remark from Mrs. Harris. At no time however, was there the slightest touch of familiarity on the part of either, although their conversation was thoroughly companionable.

"That Mrs. Harris was lookup upon as honored by Mrs. Follin's visit was easily seen by the stir that it occasioned in Cottage Lane, which is an exclusively Negro street, or rather alley, between Charlotte and Campbell streets south of Independence Avenue. All the afternoon the Harris home was the center of attraction of all the neighborhood.

Men and women stood in their own doorways, or sat at their windows and looked at the place with an air almost akin to reverence. During the day Mrs. Harris was the busiest person in Cottage Lane. Every nook and corner of the house was gone over with soap and water and when a reported for the Star went to the house early in the afternoon, expecting to find Mrs. Follin there, he found four Negro men busy with scrubbing brush, stove polish and broom. The pictures, representing the Twenty-fifth United States infantry (Negro), and the Ninth cavalry (Negro) going up San Juan hill were fairly resplendent. Not one piece of furniture had been overlooked and it is doubtful if anyone found a cleaner house in which to sleep than did Mrs. Follin last night."

[344] *Fredericksburg* (Va.) *Free Lance*, 28 Nov. 1901. An item in the 18 Jan. 1906 *Free Lance* "Crosses of Honor" mentioned: *"J. T. DeAtley, Co. E. 15th Virginia*

Cavalry."

[345] Tharp, James A. *Colleges of Medicine, Dentistry and Pharmacy, Kansas City, Missouri: Names of 3400 Graduates, 1871-1905.* (Kansas City, Mo.: The Orderly Pack Rat, 2013), 113-134.

[346] *Franklin County Tribune,* 13 Dec. 1901.

[347] Tharp, 113-134.

[348] "Sharp," *Holt County Sentinel,* 16 Feb. 1902, p. 1, c. 2. Her marriage license from October 10, 1872 (recorded in the obituary incorrectly as 1875), apparently completed by her fiancé, indicated she had been born in Missouri, when in fact she was born in Virginia. The marriage record lists that she was 18. If her birth date of May 1, 1855, was accurate, she would have been 17 years, 5 months, 9 days old on October 10, 1872. Given that her parent's names were also 'blank,' it sees clear that Thomas Sharp did not know these intimate details about his wife, and she may not have been present when the affidavit for the marriage license was completed.

[349] "Dies at Ripe Old Age," *Holt County Sentinel,* 7 Dec. 1906, p. 1, c. 6.

[350] According to a postcard from Arthur and Ida to their son, Edgar, postmarked from a bank in Harlem on 5 Sept. 1913. Roy Jackson saw this postcard at his Aunt Hazel (Jackson) Levine's home once, and recorded the details. Unfortunately a copy or transcript was not made.

[351] Schirmer, Sherry Lamb. *A city Divided: The Racial Landscape of Kansas City, 1900-1960.* (Columbia, Mo.: University of Missouri Press, 2000).

[352] Kremer, Gary R. *Race and Meaning: The African American Experience in Missouri.* (Columbia, Mo.: University of Missouri Press, 2014), 113.

[353] Coulter, Charles E. *Take Up the Black Man's Burden: Kansas City's African American Communities, 1865-1939.* (Columbia, Mo.: University of Missouri Press, 2006), 26, 30, 31.

[354] Kremer, 113.

[355] Kremer, 114.

[356] Coulter, 52-53.

[357] The Swope Park pool reopened in June 1954 as an integrated pool after having been shut down the previous two years. Attendance showed 48,301 admission fees compared to 90,146 in 1950. "Pool Segregation Put in KC Spotlight," *Kansas City Star,* 15 Jan 2002.

[358] [Jabez North Jackson obituary,] *Kansas City Journal Post,* 19 Mar 1935.

[359] Coulter, 269.

[360] Coulter, 53.

[361] Coulter, 74, 85.

[362] Coulter, 57.

[363] This is the southwest ¼ of Section 29, Township 49, Range 33. By 1925, the house where the Jacksons had lived between 1914-1917 was platted into the "New South Moreland" subdivision, Lot 2.

[364] http://www.nelson-atkins.org/art/HistPeople_Nelson.cfm and

http://www.nelson-atkins.org/images/PDF/75th%20Timeline.pdf (retrieved 11 Feb 2015).

[365] http://nreionline.com/mag/nichols-folly (retrieved 1 Feb 2015).

[366] Whitehall Condominiums apartment and condo building in 2015 is located at 323 Emmanuel Cleaver II Boulevard. Plaza Castles Condominium Building immediately west at 311. The Melbourne is the next building to the west at 303. Though the numbers are not exactly parallel to 1914 addresses, the house at 319 East 47th Street where the Jacksons lived would have been at this location between McGee, but closer the intersection at Oak Street. [SW4, SEC 29, T49, R33. In the 1940 Tax Assessment Photograph collection, this location is found in District 12, Block 80.]

[367] [SE4, SEC 30, T49, R33. In the 1940 Tax Assessment Photograph collection, this location is found in District 12, Block 112.]

[368] Coulter, 1.

[369] Coulter, 7.

[370] [SE4, SEC 30, T49, R33. In the 1940 Tax Assessment Photograph collection, this location is found in District 12, Block 114.]

[371] The house number was misprinted as 4605. Both the previous year's city directory and U.S. Census listings showed "4705."

[372] A. G. Norris was principal in 1922 when Ollie attended; the school was on the northwest corner of 13th Street and Central. Tharp, James A. Kansas City Schools in City Directories. Unpublished manuscript shared with the author, November 2015.

[373] In the 1940 Tax Assessment Photograph collection, this location is found in District 11, Block 11.

[374] http://skyscraperpage.com/cities/?buildingID=553 (retrieved 1 Feb 2015).

[375] In the 1940 Tax Assessment Photograph collection, this location is found in District 11, Block 32 or 33.

[376] NE4, SEC 30, T49, R33. In the 1940 Tax Assessment Photograph collection, this location is found in District 11, Block 338. Chris Carmody, a friend of the author, remembered a large gas explosion at that location in the 1960s. If homes were destroyed at that time, this may explain the empty lots and parking lot.

[377] "Negro Ex-Slave Dead," *St. Joseph News Press*, 18 Mar 1928. In 1905-1906, he was living at White Cloud, Doniphan County, Kansas. In 1910, Sharp was living at 1805 ½ Mulberry Street. When he completed a Declaration for Pension in 1912, he listed his residence as the National Military Home in Leavenworth, Kansas. In 1915, he lived at 836 South 18th Street, St. Joseph. From at least 1920-1928, he was living at 826 Warsaw Ave., St. Joseph.

[378] NE4, SEC 30, T49, R33. In the 1940 Tax Assessment Photograph collection, this location is found in District 11, Block 317.

[379] Missouri Death Certificate and obituary.

[380] Woodtor, 213.

[381] Willis,130.

[382] Warranty Deed dated 12 Oct 1964, from Roy W. and Nancy B. Jackson to Gerald L. and Mary K. Schwartz.

[383] Warranty Deed dated 22 Nov 1965, from Gerald L. and Mary K. Schwartz to LeRoy and Alberta F. Harris.

[384] Cameroon was once called "Biafra," and "Old Calabar" in the days of the Transatlantic Slave Trade. The author's "Paternal Lineage DNA Test Results" from Ancestry.com. "About 20% of African slaves originated in the Bight [or, bend] of Benin region during the Atlantic slave trade." http://sites.duke.edu/marronnagevoyages/nations/nago/ (retrieved 13 Feb 2015). A discussion about this Haplogroup is at, "Journey of My Ancestors," http://theskepticalafrican.blogspot.com/2008/09/journey-of-my-ancestors.html (retrieved 13 Feb 2015), where the author states, "About 60% of African American men have E1b1a Y-chromosomes, primarily because the Atlantic slave trade drew most of its individuals from western Africa and Mozambique, where E1b1a occurs in high frequencies."
The author also shared DNA with the National Geographic's Genographic Project, which identified three specific branches (M2, U175, and P277) that are associated with ancient or deep ancestry in West Africa and West-Central Africa. The M2 branch, particularly, was noted to be in high frequency in Western Africa as, "this branch accounts for most of today's African Americans who came to the Americas as part of the transatlantic slave trade."
"Africans were heavily concentrated in two areas that accounted for about 87 percent of their numbers: the Low Country of the Carolinas and Georgia, and the Tidewater region of Virginia and Maryland. The Carolinas and Georgia received more than 210,000 people, or 54.2 percent, while the Chesapeake accounted for more than 127,000 people, or 32.8 percent of all arrivals. About 28,000 people (7.0 percent) went to the area north of the Chesapeake; and the region south and west of Georgia, including Florida and Louisiana, received about 22,000 people (5.6 percent)." "The Main Areas of Destination," including an enlightening chart by date range of arrival and destination location. abolition.nypl.org/essays/us_slave_trade

[385] Heywood, Linda, Ph.D., and John Thornton, Ph.D. "Pinpointing DNA Ancestry in Africa: Most African Americans hail from just 46 ethnic groups, research shows." http://www.theroot.com/articles/culture/2011/10/tracing_dna_not_just_to_africa_but_to_1_tribe.html (viewed 14 Dec 2015).

[386] Heywood, Linda, Ph.D., and John Thornton, Ph.D. "African Ethnicities and Their Origins: These contemporary African ethnic groups have contributed most to the black population of the U.S." http://www.theroot.com/articles/culture/2011/10/african_ethnicities_and_their_origins.html (viewed 14 Dec 2015).

[387] Heywood, Linda, Ph.D., and John Thornton, Ph.D. "African Ethnicities and Their Origins: These contemporary African ethnic groups have contributed most to the black population of the U.S." http://www.theroot.com/articles/culture/2011/10/african_ethnicities_and_their_origins.html (viewed 14 Dec 2015).

Memoirs of
Roy Weldon Jackson

BORN A SLAVE

Arthur and Ida May (ANDERSON) JACKSON

By Roy Weldon Jackson

July 2006

I was born August 13, 1918. My parents Jarvis and Grace (Clifford) Jackson, who had been married in 1916, divorced when I was about one year old. My paternal grandparents, Arthur and Ida (Anderson) Jackson raised me until Grandpa Jackson died in 1931 when I was 12 years old.

Grandma, Grandpa and I lived on Boone Street (called 42nd Terrace, today) at the south edge of the old Westport area of Kansas City. Grandpa Jackson was a landscape gardener and worked for wealthy homeowners along Ward Parkway south of the Country Club Plaza. My father lived three houses up the street, which is where he lived when he married Florence Wolverton and had their child Virginia Lee.

Dad and two of my Uncles worked with Grandpa at landscape gardening ... Uncle Ed and Uncle Ollie drove the truck. I often worked with them too, and I remember customers complaining that they were working me so hard and at such a young age. I was from 10 to 12 years old then. I remember they had a large barrel with a pump hooked to a hose and my job was to manually pump the contraption to keep the pressure up on the hose so that the men could spray whatever it was they were spraying up into the trees. I got $1 a day when I worked with them.

Boone was a short street with a large field behind our house and a coal yard next door where I used to play with other neighborhood kids. I woke up each morning for school to the clock my Grandfather got when he worked grading and laying track on the Missouri Pacific Railroad. I had to be at school around 8:45 a.m. Grandma would get me up and feed me breakfast. I had a three or four block walk to Allen School at that time. I can't recall, but I may have come home for lunch.

A little more about the Regulator clock: When Nancy and I

bought our first house on Walrond, I got this clock from Aunt Hazel's attic and we cleaned it up, hung it on the wall in our bedroom and wound it up. The clock ticked so loud that we had to stop the pendulum; there wasn't any other place in the tiny house that would have made it any better so for years it hang on the wall in silence. When we moved to our present home in 1964, the clock was relegated to the garage wall. One summer in the early 1980s when David and I were really getting into genealogy, I took the clock to have its mechanism cleaned and we brought the clock inside and hung it in the kitchen. I wind it every Sunday night and it's ticking right now.

For entertainment, the Jacksons attended dances and played music. Grandpa played the violin and Dad could play lots of instruments: the guitar, mandolin, even the piano. He was what you might call the "life of the party." He could play the violin upside down, or put the bow under his leg to play it. I guess it was at one of these dances that he met my mother in 1916. As it turned out my Grandpa Clifford had met or knew Grandpa Jackson when they worked on the railroad.

Maybe he also met Florence this way, too? He and Florence Wolverton were married and baby Virginia Lee was born on June 4, 1930. I probably only saw my sister once because shortly after she was born Florence separated from my Dad and I think she even left town. Then, Grandpa Jackson died in 1931 and Grandma and I were out of a home. (Years later I was given a little beaded baby bracelet—which I still have—that had been Virginia's, and Nancy and I decided to name our first daughter Virginia Lee after my sister).

Grandma and I were shifted from one relative to another, and I would no sooner get established in school than I'd have to move and be transferred to another school. We lived with one Aunt and Uncle, then another. Sometimes I would be with one family and Grandma would be with another. I was mostly on my own as times were hard and they had their families to care for and I was in the way and taking food out of their mouths. This was the Great Depression.

Between the ages of 14-16 I delivered on a bicycle delivering for Crown Drug Store for 10 cents an hour and worked seven days a week just to get by. At times I paid for my own board and a sleeping room at a buddy's home. I'm lucky to have gotten through to 8th grade. At age 16 I joined the CCC, mostly to have a home.

Grandpa and Grandma Jackson had six children, four sons: Edgar (Ed), Jabez/Jarvis, Reginald (Reg), Oliver (Ollie) and two daughters: Hazel and Dollie. Ed, Jabez/Jarvis and Ollie were drunks who never amounted to anything. Alcoholism is a disease, I understand, and I'm glad I didn't inherit that trait from my parents.

Aunt Hazel was one that I could always count on. She and a family friend, Betty Weinstein, helped me and Nancy get off on the right foot when we set up housekeeping in 1939. I returned the favor and helped Hazel in her later years by taking her to her doctor's appointments and the like. In fact, her doctor, Dr. Moore, became our family doctor and has remained so all these years.

While Dad was lazy, he was not a "crook." He just couldn't, or wouldn't hold a job. When sober, he was very likable. One time when Nancy and I were still dating, he came by and had been drinking. I needed to put him on the streetcar just to get rid of him. Well, he only had a nickel and I wasn't going to give him the whole fare ($.10), so I borrowed a nickel from Nancy so he could make his fare. She often joked that she married me so she could get her nickel back! I let Dad know when our daughter, Virginia Lee, was born, however, that he wasn't of any use to us and to stay away... and he did.

Uncle Reg worked for the Kansas City Star newspaper for 48 years. He was married a couple of times but was up standing. Reg was the one that saw that Dad, who died at the age of 57 of "booze" whisky was buried in a decent grave with a headstone; otherwise he'd have ended up in a pauper's grave. Reg chose the location in the cemetery that was nearest the woods and said that "Jack" was a woodsman and he would enjoy being buried in the woods. Over the years the woods have, indeed, taken over the burial site and it was hard to find. When my grandson David and I went out recently and took pictures for my sister, Dad's headstone was at the edge of the forest...right where he'd like.

BORN A SLAVE

I Found a Home and Honest Work in the 3 C's (or, Civilian Conservation Corps), April 1937 to March 1938

By Roy Weldon Jackson
July 2006

Grandparents Were My Only Stability

For most of my early childhood, I had lived with my paternal grandparents, Arthur and Ida Jackson. Every once in a while, I lived with my father and mother—who had separated right after I was born in 1918—but they were never in a position to provide a space for me. So, I was shifted from home to home, school to school. Before I turned 16, I moved 18 times and attended eight Kansas City, Missouri, elementary schools before dropping out of Central Junior High School half way through ninth grade in 1935.

In the summer of 1929, at age 11, I returned to my Grandparents' who were then living at 414 Boone (now called 42nd Terrace), although my father and his second wife, Florence, lived a couple doors up the street at 418.

Two years went by and I hadn't moved.

I was enjoying attending Allen Elementary (located at 42nd and Waddel, 706 West 42nd St. to be exact). Believe it or not, at that young age, I got job as a bicycle delivery boy for Crown Drug Store on the northwest corner of Westport Road and Broadway in the Westport neighborhood of Kansas City. I worked hard and earned my own spending money. It was at this time that I tried smoking cigarettes. Grandma caught me one day, and she said, "If you're going to smoke, you can smoke in front of me." She must have known something after having raised four rambunctious boys; it just wasn't the same not having to sneak about. All in all, life seemed to be squaring up for me.

Shiftless As Great Depression Begins

One day, Grandpa said he was short of breath and was going outside for some fresh air. After a spell Grandma asked me to go outside and check on Grandpa as it was cold out. I looked out the window at my 70-year-old Grandpa Jackson sitting on the top step of the porch. He was looking out at the street. I couldn't see his reddish mustache; since his back was to me. I only saw his closely cut, white, bristly hair. At the moment I happened to look outside the frosted window. Grandpa gently leaned to the right, his shoulder and head resting against the house. I went outside to see if he had fallen asleep, but I found out he had just died.

All of the sudden on February 5, 1931, at 12 ½-years-old, I was shiftless again. So was Grandma; she lived the next 13 years shifting between her children's homes before dying in 1944.

Times were hard for everyone in those days, and they were about to get harder.

We were at the beginning of the Great Depression.

I tried living with my mother again, but she was in between husbands, and it just didn't work out. I stayed with my Aunt Hazel, then with my Aunt Dot and Uncle Bill Johnson, who took me on vacation in the summer of 1933 to the Payette National Forest in Idaho. We drove through Boise, Weiser, New Meadows, and at Warren, Idaho, drove on a one-lane road through the forest to Big Creek. A rugged old fellow named Red Fisk and his brothers (who lived at Warren) had staked out a claim between Rainbow Peak and Yellow Pine, Idaho. My Aunt, Uncle and I helped placer mine for gold. I kept my gun under my pillow, and one night I woke up to Aunt Dot saying, "Bill, Bill is that you." I looked at a grizzly shadow through the tent that honest to goodness looked like a bear, and came THIS CLOSE to firing my gun just as my Uncle, said, "Ah, be quiet." I was never so relieved, and it was a real struggle to get my finger off the trigger and release the clip. I celebrated my 15th birthday in Idaho that summer.

Soda Jerk Memories Stick in My Mind

Once back in Kansas City, I worked as a "soda jerk" at the fountain for Price's Drug Store on the northwest corner of 39th and Main (competing on the northeast corner was Crown, and on the southeast corner, Parkview Drug Stores).

I remember clearly the three-levered tap dispenser of the fountain. For each drink ordered, I'd make from scratch by "jerking the tap" and squirting a little of each one of the following: tap water; a sweet "simple syrup" that came in a bag-in-box that had to be connected to the fountain pump in the basement; and, carbonated water. Combining and mixing those along with an assortment of other fruity syrups, bitter-tasting trademark cola and root beer syrups, and even ice cream, made for an infinite variety of tasty flavored colas, trademark sodas, shakes, malts or phosphates. The area where I stood behind the counter as a "jerk" was sunken into the ground so that when customers sat at the counter, they were at my eye level.

Having funny names for drinks, or the way they were prepared

235

made the job more fun. If someone ordered a strawberry milk shake, we'd call out, *"Shake it, Make it Red."*

Some "Soda Jerk" Terms

Black And White (chocolate & vanilla)
Black Cow
Brown Cow
Bodacious Black And White
   (FRENCH vanilla ice cream)
Bottom - ice cream in a drink
Bucket of - several ingredients combined
Burn One All the Way –
   Double chocolate malt
Cha - chocolate
Chicago - pineapple juice or soda
Cow Juice - milk
Crash - cookie crumbs
Draw one - coffee
Draw one from the south - strong coffee
Forty-one - lemons or lemonade
Freeze - ice cream
Fuzzy - peaches
Gravel - nuts
Hot cha - hot chocolate

Make it Cackle – Cream nogg
Make it Red - strawberry
Mash one - mashed bananas
Mud - chocolate ice cream
Natural - 7-Up®
One on the country –
   yogurt or buttermilk
Sand – sugar sprinkles
Shake One – milkshake
Sky Juice - water
Spit on it - raspberries on top
Split one - banana split
Squeeze one - orange juice
Van - vanilla ice cream
Vanilla Coke
White cow - vanilla milkshake
81 - water for one
82 - water for two
83 - water for three (and so on)

Later I worked six days a week for $.10 an hour for the Crown Drug Store as a bicycle deliveryman. At this time, I lived with my best friend, Kenny Joyce. Kenny's father, Mr. William Joyce was a "prince," and was more like a Dad than anyone else in my life was. Besides room and board, he would buy parts if I needed something

for my delivery bike. Mr. Joyce worked for Monarch Egg Company, and he was a real mechanic. I lived with the Joyce's in 1935 when I dropped out of Central Junior High School.

About six or nine months later in February 1936, I took a sleeping room at my Aunt Dot and Uncle Bill Johnson's, and began riding my bicycle as a deliveryman for the Crown Drug Store at 39th and Indiana. I met Paul Keeling who also rode a bike making deliveries. Paul and I hung out a lot and became real buddies with lots of fun times…like hanging on to the streetcar going up the long hill of Main Street from Union Station late at night after work.

I turned 18 on August 13, 1936.

The month before, I had visited the Kansas City Relief Committee's, Missouri Relief Commission's recruitment office at 125 East 31st Street to complete my application for a six-month enrollment into the emergency conservation work program (the Civilian Conservation Corps, abbreviated "C.C.C.," but commonly called "3 C's"). I was out of work and needed a home! Fortunately for me, I was recruited about six months later.

First CCC Enrollment, April-October 1937

On April 5, 1937, I packed a small bag of clothes and the brownie camera my Uncle Reg had given me for my 18th birthday, and went by train from Kansas City's Union Station to Ft. Leavenworth, Kansas. A four-day enrollment process included getting assignments and inoculations. I was to get $30 each month, and $25 would be sent home to my Grandmother Jackson (she ended up saving my allotments, which I used when I came home to buy a car.).

I was given the serial number CC7-254784 and transferred to the ninth corps area (that included Washington, Oregon, Idaho, Montana, Utah, Nevada California, and Yellowstone Park). Between April 9 and 11, I was enroute on a transcontinental train to Company 733, Sebastopol Camp SCS-4, in Sebastopol, California, located about 11 miles west of Santa Rosa.

I don't know if it was the change in weather, but within a week of my arrival in sunny California, I was hospitalized in the camp's infirmary with tonsillitis for almost a week. After recovering, I set out on the job that I would hold for the next six months.

The CCC camps were run like the Army as far as routine and discipline went, but you didn't have to salute. We were awakened by the bugle's call, "Can't get 'em up, get 'em up, get 'em up up up," in the morning. And, they played Taps when lowering the flag at the end of each day. We had military-style clothes, rations, and barracks.

But we had fun, too. We horsed around and played endless practical jokes on one another. Anything was a joke for that matter. If it wasn't a bucket of water perched above a door, then it was a footlocker pulled out in the aisle in the middle of the night to trip an unsuspecting fella on his way to the latrine. One guy had bought a spare pair of shoes so he wouldn't have to polish and shine the ones he wore. While he was away over a weekend, some of the guys took a big, long spike and nailed his shoes to the floor (they even went underneath and bent the nails over). Those shoes were still there when we left!

One time the fellas sprinkled Post Toasties in between my sheets. Little did they know, I slept on top of the sheets to stay cool.

The most fun we had, though, were the "wars" we had after "lights out." During the day, we'd be working in the orchards and we'd pick 4 or 5 big, juicy apples for later that night. After the lights were turned out, we'd eat a little, but then begin throwing the cores at one another in the dark. All you'd hear is giggling and cussin if someone got it. The guy that got it the most was the one sleeping in the corners because they were a pretty easy target. In the morning, you could see the big, round apple juice stains on most of the headboards that were made from a cheap "beaver board."

We assisted the California State Conservation Department in making water irrigation canals (to prevent soil erosion) in the Gold Ridge apple orchard region. I used a pick and shovel, and helped lay the concrete pipes that enrollees also made in the Camp.

My 19th birthday was celebrated in Sebastapol.

On most weekends during this term of enlistment, we got to leave Camp. I mostly hitchhiked with my buddy Chuck Elmore and sometimes another guy to Santa Rosa, which was about 15 miles away.

On one trip, I met a girl named Minnie Robinson. She introduced me to her father, who was a used car lot owner. I hit it right off well with her father, and because of all the cars he had, probably got along better with him than even with Minnie. I hadn't known her long and she talked her dad into letting us take a car off the lot. Mr. Robinson walked me over to an old Studebaker. Not wanting to drive the ugly clunker, I took the keys, got in, and pretended to try to start the car by letting the engine crank over a couple times. I had my eye on the 1928 Buick, 4-door sedan parked next to it. Mr. Robinson probably didn't think that I would know how to drive the Buick (since it had a special gear shift), so he quickly gave me the keys to it after the Studebaker sputtered. Robinson didn't know that my Uncle Bill had taught me to drive on his 1928 Buick, so this car was right down my alley!

Mr. Robinson said I could take a car back to Camp, but it would have had to be parked outside the Camp and I didn't want to be responsible for it. Besides, it might have been against company policy and I might have been immediately discharged.

Another weekend leave, Elmore and I had had quite a bit to drink. You could get a gallon of the California wine for about a dollar, and it was the kind of drink that tasted kind of bitter at the beginning, but after a couple glasses, tasted pretty fine. Then, all of the sudden it'd hit you and your legs'd get weak. Well, we ended falling asleep (or passing out?) on the grass of this park one night. I can't tell you how eerie it was to wake up the next morning next to a tombstone. We had crapped out in the Santa Rosa Cemetery!

My first, six-month enrollment in the 3 C's came to an end on October 9, 1937. I was given the opportunity to re-enlist for six more months if I chose, before the War Department would have to discharge me. I thought things were going so well there in sunny Sabastopol that I re-enlisted. After all, I needed a home and had worked hard to get in the CCCs. I had a gal, and a car. I had it made.

Much to our surprise after having re-enlisted, however, Company 733 was disbanded, and 67 of us enrollees were re-assigned to Company 4762 and transferred to Camp S-263 in Coolin, Idaho, located about 32 miles north of Priest River.

I don't remember saying goodbye to Minnie. And, I can't recall ever having kept in touch with Elmore after that time.

Second CCC Enrollment, October 1937-March 1938

From October 10 and 11, our company traveled from Sebastapol by Mount Shasta on a train through Idaho to Coolin, a town with three houses, one converted to a bar. I worked for a month between October 12 and November 13 as a general laborer.

From November 14-29, we were temporarily transferred to Company 949, Camp Fort George Wright, near Spokane, Washington. We were involved with "wood procurement," set up telephone poles, and planted grass on embankments.

Meanwhile, our new barracks were being completed at Camp Drysdale in the St. Joe National Forest, near Herrick (or, St. Maries), Idaho, which is where I worked in Company 4762 through the winter between November 30, 1937 to March 26, 1938. We primarily built roads and fire routes through the forests to lookout towers.

One day, a buddy and I packed up the mountain from our camp, which was situated in a valley. We hiked quite far up, and then, wanting to get a picture of the camp below, we climbed a tall pine tree. With him on one side of the tree and me on the other, we were able to balance the tree, especially as we got way up near the top.I ended up getting some shots of the camp below, plus a pretty good panoramic shot. After we got back to camp, we looked back at about the place where we had climbed, and you could actually see the poor tree we had climbed! With some of the branches having been removed, it stood out from the others and it looked like a perfect "cross!"

Works Progress Back in Kansas City, Mo.

According to my CCC personnel file copied from microfilm at the National Personnel Records Center (Civilian Personnel Records) in St. Louis, Missouri, I left Herrick, Idaho, by train and was back at Ft. Leavenworth, Kansas, for discharge on March 31, 1938. From there I must have taken the train to Kansas City's Union Station, but I don't particularly remember.

I know that immediately upon returning home I stayed with my mother and her third (or fourth?) husband, Bert Kindler, for a short spell. But, then I ended up at my Aunt Hazel Levine's at 3401 Morrell Ave.

Still without work, I signed up and worked for Works Progress Administration (WPA). I started out digging sewer lines or pipes at 47th and Troost. Then, I worked my way into some kind of used clothing dispensing unit. I worked three days a week.

While I was away in the CCC's, my father had ruined my first car, a 1928 Whippit Cabriolet that I had stored in the garage where my Grandma Jackson was living. I had asked Grandma to watch over it for me, but I guess my Dad did as he pleased. He took it out and let the engine block freeze in the winter.

Needing transportation, I bought a 1931 Chrysler Sedan with $150 from the money my Grandmother Jackson had saved from my monthly CCC allotments.

It was this car that I, with Bill Annis and a couple gals stopped once to get some ears of corn in an obliging field. We filled the back floor up to the seat. When Bill got in the tire exploded.

Another time I was out with Paul Keeling and a couple of girls, one named Murvle. We were drinking a 1 gallon picnic jug ½ filled with slow gin and ½ with dry gin and were at Swope Park lagoon. The Deputy Sheriff came by and asked, "You girls in good company?" Murvle responded, "What's it to you flat foot?" Murvle was quite a character. She babysat for a Jewish couple who bottled their own wine. On many occasions we'd visit her while she was sitting, and enjoy some wine. Murvle filled the bottles back up with water! Murvle later married (4 Aug 1949) C. J. Trotter and we all had a paperhanging episode one night late while drinking slow gin fizzes. We'd slap the paper on the ceiling and walk across the room...and the paper'd follow to the floor. Still, the next day it looked real good after it dried.

Sometime in the fall of 1938 I met Nancy Rogers. I've written about how we met and our early married years, including World War II, in a separate recollection if you're interested.

A Short History of the Family of
Roy and Nancy (ROGERS) JACKSON

By Roy Weldon Jackson
June 2006

It was the summer or fall of 1938 when I met Nancy Rogers.

I had returned from California and Idaho to Kansas City, Missouri, near the end of March after having been discharged from serving two, six-month terms in the Civilian Conservation Corps (CCC). At first I stayed with my mother, Grace, and her third husband Bert Kindler, and I signed up to work three days a week for the Works Progress Administration (WPA). I dug sewer and other pipelines at 47th and Troost Avenue, but later worked my way into some kind of used clothing dispensing unit.

Being shifted around between family members as I had all my early life, it wasn't long before I was, once again, living with my Aunt Hazel and her husband Louis Levine at 3401 Morrell Avenue.

I had lived there before in the Spring 1932 when I was enrolled at age 14 in the sixth grade at Scarritt School. It was at that time that I had met three neighborhood girls who lived three or four doors up the street at 3413 Morrell Avenue. "Jenny" (Genevieve) Huxley seemed a bit older than I. Her sister "Little Jo" (Josephine) was younger. And, though Jo had a crush on me, I had been "sweet" on their sister Theresa who seemed closer to my age. Looking back I don't think I had any chance with either girl. They were devout Irish Catholics. Theresa wore a uniform to school and was studying the Catechism and Latin if I recall correctly.

Then, one day during the summer of 1938 I was visiting Jo, and was with her in the living room with Mrs. Huxley (I missed seeing Theresa at home during this time, and was always curious about her absence). The housekeeper and babysitter for the Salmon family--who rented the second floor of the Huxley residence--came down into the front hallway. Before she could exit the front door,

Mrs. Huxley called Nancy Rogers in to the living room and introduced us. Nancy and I were never apart after that day, except the time I spent in the Navy during World War II.

Nancy, my cousin Ruth Levine (now Mrs. Aaron Shapiro of Henderson, Nevada) and I went to Lexington so I could get permission from her father to go with her. We got along real great; all he said was not to take her into any bars. It didn't seem to us that the Salmons were too pleased about me and Nancy dating. So, Nancy asked me to visit her brother and sister-in-law, Ernie and Alma Rogers. We asked Ernie to would call Mrs. Salmon and tell her that he and Alma needed Nancy to come and help take care of their infant son. It wasn't long before Nancy was living with Alma and Ernie on 39th Street between Sterling and Crysler.

Ernie worked about a half a mile away milking cows at Olson's Dairy and I would often stop by to visit with him either before or after visiting with Nancy. I could always find him in the large dairy barn lined up with cows by listening to the sound of milk hitting the pail. Sometimes I think Ernie could milk the cows in his sleep, as I'd find him resting his head on the side of the cow with his eyes closed, but his hands busily milking.

One memorable "date" Nancy and I had, was when I was taking Nancy back to Ernie's shortly before our Midnight curfew. I went to turn my 1931 Chrysler Sedan around about half way down the hilly pasture from Ernie's, whose house was at the top of the hill, when the car failed and wouldn't start; the battery died. The only way to get the car started again was to get it back to the top of the hill so I could let it coast back down as I let out on the clutch to jump-start the car. Fortunately in those days you start a car with a hand-held crank at the front of the car. So, I put the car in reverse, got out the crank, and started maneuvering the car back up the hillside. Each crank only backed the car about ½ inch, and I had about 25 feet to get back to the street. It took an hour or so and Nancy stayed with me until I got the car started again. Needless to say, I got Nancy back home to Ernie's quite a bit late that night…probably 1:30 or 2 a.m. Nancy's mother, who was the sweetest woman alive, was staying with Ernie and Alma to visit her new grandbaby, David Rogers. She called us "scums of the road," and it surely looked that way, but it had been an innocent event. I heard about it the next day.

Nancy and I were married in Platte City, Platte County, Missouri, on January 1, 1939. I was 20 years, 5 months old and Nancy was 16 years, 6 months old. We were young but having been from broken families, we had been on our own. Nancy had worked for several years for several families as a babysitter and doing housework and cooking. So, don't let her age fool you; Nancy wasn't a girl when we married…she was a young woman. We both knew we did not want to start a family at our age. So, there was no sex until our wedding night. We both didn't believe in "shot gun" weddings. We both knew what it was like to come from broken families. So, we didn't start our family until Virginia Lee was born August 11, 1941. That was two years and eight months into our marriage. God gave us a handicapped baby, so that bonded our marriage even more.

Nancy was a woman and a real Jackson! Times were hard in those days and we never had much and I was sometimes out of work. I managed to get work here and there to pay our way though. I picked potatoes in Atherton the first summer after we were married. I worked as a deliveryman for Parkview Drug Company at its Meyer Boulevard and Prospect Avenue location. For a time I worked for Peppard Seed Company. In September 1942, I began working at Sheffield Steel Corporation in the Leed's District. Once while the steel mill was on strike for a month or more, I worked for a man who repaired roofs for an insurance company. Climbing a flimsy ladder to the roof of a 2 ½ and three-story building with a slate roof is scary, but I needed the money. Once I slid down the roof and only the chimney stopped me from going over, but then the chimney started to slowly lean away from the house. I put my arms around the chimney and it was by sheer luck that I kept the chimney from collapsing onto the man and his truck below.

Nancy and I moved several times in those early days. We lived with my mother and her husband Bert Kindler on Woodland Avenue for a couple of weeks after getting married, but soon moved to the first home of our own…a second-floor apartment at 3309 ½ 20th Street owned by the Puritans. I worked at Swope Park swimming pool and Nancy did too on Sundays and busy days. Nancy said it was easy work but hard standing on her feet all day. That summer when I turned 21, Nancy had a fishing party for my birthday and had her mother write a birthday verse for me.

When I was at Parkview Drug Store beginning sometime in 1940, we lived south in a one-room, third-floor apartment at 61st and Swope Parkway owned by the Smith family. This is where Nancy and I hosted our first Rogers family reunion, and where we were given a surprise baby shower.

We moved back to 20th Street in 1941, first to a second-floor duplex apartment in a building with four units at 3120 East 20th Street. The toilet was an outhouse, but it had running water. After Virginia was born we moved up the street to a second-floor apartment at 3315 East 20th Street in a home belonging to the Rush family. Mr. Rush made us move because he thought I was parking in his place; but it was someone else.

We then moved to a "house" at 3404 Cypress Street. It was really a shanty shack that had been on fire previously so there were burnt timbers and holes where it would rain in. The shack was owned by Clarence and Bernice Billings (who were Nancy's cousins), and we lived there rent-free. At least it was a roof over our heads. Still, we had to use an outhouse and get water from the next door neighbor's water spigot on the outside of their house. We were really poor. We knew it was time to move when Nancy notice that rats had chewed holes in the cuffs of baby Virginia's nightgown (they were attracted to the baby's saliva most likely).

Nancy never complained once.

Virginia was about 18 months old when we moved into an apartment in the home of my Aunt "Dot" (Dollie) and her husband Bill Johnson, a few months after I started working at Sheffield in September 1942. Because I was working in a steel plant doing defense-related work, I got several deferments from the draft. Things were going well when I was finally drafted in June 1944. Nancy visited with me for a few days in Chicago before I was shipped out in October. I got liberty each night and Nancy and another Navy wife spent their days together. Virginia was being taken care of by my Aunt in Kansas City. While I was in the Navy,

Nancy and Virginia moved to Lexington where they stayed with Nancy's "Poppie," but they eventually moved back to Kansas City to live with my Aunt Hazel and her husband Louis Levine. Nancy applied for a job at Newman Manufacturing Company where she got a job on a drill press making airplane parts initially, but soon her boss, Mr. Cox, transferred her to the wrapping and shipping department.

I was discharged from the Navy in July 1945, and I returned to the steel mill, which now was called Armco Steel.

We moved to 5927 Walrond and bought our first 2-bedroom home for $5,250 with my G.I. loan. We paid $39 each month until the home was paid off. Reginald Wayne was born August 1, 1949, and Betty Jean on October 2, 1950.

Needing a larger home, in 1964 we sold our house on Walrond for about $10,000 and bought our second home at 11608 East 78th Street. We paid $18,500 for the new, 3-bedroom demonstration house in the new subdivision in Raytown, Missouri, a suburb of Kansas City in Jackson County, Missouri.

I retired in 1980 with 37 years tenure at Armco. Nancy retired, too! All those years she had sent me off to work each day with a full black lunch pail, and while I was at work she raised our children, took care of our home, and all the many other daily details in between.

Nancy and I had three children: Virginia Lee, Reginald Wayne, and Betty Jean.

Virginia Lee, soon to be 63 [in 2006], was mildly affected by cerebral palsy and has always lived with Nancy and me.

Virginia Lee Jackson (1941)

Sergeant Reginald W. Jackson

Virginia is a real help around the house to her soon to be 88-year-old father and we keep one another company.Our birthdays are two days apart: hers on August 11 and mine on the 13th.

Reg was a manager of a T.V. store for many years. He was a Sergeant in the Army during the Vietnam War. He married Marcia Campbell in 1968 and they had two sons: David Wayne and Nathan Wayne. David . . . is the archivist for the Jackson County (Mo.) Historical Society, and Nathan works with computers; I can never understand what exactly he does, but it's a programmer of some kind. He and his wife, Jennifer, had their first child (our second great-grandchild). Nora Elizabeth, on June 8, 2006.

Reg and Marcia's Wedding, 1968

Reg's second marriage to Jan Whited produced one son, Brett Matthew, who works for a local oil company.

He has one son born in January earlier this year, Mason Matthew, our first great-grandchild.

Betty Jean is a retired high school special education teacher. She is married to Paul Allen who works for the FBI. They don't have any children, but have two dogs that are like their children. We plan that

Marcia with Nathan (left) and David (right)

Betty J. (Jackson) Allen)

Virginia will live with Betty after I'm gone, and Betty and Paul have a nice home to accommodate Virginia. Nancy and I saved all our married lives to build a substantial trust fund so Virginia will never want for anything. And, she has a loving family to always keep her company. Nancy and I vowed that we were going to be different than the Jacksons I've tried to fairly describe above.

We have made a good on the Jackson name and our Jackson family is a respectable family. So, really, our Jackson family is one to be proud.

Nancy and I were married 63 years when she died on March 11, 2002, at age 79 years and 8 months.

Jackson Family   September 2007

Since Roy's 2006 recollection, his family has grown!

Pictured here are Nathan and Jennifer's children:
Nora Elizabeth (left),
    born June 8, 2006;
Matthew Walter (right),
    March 2, 2008;
Megan Rooth (front),
    August 18, 2010; and,
Timothy Roy (back),
    August 27, 2012.

Brett and Cori's children are Mason Matthew, born January 17, 2006; and, Justin Robert, February 25, 2009.

Making the Grade at Potato Picking

By Roy Weldon Jackson
April 2005

Reading the Jackson County Historical Society's JOURNAL article about World War II German POWs picking potatoes in Atherton, Missouri, reminded me of my summertime job there before the War, picking potatoes in the Missouri River bottoms.

I had just gotten married to Nancy Rogers in Kansas City, Missouri, on January 1, 1939, and was out of steady work. Times were hard and work was scarce and hard to find. That summer I heard that potato workers were needed in the potato fields out east, but that it was very hard work. I ended up getting a job picking potatoes with my brother-in-law, Leonard Rogers. He and I would drive together from Kansas City east to Atherton each day.

After picking potatoes about two days the boss asked me if I would like to work in the grader. My job would be grading (or, sorting by size and quality) and sacking potatoes. He said he would give me a bonus if I would stay the whole summer with him.

I really needed the money so I took the job.

It was the hardest job I have ever had.

I had to dump one hundred pound bags of potatoes into the grader. The gunnysacks were rough burlap and handling them all day made my hands sore and swollen. It made me wish I hadn't taken the job! I needed this money so bad that I had to stick it out. After several days my hands began to toughen up and I finished out the job.

I got my bonus and the boss was happy he had found someone who would get the job done.

To this day I've never had a job that I would suffer like I did as a potato grader.

BORN A SLAVE

Nancy (ROGERS) JACKSON was a REAL Jackson

By Roy Weldon Jackson

January 1, 2009
on my 70th Wedding Anniversary

I wrote this memory because I wanted to "glorify" my wife, Nancy. I want our Jackson family...those who knew her **and** those who came along after she was gone...to know what a "REAL Jackson" she was, much better than I.

Broken Families in Childhood

Neither Nancy nor I had a stable childhood. We had to begin 'fending for ourselves' at an early age...and in the middle of the Great Depression, too. Since I was 2-years-old or so, I was passed around from one family member to another...anyone other than my parents, Jarvis and Grace (Clifford) Jackson...who separated when I was a baby. I stayed with my mother or father only occasionally...and briefly...and only at their convenience. My Grandma and Grandpa Jackson, aunts and uncles (especially my Aunt Hazel), and sometimes friends' families were the ones who took me in, and gave me a place to keep me off the streets.

Nancy's parents, George Fletcher and Annie Sharp (McCullough) Rogers, after having 11 children (Nancy was the baby), divorced. Before that, however, her parent's living situation had deteriorated, especially after the accidental drowning of Nancy's older brother, Harry, in August 1933. Nancy said her mother—who was the most loving, sweet, timid woman who ever lived—tried several times to leave her gruff, often brutal husband. But, "Poppy" (as Nancy and her siblings called their father) would always track "Mother Rogers" down, and walk behind her as she was marched back home in disgrace. I don't know what changed, but they finally were divorced on September 3, 1935, the day before their 37th wedding anniversary.

Nancy's Teenage Years

With the turmoil at home, sometime near the end of 1934 or early 1935, Nancy, age 12, left home and moved from her hometown of Lexington, Missouri, to Kansas City. She answered an ad in the newspaper for a worker for room and board, and lived at 11224 Perry Avenue with Mr. Ralph McGee and his family. There, she joined the Church of Christ at 24th and Van Brunt Boulevard. Nancy was enrolled in February 1935 in the second semester of 6th grade at Carlisle Elementary School in Independence, and re-enrolled for 7th grade that September. However, the following month, Nancy was enrolled in 7th grade at Northeast Junior High School after she went to live with the George and Ruth Salmon family at 5006 E 9th Street.

In 1936, the Salmons (and Nancy) moved to 519 Marsh Avenue. That March, Nancy's sister next oldest in age, died at age 16 from complications after an abortion ("general peritonitis" from a "retained placenta," according to the autopsy report on her death certificate). Mabel "Sissy" (Rogers) Griffin, had had a daughter, Shirley, the year before. Apparently, Sissy felt the need to terminate this pregnancy, but couldn't find help in Lexington. Sissy's death certificate says that her abortion was "presumably" performed by a Dr. Combs of Richmond, Missouri, trial pending. All Nancy ever knew—as she had likely been told—was that it had been a black doctor. Sissy had been working in a bar off Highway 24 along the Missouri River called the Peckerwood Club. (I'm sure it was because of this event that Nancy's father told me not to take her into any bars, when I asked for her hand in marriage.) For a short spell during this time, Nancy moved back to Lexington, and lived on Highland Avenue with "Poppie;" but, she didn't stay long. Nancy returned to the Salmons and started 8th grade at Northeast Junior High School that fall.

Sometime in 1937 the Salmons (and Nancy) moved to 3413 Morrell Avenue. There, Nancy finished 8th grade at Northeast Junior High School, and started 9th grade at Northeast Senior High School.

Nancy finished 9th grade, but after her first semester in 10th grade at Northeast Senior High School, Nancy dropped out of school in late 1938. (I had dropped out of school in the 9th grade in June 1935, had been working as a deliveryman for Crown Drug Stores, and had enlisted for two enrollments in the Civilian Conservation Corps (CCC)).

When Nancy Met Roy

Nancy and I met sometime that fall. The story of how we met and an overview of our 63 years together is recorded in another memory I wrote three years ago. Nancy will be gone 7 years this

March, and I love and miss her every day. Thinking about her as I do, I wanted to share some other recollections about how special she was. This is the reason for this story. We had lots of good times, but life in those days wasn't always easy by any means. Nancy was a real Jackson, and never complained even once. Most wives would have complained and rode their husbands. She was a real Jackson, a much better one than I was.

Early Married Life

When we were married on New Year's Day in 1939. We couldn't find a justice of the peace in Jackson County, so our small wedding took place in Platte County. My mother, Grace (Clifford) Kindler, signed for me as a minor. Nancy and I stayed with my mother and her husband, Bert Kindler, for the first couple of weeks.

Then, we moved into our first home and rented a second-floor apartment in the Puritan's home at 3309 ½ 20th Street (two doors from the Weinstein's...Betty Weinstein was Harold Levine's aunt). I had $20 saved up—a lot of money in those days—and we spent it all! But, we got everything we needed to set up housekeeping. My Aunt Hazel Levine and Betty Weinstein had some pull with the store owner, Mr. Worbey, who gave us a good deal for our money. Plus, he also gave us from $50-75 of furniture on time (credit). This wasn't the usual practice then, as it is today. This was before credit cards, which neither Nancy or I have ever had. With rare exceptions, we have always paid cash for anything we've ever needed or wanted. We loaded up the old 1931 Chrysler sedan so full that I could hardly see to drive. When he was setting up his first home in 1999, Nancy gave our grandson, David, the floor lamp Nancy and I got on time that day, and that we had used our first 60 years together. Oh, this was the place where our good friend and prankster, Bill Annis, visited one night and thought he was being funny by stomping up the stairs at 10 o'clock at night. He got us kicked out of the Puritan's home.

We moved to 61st and Swope Parkway to a third floor apartment in the Smith's home. I worked for a time (and so did Nancy) at the Swope Park Swimming Pool, and later the Parkview Drug Store at Meyer and Prospect Boulevards. We hosted our first Rogers family reunion there in that one large room with hardwood floors. The annual reunions were in honor of Mother Rogers, and were hosted on or near her birthday (March 29) by her surviving 11 children. And, in the summer of 1941, we were given a surprise baby shower there.

In those very early days after we were married, Nancy's father came to visit us several times. He was a heavy eater. I didn't mind what he ate, as I really enjoyed having him visiting us. Nancy really fed him, even needing to run a grocery bill on credit. One time while he was visiting, I was leaving for work when Nancy said she was going to bake a peach cobbler. All day long, I thought about her making that cobbler in that deep iron skillet, and couldn't wait to have some when I got home. So, that night after supper, I asked Nancy for a piece of pie. Nancy said it was all gone, "Poppie" had eaten it all. I said, "You could have saved me one lousy piece, and let him have the rest!" Nancy and I had our first argument over that pie.

As I've said before, times were hard in those days and we never had much and I was sometimes out of work. I managed to get work here and there to pay our way though. We moved back to 20th Street in 1941, first to a second-floor duplex apartment in a building with four units at 3120 East 20th Street. The toilet was an outhouse, but it had running water. After Virginia was born we moved up the street to a second-floor apartment at 3315 East 20th Street in a home belonging to the Rush family. Mr. Rush made us move because he thought I was parking in his place; but it was someone else.

Nancy and I were really down and out when we moved to a "house" at 3404 Cypress Street. It was really a shanty shack that had been on fire previously so there were burnt timbers and holes where it would rain in. We had to use an out house that was about 100 feet from the house. We had to use a 'thunder pot' (chamber pot) at night, and when it rained. And, the next door neighbor allowed us to get fresh water from the water spigot on the outside of their house. Imagine Nancy wearing denim coveralls, carrying water like that, using a two-burner kerosene stove to cook on, feeding and nursing baby Virginia, and washing cloth diapers (and our clothes, too) on a washboard by hand. She took this shack in stride, and never complained once! Nobody knew all the things she dealt with. We were really poor, but the shack was rent free. It was owned by Clarence C. and Bernice (Toms) Billings (who were Nancy's cousins). At least it was a roof over our heads. We knew it was time to move when Nancy noticed that rats had chewed holes in the cuffs of Virginia's nightgown (they were attracted to the baby's saliva most likely). Fortunately, I got a job at Peppard Seed Company, and we moved.

Nancy had to have her teeth pulled not too long after we were married. This old dentist pulled her teeth one by one and she never made a sound. I cringed at the sight. Boy what a gal! The dentist made the false teeth. She put them in never complained once. She was a great Jackson. I complained plenty when my teeth and false teeth hurt!

Life Looking Up

After I was discharged from the Navy in 1945, Nancy, Virginia, and I moved to 5927 Walrond and bought our first house for $5,250 with my G.I. loan. We paid $39 a month. I got a steady job at Sheffield, later Armco Steel, and for the first time, things were looking up. This is where we raised our family. I should say, this is where NANCY raised our three children, Virginia, Reggie and Betty.

Now that I think about it, "What was Nancy's thoughts about having children?" I'll never know what she must have gone through. And, I'll never know what pain. I was working, and never gave her any encouragement. Certainly, expecting fathers weren't allowed in the delivery rooms like they are today. We just really loved one another, and stuff like that wasn't talked about then, I guess.

Nancy was a great mother. And, she was a great cook. She sent me off to work each day with a full, black lunch pail, and always had our dinner ready when I came home from work. All I did was work at the steel mill. I brought home my paychecks and turned them over to her. She ran the house, raised the kids, and sent them to school, as I was very tired when I got home from work. Oh yes,  Nancy also did all the yard work, pushing a grass mower, planting flowers, trimming the hedges, and even painting the house.

Nancy learned to drive after we moved to Walrond. Then, she drove the kids to school, and did all the grocery shopping, too. We went up to get a car that I had picked out, and for some reason they couldn't find it. As we were waiting for my car, Nancy saw the 1956 Crown Victoria and said, "That's what I call a beautiful car." The salesman said, "Come let me show it to you." So, we bought the car that Nancy liked. It came to be her car; she really loved that car. We had it for more than 30 years, and when we sold it, it looked and smelled as good as it did the day we bought it.

Make Good on the Jackson Name

Nancy and I vowed that we were going to lead different lives than our parents. We made good on the Jackson name, and our Jackson family is a respectable family. So, really, our Jackson family is one to be proud.

Farewell, Never Goodbye

Nancy and I were married 63 years when she died on March 11, 2002. In the hospital the day before, she was heavily sedated with morphine and unresponsive. I sat in a chair beside Nancy as she lay curled up on the hospital bed. I whispered in her ear, "*I love you, I love you, I love you.*" To my surprise and delight, she opened her eyes and said, "*I love you.*" That was the last thing we ever said to one another and I was SO glad we had that one last farewell.

Genealogies

BORN A SLAVE

Descendants of
Arthur and Ida May (ANDERSON) JACKSON

More extensive genealogical data is archived in the author's personal research collection. To protect their privacy, given names are listed for living descendants (or, those suspected to still be living) at the time of this publication.

1-Arthur JACKSON
b: 4 Mar 1856, (or 4 Mar 1858), Charleston, Kanawha, Virginia
d: 5 Feb 1931, 414 Boone St (42nd Terr), Kansas City, Jackson, Missouri
+Melissa E. ANDERSON
b: 15 Jun 1860, Neosho, Kansas Territory
m: 25 Oct 1884, Interracial marriage/not permitted to legally marry
              [Holt, Missouri]
d: 3 Apr 1888, White Cloud, Doniphan, Kansas
+Ida May ANDERSON
b: 5 May 1869, Saint Deroin (Historical), Nemaha, Nebraska
m: 18 Sep 1888, Interracial marriage/not permitted to legally marry
              [White Cloud, Doniphan, Kansas]
d: 15 Sep 1948, Kansas City, Jackson, Missouri
.... **2-Mary E. JACKSON**
    b: 1889, White Cloud, Doniphan, Kansas
    d: (at birth)
.... **2-Edgar Walter JACKSON**
    b: 1 Sep 1891, White Cloud, Doniphan, Kansas
    d: 16 Aug 1930, Kansas City, Jackson, Missouri
.... **+Dulcie ROSECRANS**
    b: 10 May 1896, Missouri
    m: 2 Oct 1916, Kansas City, Jackson, Missouri
    d: 25 Nov 1993, El Dorado, El Dorado, California
.... **2-Jabez Roy "Javies/Javis/Davis/Jarvis" JACKSON**
    b: 7 Apr 1895, White Cloud, Doniphan, Kansas
    d: 22 Jun 1952, Kansas City, Jackson, Missouri
.... **+Grace CLIFFORD**
    b: 17 Oct 1899, Joplin, Jasper, Missouri
    m: 2 Oct 1916, Kansas City, Jackson, Missouri
    d: 6 Apr 1949, Kansas City, Jackson, Missouri
.... **3-Roy Weldon JACKSON**
        b: 13 Aug 1918, Kansas City, Jackson, Missouri
.... **+Nancy Beatrice ROGERS**
        b: 6 Jun 1922, Lexington, Lafayette, Missouri
        m: 1 Jan 1939, Platte City, Platte, Missouri
        d: 12 Mar 2002, Kansas City, Jackson, Missouri

. . . . 4-**Reginald Wayne JACKSON**
            b: 1 Aug 1949, Kansas City, Jackson, Missouri
            d: 10 Dec 2012, Archie, Cass, Missouri
. . . . +**Marcia Ann CAMPBELL**
            m: 6 Jul 1968, Kansas City, Jackson, Missouri
. . . . 5-**David Wayne JACKSON**
. . . . +**Russell James HOWERTON**
. . . . 5-**Nathan Wayne JACKSON**
. . . . +**Jennifer ROOTH**
. . . . 6-**Nora Elizabeth JACKSON**
. . . . 6-**Matthew Walter JACKSON**
. . . . 6-**Megan Rooth JACKSON**
. . . . 6-**Timothy Roy JACKSON**
. . . . +**Janice E WHITED**
. . . . 5-**Brett Matthew JACKSON**
. . . . +**Cori PARKER**
. . . . 6-**Mason Matthew JACKSON**
. . . . 6-**Justin Robert JACKSON**
. . . . 4-**Virginia Lee JACKSON**
. . . . 4-**Betty Jean JACKSON**
. . . . +**Florence WOLVERTON**
    b: 1902/3, Colorado
    m: 24 Apr 1924, Independence, Jackson, Missouri
. . . . 3-**Virginia Lee JACKSON**
. . . . +**Joel FITZWATER**
. . . . 2-**Hazel Mae JACKSON**
    b: 21 May 1899, White Cloud, Doniphan, Kansas
    d: 30 Aug 1985, Kansas City, Jackson, Missouri
. . . . +**Max LEVINE**
    m: ca 1923
    d: 4 Jul 1928, Richmond, Ray, Missouri
. . . . 3-**Ruth May LEVINE**
        b: 19 Jul 1923, Kansas City, Jackson, Missouri
        d: 22 Apr 2013, Henderson, Clark, Nevada
. . . . +**Aaron SHAPIRO**
        b: 22 Apr 1920
        d: 1 Jul 1993, Henderson, Clark, Nevada
. . . . +**Louis LEVINE**
    b: 1908/9, Missouri
    m: 31 Oct 1929, Kansas City, Jackson, Missouri
. . . . 3-**Max LEVINE**
. . . . +**Doris**
. . . . 4-**Deborah "Debbie" LEVINE**
. . . . +**Michael "Mike" MILLER**

. . . . 5-Joseph "Joe" MILLER
. . . . 4-Jay LEVINE
. . . . 2-Dollie Frances JACKSON
      b: 8 Dec 1901, White Cloud, Doniphan, Kansas
      d: 15 Feb 1959, 3421 Garner, Kansas City, Jackson, Missouri
. . . . +William Weldon JOHNSON
      b: 16 Dec 1894 (or 1897), Wayne, Illinois
      m: 17 Feb 1920, (1920K0088856), Jackson, Missouri
      d: 11 Jul 1970, Baptist Memorial Hospital, Kansas City, Jackson, Missouri
. . . . 3-Mary Ida JOHNSON
          b: 6 Mar 1923, Kansas City, Jackson, Missouri
          d: 26 Feb 2014, Lathrop, Clinton, Missouri
. . . . +Theodore "Ted" BENTLEY
. . . . 4-Susan Mary BENTLEY
. . . . +Craig BRECKENRIDGE
. . . . 5-Blake Alan BRECKENRIDGE
. . . . 5-Brianna Sue BRECKENRIDGE
. . . . 4-Alice Louise BENTLEY
. . . . +Michael "Mike" WHITE
. . . . +Harold Arthur EVANS
. . . . 4-Brian Arthur EVANS
. . . . +Evelyn HARRIS
. . . . 5-Brian Arthur "Sonny" EVANS
. . . . 5-Robert E. "Bobby" EVANS
. . . . 3-Dorothy Frances JOHNSON
          b: 31 Aug 1927, Kansas City, Jackson, Missouri
          d: 13 Aug 2011, Lees Summit, Jackson, Missouri
. . . . +John Frederick RITTERMEYER
          b: 7 Aug 1924, Kansas City, Jackson, Missouri
          m: 2 Jun 1946, Kansas City, Jackson, Missouri
          d: 25 Jun 1986, Kansas City, Jackson, Missouri
. . . . 4-William Ernest RITTERMEYER
. . . . +Martha Sue KIVETT
. . . . 5-Shara Christine RITTERMEYER
. . . . 5-Jason Eric RITTERMEYER
. . . . 4-Gary Ray RITTERMEYER
. . . . +Rebecca Sue CRANE
. . . . 2-Reginald Brewster JACKSON
      b: 19 May 1905, Hiawatha, Brown, Kansas
      d: 27 Aug 1982, Saint Mary's Hospital, Roeland Park, Johnson, Kansas
. . . . +Violet BROWN
      m: 14 Jan 1924, Kansas City, Jackson, Missouri
. . . . +Irene [--?--]
      m: by 1938

. . . . +**Ida**

     m: by 1947, Kansas City, Jackson, Missouri

. . . . +**Clideen WEINGAND**

     b: 10 Sep 1916

     d: 16 Apr 2009, Wichita, Sedgwick, Kansas

. . . . 2-**Oliver Wadsworth "Ollie" JACKSON**

     b: 3 Oct 1908, Hiawatha, Brown, Kansas

     d: 31 Oct 1965, Wichita, Sedgwick, Kansas

. . . . +**Marvel [--?--]**

     m: by 1938

. . . . +**Ruth KINSTLER**

     b: 1907/8

     m: 20 Apr 1939, Kansas City, Jackson, Missouri

. . . . +**Mavis [--?--]**

Descendants of
Thomas "Tom" and
Mary "Mollie" Jackson (Pryor/Prior) SHARP

More extensive genealogical data is archived in the author's personal research collection. To protect their privacy, given names are listed for living descendants (or, those suspected to still be living) at the time of this publication.

1-**Thomas "Uncle Tom" SHARP**
b: 3 May 1837, Abe and Ad (brothers) Sharp family plantation, Anderson, Kentucky
d: 17 Mar 1928, Saint Joseph, Buchanan, Missouri
+**Mary E. "Mollie" JACKSON – PRYOR/PRIOR**
b: 1 May 1855, Charleston, Kanawha, Virginia
m: 10 Oct 1872, Falls City, Richardson, Nebraska
d: 16 Feb 1902, Forest City, Holt, Missouri
.... 2-**Catherine A. "Kate/Katie" SHARP**
b: 21 Jul 1873, Craig, Holt, Missouri
d: 14 Aug 1941, Saint Joseph, Buchanan, Missouri
.... +**William M. "Will" HAYES**
b: 17 Dec 1873, Forbes, Holt, Missouri
m: by 1901
d: 22 Jan 1933, Saint Joseph, Buchanan, Missouri
.... 3-**Allie M. HAYES** [adopted]
b: 6 Jan 1905, Kansas
d: 16 May 1975, Saginaw, Saginaw, Michigan
.... +**Tony AUTRY**
b: 1907, Louisiana
m: by 1940
.... 2-**William "Henry" SHARP**
b: 25 Jan 1875, Craig, Holt, Missouri
d: 28 Dec 1935, Saint Joseph, Buchanan, Missouri
.... +[--?--]
d: post 28 Dec 1935
.... 2-**Hattie SHARP**
b: 18 Jan 1877, Craig, Holt, Missouri
d: Apr 1880
.... 2-**James Arthur SHARP**
b: 11 Feb 1881, Craig, Holt, Missouri
d: 3 Jan 1933, Buchanan County Jail, Saint Joseph, Buchanan, Missouri
.... +[--?--]
d: or divorced before 3 Jan 1933

BORN A SLAVE

Descendants of
Richard Ludlow JACKSON, Sr., and
Lucinda Edwards (DEATLEY) JACKSON

More extensive genealogical data is archived in the author's personal research collection. To protect their privacy, given names are listed for living descendants (or, those suspected to still be living) at the time of this publication.

1-Richard Ludlow JACKSON, Senior
b: 9 Jul 1797, Fredericksburg, Spotsylvania, Virginia
d: 10 Aug 1863, Gray's Summit, Boles Township, Franklin, Missouri
    [Re-interred in 1901 in Elmwood Cemetery, Kansas City, Jackson, Missouri]
+Lucinda Edwards DEATLEY
b: 11 Feb 1811, Westmoreland, Virginia
m: 24 Nov 1828, Westmoreland, Virginia
d: 29 Nov 1906, Mound City, Holt, Missouri
. . . . **2-George? JACKSON**
    b: 1829, Charles, Maryland
    d: before 1840
. . . . **2-Virginia Catherine JACKSON**
    b: 25 Oct 1833, Charles, Maryland
    d: 1 Oct 1873, Holt, Missouri
. . . . **+George W. THOMAS**
    b: 1829/30, Virginia
    m: 3 Nov 1853, Kanawha, Virginia
. . . . **3-Anna P. "Annie" THOMAS**
        b: 6 Oct 1856, Kanawha, Virginia
        d: 22 Mar 1900, Springfield, Greene, Missouri
. . . . **+Louis William ISBELL Sr**
        b: Jan 1854, Arkansas
        m: ca 1881
. . . . **4-Virginia Adele ISBELL**
            b: 7 Aug 1882, Parsons, Labette, Kansas
            d: 11 Nov 1962, Palo Alto, California
. . . . **+Ezra William OBER Jr**
            b: 3 Oct 1874, Kansas
            d: 11 Sep 1937, Kansas City, Jackson, Missouri
. . . . **5-Ezra William OBER, III**
                b: 30 Aug 1905, Kansas
                d: 26 Apr 1980, Carmel By the Sea, Monterey, California
. . . . **+Jane HARWOOD**
                b: 13 Jul 1901, Kansas City, Jackson, Missouri

> d: 18 Jan 1991, Carmel-By-The-Sea, Monterey, California
.... 6-**William H. OBER**
> b: 9 Feb 1932
> d: 3 Jun 2001 Carmel-By-The-Sea, Monterey, California
.... 5-[--?--] **OBER**
.... +**R. D. BAKER**
.... 4-**Louis William ISBELL Jr**
> b: Mar 1885, Kansas
.... 4-**Jackson Thomas ISBELL**
> b: 3 Sep 1893, Parsons, Labette, Kansas
> d: 25 Feb 1969, San Mateo, San Mateo, California
.... +**Caroline B.**
> b: 1893, Kansas
> m: by 1920
.... 3-**Matthew Ludlow THOMAS**
> b: 5 Feb 1857, Kanawha, Virginia
> d: 12 Apr 1926 Bayard, Morrill, Nebraska
.... +**Angeline "Annie" M. WHITE**
> b: Oct 1867, Missouri
> m: 30 Nov 1880, Cuyahoga, Ohio
.... 4-**Cecil A THOMAS**
> b: Sep 1888, Nebraska
.... 4-**John THOMAS**
> b: Feb 1890, Nebraska
> d: Unknown, Bayard, Morrill, Nebraska
.... 4-**Ruth THOMAS**
> b: Nov 1892, Nebraska
.... 4-**Ethel THOMAS**
> b: Jan 1895, Nebraska
.... 4-**William Andrew "Willie" THOMAS** (WWI veteran)
> b: 14 Sep 1896, Nebraska
> d: 13 May 1980, Hastings, Adams, Nebraska
.... +**Marie MINCH**
> m: 29 Nov 1917 Hastings, Adams, Nebraska
.... 5-**Harold M THOMAS**
> b: 1919 Bayard, Morrill, Nebraska
> d: 1943 Aleutian Islands (Alaska) {UF Catherine Archipelago}
> marker in Bayard Cemetery, Bayard, Morrill, Nebraska
.... 5-**Audrey M THOMAS**
> b: 1921 Hastings, Adams, Nebraska
.... 4-**Cordie THOMAS**
> b: Feb 1899, Nebraska
.... 4-**Thelma THOMAS**
> b: 1901, Nebraska

. . . . **4-Myrl THOMAS**
        b: 1903, Nebraska
. . . . **3-William Andrew THOMAS**
        b: 10 Oct 1860, (or 5 Oct; Bowen Bible), Virginia
        d: 11 Feb 1892, Kansas City, Jackson, Missouri
. . . . **+Cordelia "Delia" ROWLAND**
        b: 4 Nov 1867, Bigelow Township, Holt, Missouri
        m: 8 Sep 1884, Holt, Missouri
        m2): **Samuel V. LEAR**
        d: 13 May 1941, White Cloud, Doniphan, Kansas
. . . . **4-Ernest Edgar THOMAS**
        b: 18 Nov 1885, White Cloud, Doniphan, Kansas
        d: 9 Mar 1952, Saint Joseph, Buchanan, Missouri
. . . . **+Goldie M. WALTERHOUSE**
        b: 28 Apr 1890, Missouri
        m: 29 Jul 1907
        d: Nov 1978 Saint Joseph, Buchanan, Missouri
. . . . **4-William Howard THOMAS**
        b: 2 Dec 1888, Kansas
        d: 28 May 1965, Santa Barbara, Santa Barbara, California
. . . . **+Bessie Viola "Ola" CHRISTIAN**
        b: 1 Jun 1889, Gentry, Missouri
        m: 3 Mar 1909
        d: 23 Aug 1929, Colorado Springs, El Paso, Colorado
. . . . **5-Harold THOMAS**
        b: Jan 1910, White Cloud, Doniphan, Kansas
. . . . **5-Kenneth THOMAS**
        b: 1911/2, Kansas
. . . . **5-Robert THOMAS**
        b: 1913/4, Kansas
. . . . **5-Sarah Vivian THOMAS**
        b: 27 Jun 1916, White Cloud, Doniphan, Kansas
        d: 27 Apr 1987, Colorado Springs, El Paso, Colorado
. . . . **+Herbert Leo CORDER**
        b: 20 Apr 1914, Ramah, El Paso, Colorado
        d: 15 Oct 2003, Colorado Springs, El Paso, Colorado
. . . . **6-Phyllis Darlene CORDER**
. . . . **+William Leo KINDER**
. . . . **+GANN**
. . . . **6-Leona Nadine CORDER**
        b: 7 Oct 1939, Colorado Springs, El Paso, Colorado
        d: 1 Aug 2006
. . . . **+Kenneth John GOOD**
        b: 11 Mar 1938, Ephrata, Lancaster, Pennsylvania

                    d: 31 Jan 1987, Colorado Springs, El Paso, Colorado

.... 6-**Viola Thadine CORDER**
                    b: 7 Nov 1941, Colorado Springs, El Paso, Colorado

.... +**Wayne FINCHER**

.... +**Larry William MORRISON**

.... 5-**Loyd J. THOMAS**
                    b: 1918, White Cloud, Doniphan, Kansas
                    d: 23 Sep 1928, Colorado Springs, El Paso, Colorado

.... +**Dora A.**
                    b: 1887, Kansas

.... 4-**Mary Gladys THOMAS**
                    b: 25 Dec 1890, Bigelow Township, Holt, Missouri
                    d: 20 Jan 1956, Fresno, Fresno, California

.... +**Gilbert BOWEN**
                    b: 21 Jun 1880, White Cloud, Doniphan, Kansas
                    m: 28 Aug 1907, Hiawatha, Brown, Kansas
                    d: 24 Oct 1961, White Cloud, Doniphan, Kansas

.... 5-**Nancy Ann Cordelia BOWEN**
                    b: 29 Mar 1912, White Cloud, Doniphan, Kansas
                    d: 23 Aug 1973, Saint Joseph, Buchanan, Missouri

.... +**Mark Ethelbert ZIMMERMAN Jr.**
                    b: 11 Jun 1909, White Cloud, Doniphan, Kansas
                    d: 8 Nov 1993, Highland, Doniphan, Kansas

.... 6-**Anna Marie ZIMMERMAN**
                    b: 26 Aug 1931, White Cloud, Doniphan, Kansas
                    d: 8 May 2011, Topeka, Shawnee, Kansas

.... +**James Maxwell HERRING**
                    b: 18 Feb 1931, Sparks, Doniphan, Kansas
                    m: 28 Sep 1951, Highland, Doniphan, Kansas
                    d: 12 Aug 2008, Topeka, Shawnee, Kansas

.... 7-**Angela Nan HERRING**
                    b: 4 Jan 1955, Higland, Doniphan, Kansas
                    d: 7 Mar 2013, Lawrence, Douglas, Kansas

.... +**[--?--] HEWITT**

.... 8-**Tammy HEWITT**
                    +**[--?--] MASTERS**

.... 8-**Matthew J. HEWITT**

.... 8-**Michael J. HEWITT**

.... +**Crystal**

.... +**Francene K. BEALL**

.... 7-**James Mark HERRING**

.... 7-**Jere Matthew HERRING**

.... 6-**Mark Earl ZIMMERMAN**
                    b: 4 Apr 1936, White Cloud, Doniphan, Kansas

                     d: 21 Oct 1977, Sulphur, Murray, Oklahoma

................**+Almira PARSONS**

                  m: 31 May 1958

...................**7-Chirsty Marca ZIMMERMAN**

...................**7-Cindy ZIMMERMAN**

                  b: 11 Mar 1962

                  d: 21 Mar 1962

...................**7-Mark Elwain ZIMMERMAN**

...................**7-Matthew Earl ZIMMERMAN**

...................**7-Michael Evans ZIMMERMAN**

....**2-Dr John Wesley JACKSON**

    b: 6 Nov 1834, Charles, Maryland

    d: 13 Mar 1890, Kansas City, Jackson, Missouri

....**+Virginia Carter "Jennie" NORTH**

    b: 16 Jul 1842, Labadie, Franklin, Missouri

    m: 10 Oct 1867, Franklin, Missouri

    d: 2 Dec 1917, Kansas City, Jackson, Missouri

........**3-Dr. Jabez North JACKSON**

        b: 6 Oct 1868, Labadie, Franklin, Missouri

        d: 18 Mar 1935, Kansas City, Jackson, Missouri

........**+Virlea WAYLAND**

        b: 23 Nov 1877, Glasgow, Howard, Missouri

        m: 12 Oct 1899

        d: 5 Mar 1921, Kansas City, Jackson, Missouri

............**4-Virginia JACKSON**

           b: 17 Jan 1902, Kansas City, Jackson, Missouri

           d: 18 Jan 1969, Kansas City, Jackson, Missouri

............**+Thomas Greenwood MACLAUGHLIN**

           b: 27 Jun 1896, Peoria, Peoria, Illinois

           m: 10 Jan 1923, Kansas City, Jackson, Missouri

           d: 23 Sep 1990, Kansas City, Jackson, Missouri

................**5-Virlea MACLAUGHLIN**

               b: 8 Oct 1925, Kansas City, Jackson, Missouri

               d: 9 Jun 1996, Kansas City, Jackson, Missouri

................**+Beverly Helm PLATT, Sr.**

               b: 16 Feb 1919 Kansas City, Jackson, Missouri

               m: 1947

               d: 19 Nov 2015; buried Kansas City, Jackson, Missouri

................**6-Thomas MacLaughlin "Tom" PLATT**

................**6-Beverly Helm PLATT, Jr.**

................**6-Stephen PLATT**

                +Susan BOWERS

....................**7-Stephanie PLATT**

                  +[--?--] ZETTL

. . . . 7-**Meredith PLATT**
. . . . +[--?--] **THIEGART**
. . . . 5-**Jabez Jackson "Jay" MACLAUGHLIN**
        b: 27 Jul 1929, Kansas City, Jackson, Missouri
        d: 5 Nov 2014, Leawood, Johnson, Kansas
. . . . +**Joanna MITCHELL**
        m: 1955
        d: 2013, Leawood, Johnson, Kansas
. . . . 6-**Jim MACLAUGHLIN**
. . . . 6-**Virginia MACLAUGHLIN**
. . . . +**Whit MCCOSKRIE**
. . . . 4-**Margaret Elizabeth JACKSON**
        b: 7 Oct 1906, Missouri
        d: 10 Dec 1958, Kansas City, Jackson, Missouri
. . . . +**Herbert A. SCHAEFER**
        m: 20 Aug 1928, Kansas City, Jackson, Missouri
. . . . +**John T. HARRIS**
        b: 4 Jun 1870, Canada
        d: 16 Feb 1925, Pittsburgh, Allegheny, Pennsylvania
. . . . 5-**Hillary HARRIS**
. . . . +[--?--]
. . . . 5-**John Jackson HARRIS**
. . . . 5-**Kenneth Thomas HARRIS**
. . . . 5-**Sally HARRIS**
. . . . +**Bruce T. WOLFE**
. . . . 5-**Sue HARRIS**
. . . . +**Florence Hinkle STOREY**
        b: 24 Jul 1883
        m: 27 Oct 1925, Jackson, Missouri
        d: 17 Oct 1967, Kansas City, Jackson, Missouri
. . . . 3-**Dr. Walter Emmett JACKSON**
        b: 24 Oct 1870, Labadie, Franklin, Missouri
        d: 24 Oct 1934, Kansas City, Jackson, Missouri
. . . . 2-**Lucy Christina JACKSON**
        b: 24 Dec 1838, Charles, Maryland
        d: 20 Nov 1922, Kansas City, Jackson, Missouri
. . . . +**Charles Swanson ARMSTRONG**
        b: 31 Dec 1834, Pennsylvania
        m: 23 Apr 1879, Franklin, Missouri
        d: 17 Mar 1918, Mound City, Holt, Missouri
. . . . 2-**Thomas B. JACKSON**
        b: 14 Mar 1840, (or Virginia), Charles, Maryland
        d: 2 Apr 1903, Stella Township, Woods, Oklahoma Territory
. . . . +**Mary C. [--?--]**

b: 1845, Ohio
m: 1876
d: 1880–1900
.... 3-**Jasper L. JACKSON**
    b: 1877, Missouri
.... 3-**Jesse S. JACKSON**
    b: 19 Feb 1877, Missouri
    d: Mar 1973, Norwood, Wright, Missouri
.... +**Ida M. WINIGER**
    b: 4 Nov 1875, Belvidere, Boone, Illinois
    d: 29 Jun 1959, Mansfield, Wright, Missouri
.... 2-**Richard Ludlow "Dick" JACKSON, Jr**
    b: 13 Sep 1843, Charleston, Kanawha, Virginia
    d: 3 Aug 1915, Haley, Bowman, North Dakota
.... +**Laura Elizabeth JOHNSON**
    b: 1852, Ohio
    m: 28 Jan 1872, Des Moines, Polk, Iowa
    d: 7 Apr 1890, Northwest End of the West Short Pines, Harding, South Dakota
.... 3-**Annie Laura JACKSON**
    d: pre 1911
.... 3-**Joseph P. JACKSON**
    d: pre 1911
.... 3-**Edwin Carlton "Eddie" JACKSON**
    d: pre 1883, Holt, Missouri
.... 3-**Lucy Virginia JACKSON**
    d: pre 1911
.... 3-**Henry Lee "Harry" JACKSON**
    b: 1873/4, Missouri
    d: before 1880, Holt, Missouri
.... 3-**Edgar Ludlow "Ed" JACKSON**
    b: 23 Jan 1879, Holt, Missouri
    d: 1 Jul 1966, Baker, Fallon, Montana
.... +**Elizabeth Moore "Lizzie" FELT**
    b: 1886/7, South Dakota
    m: 9 Jan 1907, Dickinson, Stark, North Dakota
    d: 11 May 1957, Fallon, Prairie, Montana
.... 4-**Infant JACKSON**
    b: 20 Sep 1907, North Dakota
    d: Oct 1907
.... 4-**Mildred J. JACKSON**
    b: 20 Sep 1907, North Dakota
    d: 9 Feb 1989, Darby, Ravalli, Montana
.... +**Mack Francis NICCUM**
    b: 21 Dec 1907, Grundy, Missouri

m: 11 Dec 1930, Glendive, Dawson, Montana
d: 26 Feb 2002, Baker, Fallon, Montana
. . . . 5-**Jim Pat NICCUM**
. . . . 4-**Loleta J. "Loli" JACKSON**
b: 7/14 Apr 1909, South Dakota
d: 7 Apr 1999, Baker, Fallon, Montana
. . . . +**James A/J "Jim" GILLAN**
b: 1909, Montana
m: by 1935
d: 2 Oct 1974, Medford, Jackson, Oregon
. . . . 5-**Garth GILLAN**
. . . . 3-**Maude Wheeler "Bertie" JACKSON**
b: 4 Oct 1880, Holt, Missouri
d: May 1968, Spearfish, Lawrence, South Dakota
. . . . +**John R. DODGE**
b: Jul 1878, Missouri
m: 1899/1900
buried: 1918, Lewistown, Fergus, Montana
. . . . 4-**Laura M. DODGE**
b: 1900/1, North Dakota
. . . . +**[--?--] WEBER**
. . . . 5-**George Roy WEBER**
b: 7 Oct 1925, Montana
d: 18 May 1944
. . . . 5-**James E. WEBER**
. . . . 4-**John M. DODGE**
b: 1902/3, North Dakota
. . . . 3-**John Richard "Dick" JACKSON**
b: 3 Oct 1883, Camp Crook, Dakota Territory
d: 3 Aug 1963, Rapid City, Pennington, South Dakota
. . . . +**Arta Arzola "Kit" GARDNER**
b: 28 May 1884, Akron, Plymouth, Iowa
m: 1907/8
d: 8 May 1976, Spearfish, Lawrence, South Dakota
. . . . 4-**Neva Dell JACKSON**
b: 9 Aug 1914, Buffalo, Harding, South Dakota
. . . . +**Dale Edward MESSER**
b: 10 Oct 1907, Badger, Kansas
m: 26 Nov 1938, Rapid City, Pennington, South Dakota
d: 5 Apr 1977, Hot Springs, Fall River, South Dakota
. . . . 5-**Carole MESSER**
. . . . +**Carl Francis OBERLITNER**
. . . . +**Kelly [--?--]**
. . . . 3-**Franklin Cleveland "Frank" JACKSON**

b: Oct 1884, South Dakota
d: Sep 1970, Winnett, Petroleum, Montana
. . . . +**Katherine A. KENNEDY**
b: 1878, New York
m: 1907/8
d: 1964
. . . . 4-**Katherine Mabel "Patty" JACKSON**
b: 1908/9, North Dakota
m**: [--?--] MULLIN**
d: before 19 Apr 2000
. . . . 4-**Francis "Bud" JACKSON**
b: 1910, North Dakota
d: after 19 Apr 2000, Dillon, Beaverhead, Montana
. . . . 4-**Richard L. "Dick" JACKSON**
b: 1915, Montana
d: before 19 Apr 2000
. . . . 4-**Dorothy Mae "Dot" JACKSON**
b: 4 Jan 1916, Heath, Fergus, Montana
d: 19 Apr 2000 Roundup, Musselshell, Montana
. . . . +**Cosby Everet "Coty" MESERVE**
b: 18 Jul 1912, Windham, Fergus, Montana
m: 17 Jul 1933, Lewistown, Fergus, Montana
d: 26 Jul 1992, Winnett, Petroleum, Montana
. . . . 5-**William Wade "Bill/Billy" MESERVE**
b: 6 May 1935, Lewistown, Fergus, Montana
d: 15 Feb 2009, Winnett, Petroleum, Montana
. . . . +**Mary O'DRISCOLL**
m: 24 Jul 1978, Lewistown, Fergus, Montana
. . . . 6-**Kari MESERVE**
. . . . +**Jeff ALTENBERG**
. . . . 7-**Hayden ALTENBERG**
. . . . 7-**Sara ALTENBERG**
. . . . 7-**Kady ALTENBERG**
. . . . 6-**Paulette MESERVE**
. . . . +**Grant GERSHMEL**
. . . . 7-**Paige GERSHMEL**
. . . . 6-**Dottie MESERVE**
. . . . +**Tim KISER**
. . . . 7-**Carter KISER**
. . . . 6-**Cotty MESERVE**
. . . . +**Annette**
. . . . 7-**Taylor MESERVE**
. . . . 4-**Ernest Kennedy JACKSON**

> d: before 19 Apr 2000
.... 3-**James Poke JACKSON**
> b: 13 Oct 1886, South Dakota
> buried: 1927 Lewistown, Fergus, Montana
.... 3-**William JACKSON**
> b: Apr 1890, Haley, Bowman, North Dakota
> d: Apr 1890, Northwest End of the West Short Pines, Harding, South Dakota
.... 2-**Dr James Polk JACKSON**
> b: 16 Apr 1845, Charleston, Kanawha, Virginia
> d: 22 Nov 1901, Kansas City, Jackson, Missouri
.... +**Gertrude M. GROGAN**
> b: 30 May 1861, Saint Clair, Allegheny, Pennsylvania
> m: 1 Dec 1886, Kansas City, Jackson, Missouri
> d: 26 Nov 1948, Kansas City, Jackson, Missouri
.... +**Elizabeth "Lizzie" ROBERTS**
> b: 1855/6, Missouri
> m: 9 Nov 1867, Franklin, Missouri
> d: 1884, Kansas City, Jackson, Missouri
.... 3-**Edna Earle JACKSON**
> b: 1876, Mound City, Holt, Missouri
> d: 24 Sep 1899, Fowler, Otero, Colorado

Descendants of
William H. and Catherine (LUDLOW) JACKSON

[Seeking submissions from descendants for a future edition.]

Descendants of
James E. DEATLEY

[Seeking submissions from descendants for a future edition.]

BORN A SLAVE

Illustrations

15   David W. Jackson, great great grandson of Arthur Jackson. High school graduation, 1987. Unless noted, images courtesy the Roy and Nancy Jackson family archives, as copied with their permission by their grandson, David W. Jackson, 1991/2006/2007.

19   Roy W. Jackson, grandson of Arthur Jackson, World War II.

21   Ida May (Anderson) and Arthur Jackson, ca. 1922. This is the only photograph that the Jackson family seems to have of Arthur. Next to Ida, Arthur has darker skin tones. For many years the rationale that Arthur had darker complexion because he was a landscape gardener placated the accusation that Arthur was of African descent. Another deflection was that Arthur must have been part Native American Indian. Historical documentation and DNA testing confirms that Arthur's direct, ancient paternal ancestry migrated from Africa. If he were mulatto, any European genes would have come from any one of Arthur's mother's ancestral lines.

22   414 Boone Street (today, 42nd Terrace), Kansas City, Missouri, where Arthur, Ida, and their grandson, Roy lived in 1931 when Arthur died while sitting on the front porch. Courtesy Missouri Valley Special Collections, Kansas City Public Library, Kansas City, Missouri, 1940 Tax Assessment Photograph Collection. "In 1940, the Works Progress Administration, in conjunction with the Jackson County Tax Assessor's office and other local agencies, provided the manpower and partial funding for a photographic survey of all standing buildings in Kansas City, Missouri. The project produced thousands of images of residences, businesses, schools, churches, and government buildings, including many structures that are no longer in existence or would not have otherwise been photographed. The images consisted of small, black-and-white contact prints mounted on block record cards. Each card represented one city block and contained all photographs of properties within those block boundaries. For the purpose of identification, an indexing system by district-block-parcel was created, which allowed for complete accounting of every property in the city. The identification number was displayed on a sign in front of each building photographed, and a WPA worker is typically seen

283

holding the sign or standing nearby in the frame. After the tax assessment images were no longer useful for property valuations, they came into the possession of the Historic Preservation Commission of Kansas City (formerly the Landmarks Commission). In 2012, the collection was donated to the Kansas City Public Library and housed in Missouri Valley Special Collections. The photographs were digitized by the Library with the intention to make them more accessible to researchers and property owners. The collection consists of more than 40,000 images of Kansas City residences and buildings in 1940. Each photographic print is approximately 1"x1.5", mounted on 12"x18" cards, and organized by block. There may be only one image mounted on a card or as many as several dozen. There are 4,241 block cards in the collection, as well as 55 districts maps. Many of the cards also contain individual block maps, which are useful for locating a particular parcel. The collection does not include all photographs that were taken as part of the 1940 tax assessment project. Several hundred block cards are missing from the original survey. Many other individual property photos were previously removed or otherwise missing before the Library took possession of the collection. The large numbers of photographs that remain, however, provide a unique snapshot of 1940 Kansas City." cdm16795.contentdm.oclc.org/cdm/landingpage/collection/kcpltax

23   Pate's Addition included Steptoe Street (today, 43rd Terrace) that ran 4 blocks west of Broadway to Summit. *Plat Book of Jackson County, Missouri.* (Kansas City, Mo.: Berry Publishing Co., 1911).

25-26   E. Ingraham and Company Regulator wall clock once belonging to Arthur and Ida Jackson.

27   David W. Jackson at the Antiques Roadshow® Kansas City, Missouri, 10 August 2013.

29   Jabez "Jarvis" Jackson (right) with an unidentified friend, Swope Park, Kansas City, Missouri, ca. 1920.

31   Virginia Lee Jackson, daughter of Jabez "Jarvis" and Florence (Wolverton) Jackson, as Roy knew his half-sister in 1930.

33   Allen School. Missouri Valley Special Collections, Kansas City Public Library, Kansas City Missouri, School District Records, SC23, Series II, Box 1, Folder 2; ID 10010936.

34   Parkview Drug Store where Roy was a bicycle delivery boy, was

located on the corner at the far left just out of this view at the northwest corner of Westport Road and Broadway. This was the view looking north from that intersection on June 7, 1948. Missouri Valley Special Collections, Kansas City Public Library, Miscellaneous Landmarks Commission Photographs, P34-4, Box 1, Folder 30, #1B; ID 10018575.

35   Streetcar Bridge over Broadway at 43rd Street, Kansas City, Missouri, as it appeared in 1985 (since demolished).

36   Above: Streetcar bridge at 43rd Street from below, looking north from southeast corner of 43rd and Broadway, 1977. Courtesy Missouri Valley Special Collections, Kansas City Public Library, Kansas City, Missouri, Randy Storck, photographer, General Collection (P1), Bridges--Broadway at 43rd, Number 2; ID 10001088.

36   Below: Office of the Wiedenann & Simpson coal yard, 1940. Courtesy Missouri Valley Special Collections, Kansas City Public Library, Kansas City, Missouri, 1940 Tax Assessment Photograph Collection.

37   Sanborn Fire Insurance map showing the neighborhood at 43rd and Wornall, including the block where Arthur, Ida, and Roy Jackson lived at 414 Boone when Arthur died in 1931. Courtesy Missouri Valley Special Collections, Kansas City Public Library, Kansas City, Missouri.

39   Arthur Jackson's Missouri Death Certificate, Courtesy Missouri State Archives.

40   An image of the CCC Camp where Roy W. Jackson served in Sebastopol, California.

43   Dr. Jabez North Jackson, courtesy Sally Harris Wolfe, his granddaughter. Used with permission from the John T. Harris Family Home   Page: familytreemaker.genealogy.com/users/w/o/l/Sally--Wolfe/

45   Indian-head Liberty nickel, 1931, the year Arthur Jackson died. Anonymous.

75   A typical American slave family in front of a rather atypical slave dwelling. Most slave quarters were less substantially constructed, generally log cabins, built cheaply of perishable materials, in much the same way as the houses of poorer white Virginians. Courtesy National Museum of African American History and Culture, Smithsonian Institution, Washington, D.C.

79   Slave Populations in Virginia, ca. 1860. Charleston in Kanawha County had a slightly higher concentration of slaves than surrounding counties; but, nothing compared to eastern Virginia counties where the Jacksons had migrated from between 1841-1842. slaveryinamerica.org/geography/slave_census_VA_1860.htm.

82   Large group of slaves(?) standing in front of buildings on Smith's Plantation, Beaufort, South Carolina. Timothy H. O'Sullivan (1840-1882), photographer. Library of Congress Prints and Photographs Division Washington, D.C. Reproduction Number: LC-USZ62-67819 (b&w film copy neg.) Call Number: LOT 4205 <item> [P&P].

86   Southeast Missouri Farms. Negro FSA (Farm Security Administration) client cultivating in field of corn. Russell Lee, (1903-1986)1, photographer. Library of Congress Prints and Photographs Division Washington, DC. Reproduction Number: LC-USF33-011558-M4 (b&w film nitrate neg.) LC-DIG-fsa-8a23284 (digital file from original neg.). Call Number: LC-USF33- 011558-M4 [P&P].

87   Slave quarter. Historic American Buildings Survey, Theodore LaVack, Photographer. November, 1936. - The Cedars, Slave Cabin, Barnhart, Jefferson County, Missouri. Library of Congress Prints and Photographs Division Washington, D.C. Call Number: HABS MO, 50-BARN, 1A—1.

88   Slave cabin. sonofthesouth.net/slavery/slavery-us-constitution.htm.

90   1853 Marriage record of George W. Thomas and Virginia Catherine Jackson. Courtesy Kanawha County Recorder of Deeds.

92   Arthur Jackson's mother, like this slave girl, may have served "her white family" as a personal servant, nurse and/or nanny, while raising at least two of her own children (Arthur and Mollie) from two different partners. Pictured here is Mary Allen Watson, 15, June, 1866, Disbrow & Few, Photographers, Albion, NY. Library of Congress Prints and Photographs Division Washington, D.C. Reproduction Number: LC-DIG-ppmsca-11038 (digital file from

original item, front) LC-DIG-ppmsca-11039 (digital file from original item, back). Call Number: LOT 14022, no. 90 [P&P].

93   John Wesley Jackson, in his 20s, son of Richard L. and Lucinda Edwards (Deatley) Jackson, Sr. Courtesy Sally Harris Wolfe, great granddaughter of Dr. John Wesley Jackson. Used with permission from the John T. Harris Family Home Page: familytreemaker.genealogy.com/users/w/o/l/Sally--Wolfe/

95   Birth record of Matthew L. Thomas, February 5, 1857. Courtesy Recorder of Deeds, Kanawha County, West Virginia.

98   Map of Franklin County, Missouri, undated. Boles Township is in the northeast corner of the county. Anonymous.

101   Five generations on Smith's Plantation, Beaufort, South Carolina. Library of Congress Prints and Photographs Division Washington, D.C. Reproduction Number: LC-DIG-ppmsc-00057 (digital file from original) LC-B8171-152-A (b&w film copy neg.). Call Number: LOT 4205 [item] [P&P].

102-107 Bird's Eye Views of Missouri, from 1860 U.S. Census Bureau data. Leigh, E. M.D. *Bird's-Eye Views of Slavery in Missouri*. (St. Louis, Mo.: Keith & Woods, C. C. Bailey, James M. Crawford, C. Witter, 1862).

113   Virginia (North) Jackson, wife of John W. Jackson, courtesy Sally Harris Wolfe, her great granddaughter. Used with permission from the John T. Harris Family Home Page: familytreemaker.genealogy.com/users/w/o/l/Sally--Wolfe/

120   Emancipation Proclamation by famous cartoonist and illustrator, Thomas Nast. His vivid illustration that formed the basis for this print–with one essential difference–originally appeared in *Harper's Weekly* on January 24, 1863.

121   Come and Join Us Brothers. U.S. Colored Troop Recruitment broadside. 1863-1865. Courtesy of Rare Book, Manuscript, and Special Collections Library at Duke University, as published at usgennet.org/usa/mo/county/stlouis/ct.htm.

131   Emancipation Proclamation by the Governor of the State of Missouri.
         E. Knobel, artist. One of two large commemorative prints marking the
         ordinance issued by Missouri governor Thomas C. Fletcher,
         proclaiming the immediate emancipation of slaves in that state. The
         Missouri ordinance was issued on January 11, 1865, three weeks
         before the Thirteenth Amendment to the U.S. Constitution was
         proposed by Congress. Library of Congress Prints and Photographs
         Division Washington, D.C. Reproduction Number: LC-DIG-pga-
         01806 (digital file from original print) LC-USZ62-91379 (b&w film
         copy neg.). Call Number: PGA - Knobel--Emancipation
         Proclamation... (D size) [P&P].

135   Section 31, Township 44, Range 2 East, in the Franklin County,
         Missouri Atlases: 1878 (top); 1898 (middle); and, 1930 (bottom).

136   Section 31, Township 44, Range 2 East, in the Franklin County,
         Missouri, Plat Book, 1961.

142   Tri-State area of Holt County, Missouri; Richardson County,
         Nebraska; and Doniphan County, Kansas. Anonymous.

144   Levee and steamboat, undated, Town of Washington, Franklin
         County, Missouri. Library of Congress Prints and Photographs
         Division Washington, D.C. 2054. Reproduction and Call Number:
         HABS MO,36-WASH,17-2.

146   *Holt County Sentinel*, 3 Aug 1877.

148   1880 U.S. Census, Bigelow, Holt County, Missouri. This is the
         document that connected Arthur Jackson with his former slaveholding
         family, ancestors of Dr. Jabez North Jackson.

149   Downtown Sedalia, Missouri, Ohio Street, looking south, from a
         postcard in the author's possession.

150   University Medical College and Hospital, corner of 19th Street and
         Campbell, Kansas City, Missouri. Postcard courtesy Kansas City
         Public Library.

151   Dr. Jabez North Jackson, courtesy Sally Harris Wolfe, his
         granddaughter. Used with permission from the John T. Harris Family
         Home Page: familytreemaker.genealogy.com/users/w/o/l/Sally--
         Wolfe/

152   East side of Broadway, looking north from 15th to 16th Streets. Courtesy Jackson County (Mo.) Historical Society Archives, Albert Schoenberg (1886-1965) Realty and Investment Company Records.

153   Giles A. Briggs farm where Arthur and Melissa Jackson lived is in the Southwest ¼ of Section 18, just south of the Iowa Reservation. Melissa may have been buried in the cemetery denoted with a Christian cross "†" just west of White Cloud. Giles Briggs (1816-1898) and Eliza (O'Banion) Briggs (1824-1898) are in the Olive Branch Cemetery. *Doniphan County, Kansas, Atlas*, 1878, by J. S. Birch, Chicago. Detailed here is Township 1 South, Range 19 East.

155   John Wesley Jackson (reversed vertically), courtesy Sally Harris Wolfe, his great granddaughter. Used with permission from the John T. Harris Family Home Page: familytreemaker.genealogy.com/users/w/o/l/Sally--Wolfe/.

156   Dr. Jabez North Jackson in military uniform and regalia, courtesy Sally Harris Wolfe, his granddaughter. Used with permission from the John T. Harris Family Home Page: familytreemaker.genealogy.com/users/w/o/l/Sally--Wolfe/.

157   Dr. Jabez Jackson was identified as a member of the Jackson County Medical Society (today, Metropolitan Medical Society). In the composite below, courtesy the Jackson County Historical Society Archives, J. N. Jackson is on the far right, fourth down. [Directly to the left on the same row is Dr. Bennett Clarke Hyde, who, in 1910 would be charged and tried three times for murder of prominent Kansas City and Independence Swope family members, whom Dr. Hyde was connected through marriage.]

159   Dr. Jabez North Jackson, courtesy Sally Harris Wolfe, his granddaughter. Used with permission from the John T. Harris Family Home Page: familytreemaker.genealogy.com/users/w/o/l/Sally--Wolfe/.

160   Thomas "Tom" Sharp. *St. Joseph Gazette*, 17 June 1923; and syndicated in the *Holt County Sentinel* in the days following, p. C2, "Slavery Days: An Interesting Sketch of Tom Sharp, a Former Holt County Slave."

161   Lucinda Edwards (Deatley) Jackson, as published in, "Their Fathers were Soldiers: Reminisces of the Revolutionary Period by Two True Daughters," *Kansas City* (Mo.) *Star*, 31 Jan 1898, 9.

162   Jackson tombstone, Elmwood Cemetery, courtesy Sally Harris Wolfe, granddaughter of Dr. Jabez North Jackson. Used with permission from the John T. Harris Family Home Page: familytreemaker.genealogy.com/users/w/o/l/Sally--Wolfe/.

165   Dr. Jabez North Jackson, courtesy Sally Harris Wolfe, his granddaughter. Used with permission from the John T. Harris Family Home Page: familytreemaker.genealogy.com/users/w/o/l/Sally--Wolfe/.

167   319 East 47th Street, where the apartment and now condominium/apartment buildings now known as Whitehall and Plaza Castles buildings have stood since these images were taken in 1940. Courtesy Missouri Valley Special Collections, Kansas City Public Library, Kansas City, Missouri, 1940 Tax Assessment Photograph Collection.

168   Rear view of Oak Hall, residence of William Rockhill Nelson, as it appeared in 1890. The grand home was razed and groundbreaking for the art museum was on June 16, 1930. Arthur Jackson and his family had this view from the home they rented on 47th Street to the south and *west* of the Nelson home between 1914-1917. To the south and *east* of Oak Hall, Nelson had constructed nearly 100 rental houses of varying sizes around 1908. Photo taken from Picturesque and Descriptive Kansas City, Missouri , courtesy of Kansas City Public Library Missouri Valley Special Collections (Q 090.8 A78), p. 82; General Collection (P1), Residences--William R. Nelson, #19; ID 10016995.

168   1925 Atlas of Jackson County, Missouri, showing the southwest ¼ of Section 29, Township 49, Range 33. By 1925, the house where the Jacksons had lived between 1914-1917 was platted into the "New South Moreland" subdivision, Lot 2. Out of view on the northeast corner was the 20-acres where Oak Hall was still situated when this map was created. E. C. White School (where Arthur and Ida's son, Reginald, and later grandson, Roy would attend school) was three city blocks south and west.

170   Today (2015) a modern parking structure and a ca. 1920s Tudor-style apartment house is located where the Jacksons lived at 4724 Summit, between September 1918 to 1919.

172   4605 W Prospect Place (Jarboe) in 2015.

Bibliography

Monographs

Ambler, Charles Henry. *A History of West Virginia.* (Prentice-Hall, 1933).

Andrews, William W., ed. *From Fugitive Slave to Free Man: The Autobiographies of William Wells Brown.* (Columbia, Mo.: University of Missouri Press, 2003).

Berry Publishing Co. *Plat Book of Jackson County, Missouri.* (Kansas City, Mo.: Berry Publishing Co., 1911).

Bird, J. S. *Historical Plat Book of Doniphan County, Kansas.* (Chicago: J. S. Bird, 1878).

Born in Slavery: Slave Narratives from the Federal Writers' Project, 1936-1938. Ohio Narratives, Volume XII. Part of the larger work, *Slave Narratives: A Folk History of Slavery in the United States from Interviews with Former Slaves.* (Washington, D.C.: Library of Congress, Manuscripts Division, 1941).

Brink, McDonough and Co. *An Illustrated Historical Atlas of Holt County, Missouri.* (Philadelphia, Pa.: Brink, McDonough and Co., 1877).

Burke, Diane Mutti. *On Slavery's Border: Missouri's Small Slaveholding Households, 1815-1865.* (Athens, Ga.: University of Georgia Press, 2010).

Butler Stuart Lee, *Guide to Virginia Militia Units in the War of 1812* (Athens, Ga.: Iberian Publishing Co., 1988), 211-214.

Caldwell, A. B., ed. "William Jackson." *History of the American Negro*. West Virginia Edition. Volume VII. (Atlanta, Ga.: A. B. Caldwell Publishing Co., 1923)

Callahan, James Morton. *The Semi-Centennial History of West Virginia*. (Charleston, Wv.: Semi-Centennial Commission of West Virginia), 1913.

Coggswell, Gladys Caines. *Stories from the Heart: Missouri's African American Heritage*. Missouri Heritage Reader series. (Columbia, Mo.: University of Missouri Press, 2009).

Conley, Phil Mallor, ed. *The West Virginia Encyclopedia.* (Charleston, Wv.: West Virginia Publishing Co., 1929).

Conrad, Howard Louis. "John W. Jackson." *Encyclopedia of the History of Missouri*. Volume 3. (St. Louis, Mo.: The Southern History Company, 1901).

Coulter, Charles E. *Take Up the Black Man's Burden: Kansas City's African American Communities, 1865-1939*. (Columbia, Mo.: University of Missouri Press, 2006).

Crozier, William Armstrong, ed. *Spotsylvania County Records, 1721-1800: Being Transcriptions from the Original Files at the County Court House....* (Baltimore, Md.: Southern Book Co., 1955).

Dunaway, Maxine. *Missouri Military Land Warrants: War of 1812.* (Maxine Dunaway, 1985).

Dunaway, Wilma A. *Slavery in the American Mountain South.* (Cambridge Univ. Press, 2003).

Eubank, H. Ragland. *The Authentic Guide Book of Historic Northern Neck Virginia.* (Richmond, Va.: Whittet & Shepperson, 1934).

Frazier, Harriet C. *Slavery and Crime in Missouri, 1773-1865.* (Jefferson, N.C.: McFarland and company, Inc., Publishers, 2001).

Glanker, Bill. "From Slavery to Freedom: The Slaves of Valentine Hunter." *The Missouri State Archives: Where History Begins.* (Jefferson City, Mo.: Robin Carnahan, Secretary of State in partnership with the Friends of the Missouri State Archives, 2012).

Goodspeed Publishing Co. *History of Franklin, Jefferson, Washington, Crawford, and Gasconade Counties, Missouri.* (Chicago: Goodspeed Publishing Co, 1888).

Greene, Lorenzo J., Gary R. Kremer, and Antonio F. Holland. "From Sunup to Sundown: The Life of the Slave." *Missouri's Black Heritage.* Revised. (Columbia, Mo.: University of Missouri Press, 1993).

Hixson, W. W. *Plat Book, Franklin County, Missouri.* (Rockford, Il: W. W. Hixson and Company, 1930).

Howell, Donna Wyant. *I Was a Slave: True Life Stories Dictated by Former American Slaves in the 1930's. Book 5: The Lives of Slave Children.* Voice of Will Daily. (Washington, D.C.: American Legacy Books, 2004).

Jackson, David W. *Direct Your Letters to San Jose: The California Gold Rush Letters and Diary of James and David Lee Campbell, 1849-1852.* (Kansas City, Mo.: The Orderly Pack Rat, 2000).

Jackson, David W. *Kansas City Chronicles: An Up-to-Date History*. (Charleston, Sc.: The History Press, 2010).

Jackson, David W. and Paul Kirkman. *LOCK DOWN: Outlaws, Lawmen and Frontier Justice in Jackson County, Missouri*. (Independence, Mo.: Jackson County Historical Society, 2009, 2012).

Kiel, Herman Gottlieb. *Centennial Biographical Dictionary of Franklin County, Missouri*. Reprinted; originally published in 1925. (Washington, Mo.: Washington Historical Society). [Kiel's archival files were also accessed (particularly the 1874 and 1878 medical directories), courtesy Judy Schmidt, compiler, Washington Historical Society.]

History Publishing Co. *History of Holt County, Missouri*. (St. Joseph, Mo.: History Publishing Co., 1917).

Kremer, Gary R. *Race and Meaning: The African American Experience in Missouri*. (Columbia, Mo.: University of Missouri Press, 2014).

Leigh, E. M.D. *Bird's-Eye Views of Slavery in Missouri*. (St. Louis, Mo.: Keith & Woods, C. C. Bailey, James M. Crawford, C. Witter, 1862).

McClain, Carlton Dubois. *Mulattoes in the Postbellum South and Beyond: The Invisible Legacy of an Afro-European People, Custom, and Class in Americas' Binary and Three-Tier Societies*. (n.p.: Carlton Dubois McClain, 2014).

Missouri Adjutant General. *Annual Report of the Adjutant General of Missouri for 1864* (Jefferson City, Mo.: W.A. Curry, Public Printer, 1865).

Missouri State Legislature. *Missouri Session Laws*, 1829; 1840-1841; 1846.

National Historical Publishing Co. *History of Atchison and Holt Counties, Missouri.* (St. Joseph, Mo.: National Historical Publishing Co., 1882).

National Society Daughters of the American Revolution. *Lineage Book.* Volume LVII, 1906. Application No. 14354 of Mrs. Virginia Adele Ober, 56440.

Nolen, Rose M. *Hoecakes, Hambone, and All That Jazz.* Missouri Heritage Reader series. (Columbia, Mo.: University of Missouri Press, 2003).

Ogle, George A. *Standard Atlas of Franklin County, Missouri.* (Chicago, Il.: George A. Ogle & Co., 1898).

Ogle, George A. *Standard Atlas of Holt County, Missouri.* (Chicago, Il.: George A. Ogle & Co., 1918).

Postma, Johannes. *The Atlantic Slave Trade.* (Westport, Ct.: Greenwool Press, 2003).

Quarles, Benjamin. *The Negro in the Civil War.* (New York: Russell & Russell, 1968).

Rawick, George P., ed. *The American Slave: A Composite Autobiography.* Volume 16(b). (Westport, Ct.: Greenwood Publishing, 1972).

Rawick, George P., ed. *The American slave: A Composite Autobiography, Supplement II.* Volumes 4 and 5. 1(Westport, Ct.: Greenwood Publishing, 1979).

Rodriguez, Junius P., ed. *Slavery in the United States: A Social, Political and Historical Encyclopedia.* Volume 1. (Santa Barbara, Ca.: ABC-CLIO, 2007).

St. Louis Publishing Co. *Atlas Map, Franklin County, Missouri.* (St. Louis, Mo.: St. Louis Publishing Co., 1878).

Schirmer, Sherry Lamb. *A City Divided: The Racial Landscape of Kansas City, 1900-1960.* (Columbia, Mo.: University of Missouri Press, 2000).

Sims, Edgar Barr. *Making a State: Formation of West Virginia.* (Charleston, Wv.: E.B. Sims, 1956).

Stinson, Helen S. *A Handbook for Genealogical Research in West Virginia. County: Kanawha.* (Charleston, Wv.: Kanawha Valley Genealogical Society, 1992).

Switala, William J. *Underground Railroad in Delaware, Maryland, and West Virginia,* (Mechanicsburg, Pa: Stackpole Books, 2004).

Sylvester, Theodore L. and Sonia Benson, eds. *Slavery Throughout History: An Almanac.* (Detroit, Mi.: UXL, an imprint of the Gale Group, 2000).

Tharp, James A. *Colleges of Medicine, Dentistry and Pharmacy, Kansas City, Missouri: Names of 3400 Graduates, 1871-1905.* (Kansas City, Mo.: The Orderly Pack Rat, 2013).

Trexler, Harrison Anthony, Ph.B. *Slavery in Missouri, 1804-1865.* Johns Hopkins University Studies in Historical and Political Science, Series 32, No. 2. (Baltimore, Md.: Johns Hopkins Press, 1914).

U.S. Congress. *Congressional Record.* "Message from the President of the United States transmitting a letter from the

Secretary of the Interior relative to the sale of the Sac and Fox and Iowa Indian Reservations." (Washington, D.C.: Government Printing Office): Vol. 2336, Ex. Doc. No. 70.

U. S. Pension Bureau. *List of Pensioners* for Holt County, Missouri, January 1, 1883.

Weant, Kenneth E. *Civil War Records: Missouri Enrolled Militia Infantry Regiments.* Volume 7. (Arlington, Tx.: K. E. Weant, ca. 2010).

Willis, Deborah, and Barbara Krauthamer. *Envisioning Emancipation: Black Americans and the End of Slavery.* (Philadelphia, Pa.: Temple University Press, 2013).

Witherspoon, Dorothy Wofford. *Researching Slave Ancestry: A Case Study of Ben Stanley Jordan and Anna Laudermilk Jordan.* (Heritage Publications, 2010).

Woodtor, Dee Parmer, Ph.D. *Finding A Place Called Home: A Guide to African American Genealogy and Historical Identity.* (New York: Random House, 1999).

Wright, T. R. B. *Westmoreland County, Virginia : Parts I and II : A Short Chapter and Bright Day in its History* (Richmond, Va.: Whittet & Shepperson, printers, 1912).

Archival Matter

Franklin County, Missouri, Probate Court. Richard L. Jackson (deceased August 10, 1863) Estate, August 1863 Term. [Missouri State Archives microfilm roll number C40570. Originals are maintained and preserved by the Washington Historical Society, Franklin County, Missouri.]

Franklin County, Missouri, Recorder of Deeds. Deed Books.

Franklin County, Missouri, Tax Record Books, 1860, 1862, and 1863. [The originals are maintained and preserved with the Four Rivers Genealogical Society, Washington, Franklin County, Missouri, with gratitude to Sue Lampe.]

Jackson County, Missouri, Recorder of Deeds. Deed and Marriage Books.

Jackson, David W. Personal Papers, family archives and genealogical research, 1980-present.

Kanawha County, (West) Virginia, Circuit Court file. "Index cards to court records, Kanawha County, West Virginia: 1754-1933," [Microfilmed by the Family History Center (LDS film 249656) from originals at the West Virginia University Library, Morgantown, West Virginia. This index is to the loose papers, also at the West Virginia University Library.]

Kanawha County, (West) Virginia, County Clerk. Deed and Marriage Books.

Missouri Secretary of State. "Missouri Digital Heritage" database of soldiers' records that covers the War of 1812 through World War I, as abstracted from Record Group: *"Office of the Adjutant General,"* Series: *"Record of Service Card, Civil War, 1861-1865,"* Box: 43, Reel: S00873.

Missouri State Census, 1868. Claggett, Steven F. *1868 Census, Franklin County, Missouri (Surviving Records).* (Washington, Mo.: Four Rivers Genealogical Society, September 2007), Preface and Introduction. [The original census scheduled are maintained and preserved by the Washington Historical Society.]

National Archives and Records Administration (NARA). Civil War pension application file for Thomas Sharp, Private; Co. G, 68th U.S. Colored Volunteer Infantry; Soldier's Certificate 470291)

National Archives and Records Administration (NARA). Record Group 105, *Records of the Bureau of Refugees, Freedmen, and Abandoned Lands (Freedmen's Bureau)*:

Field Office Records

Series M1908, *Records of the Field Offices for the State of Missouri, Bureau of Refugees, Freedmen, and Abandoned Lands, 1865–1872.* 24 rolls.

Other Records

M803, *Records of the Education Division of the Bureau of Refugees, Freedmen, and Abandoned Lands, 1865–1871.* 35 rolls.

M1875, *Marriage Records of the Office of the Commissioner, Washington Headquarters of the Bureau of Refugees, Freedmen, and Abandoned Lands, 1861–1869.* 5 rolls.

M1894, *Descriptive Recruitment Lists of Volunteers for the United States Colored Troops for the State of Missouri, 1863–1865.* 6 rolls.

M1895-06, *Washington Recruiting Station, December 1863-March 1864.*

National Archives and Records Administrations (NARA). Washington, D.C. *Consolidated Lists of Civil War Draft Registration Records (Provost Marshal General's Bureau; Consolidated Enrollment Lists, 1863-1865).* Record Group: 110, Records of the Provost Marshal General's Bureau (Civil War).

National Archives and Records Administration (NARA). Record Group M776, Internal Revenue Assessment Lists for the State of Missouri, 1862-1866. Division 8, District 2, Franklin County, Missouri, April 1863.

National Archives and Records Administration (NARA). Thomas Sharp military file and pension file (Application No. 38987; Certificate No. 470291).

Nebraska State Census, 1885.

U.S. Census Bureau.

1830 Census	Westmoreland County, Virginia (Population)
1840 Census	Charles County, Maryland (Population)
1850 Census	Kanawha County, Virginia (Population, Slave, Agricultural)
1860 Census	Kanawha County, Virginia (Population, Slave) Franklin County, Missouri (Population, Slave, Agricultural)
1870 Census	Charleston County, West Virginia (Population) Fairfax County, West Virginia (Population)
1880 Census	Kanawha County, West Virginia (Population) Holt County, Missouri (Population)

Westmoreland County, Virginia, County Clerk. Fiduciaries and Accounts Book 19. DeAtley Estate. Courtesy, Francesca Henle Taylor, Genealogy Volunteer.

Newspapers (grouped by county)

Buchanan County, Missouri

St. Joseph Gazette, 17 June 1923; and syndicated in the Holt County Sentinel in the days following, p. C2, "Slavery Days: An Interesting Sketch of Tom Sharp, a Former Holt County Slave."

St. Joseph Gazette, 5 Sep 1923

St. Joseph News Press

"Negro Ex-Slave Dead," 18 Mar 1928
"Found Dead in Jail," 3 Jan 1933

Doniphan County, Kansas

Weekly Kansas Chief, (Troy, Ks.)

20 Oct 1887
10 Nov 1887
8 Dec 1887
12 Apr 1888
28 Sept 1892

Franklin County, Missouri

Daily Missouri Republican (St. Louis, Missouri),
28 Mar. 1863, p. 1, c. 1.

German newspaper, Washington, Mo., 27 May 1880.

Franklin County Observer, 24 Jan and 14 Mar 1890.

"Slaves In Missouri In 1860: There Were 114,000 in the State,
One County Only Had No Slaves." *Howard County* (Mo.)
Advertiser, 9 Jan 1903.

Fredericksburg, Spotsylvania County, Virginia

Free Lance

28 Nov 1901
"Crosses of Honor," 18 Jan 1906

Free Lance Star, 29 Mar 1929

Holt County, Missouri

Holt County Sentinel

26 Mar 1869

24 Mar 1871
26 May 1871
"Field Notes from Bigelow Township," 18 Jul 1873; also 7 Mar
17 Apr 1874
17 Mar 1875
2 Apr 1875
"Take Notice," 5 May 1876
30 June 1876
4 Aug 1876
3 Aug 1877
23 Feb. 1877
"Mound City," 12 Sept 1884
30 Sep 1892
"Sharp," 16 Feb 1902
"Dies at Ripe Old Age," 7 Dec 1906
"November 12, 1870," 15 Nov 1907

Jackson County, Missouri

Kansas City Star

"Dr. J. W. Jackson Dead." 13 Mar 1890
"Their Fathers were Soldiers: Reminisces of the
   Revolutionary Period by Two True Daughters,"
   31 Jan 1898
"Death of Dr. J. P. Jackson," 22 Nov 1901
"Visits her Former Slave," 6 Dec 1901
"Negro Nomenclature." 5 Oct 1905
"Leases Boyhood Homesite," 12 Jun 1932
"Pool Segregation Put in KC Spotlight," 15 Jan 2002

Kansas City Journal Post

[Jabez North Jackson obituary], 19 Mar 1935

Kanawha County, West Virginia

"Law! Law! Law!" *Kanawha Valley Star*, 2 Mar 1858, 2.

Westmoreland County, Virginia

Trebay, Guy. "Virginia's Lost History: Exploring the Lost History of Virginia's Northern Neck" *New York Times*, 25 Nov 2012. Also: hailtoyou.wordpress.com/2010/ 11/24/the-blackest-surnames-in-the-usa/

Periodicals

Claggett, Steve. "Civil War in Franklin County." *Four Rivers Genealogical Society* (August 2014).

Mattox, JoeLouis. "Taking Steps to Record Steptoe, Westport's Vanishing African American Neighborhood," *Jackson County Historical Society JOURNAL* (Autumn 2004).

"Slave Owners Spotsylvania County, 1783 (Continued)," *The Virginia Magazine of History and Biography* (Jan. 1897).

Audio Visual

Thompson, Rodney M., and St. Luke's Health System. "A Step Above the Plaza."

Internet Resources

"100 Milestone Documents." ourdocuments.gov/doc.php?flash=true&doc=35

"African Ethnicities and Their Origins: These contemporary African ethnic groups have contributed most to the black population of the U.S." Heywood, Linda, Ph.D., and John

Thornton, Ph.D. http://www.theroot.com/articles/culture/
2011/10/african_ethnicities_and_their_origins.html
(viewed 14 Dec 2015).

Ancestry.com

Antislavery.org and Freetheslaves.net (retrieved 1 Feb 2015)

archives.gov/research/african-americans/freedmens-
bureau/missouri.pdf (retrieved 27 Jan 2015)

Biography of the Honorable Henry J. (Jefferson) Samuels,
Archives & History Library, The Cultural Center, Charleston,
West Virginia; transcribed from handwriting by Harry E.
Pontius, as viewed 5 April 2013 at: wvencyclopedia.org/
articles/456

"The Civil War in Missouri." 1861. mocivilwar.org/
history/1861.html (retrieved 30 Aug 2012)

"The Civil War in Missouri." 1862. mocivilwar.org/
history/1862.html (retrieved 30 Aug 2012)

"The Civil War in Missouri." 1863. mocivilwar.org/
history/1863.html (retrieved 30 Aug 2012)

"The Civil War in Missouri." 1864. mocivilwar.org/
history/1864.html (retrieved 30 Aug 2012)

Danforth, Nelson. Slave Narrative--Missouri. Transcripts compiled
from the WPA Writer's Projects, 1936-1938. George P. Rawick
Papers, Series 5. State Historical Society of Missouri, St. Louis
Research Center. law.wustl.edu/staff/taylor/SLAVES/
danforth.htm (retrieved 30 Aug 2012)

Elmwoodcem-kc.org

Emancipation Proclamation. en.wikipedia.org/wiki/
Emancipation_Proclamation (retrieved 30 Aug 2012)

examiner.com/list/untangling-the-genealogy-of-the-former-slave-
holder-and-enslaved (retrieved 6 Nov 2013)

Federal Non-Population Census Schedules, 1850-1880
archives.gov/research/census/nonpopulation/reference-report-
1850-1880.pdf (retrieved 27 Aug 2012)

Findagrave.com

Foster, Robin. "Untangling the genealogy of the former
slaveholder and enslaved."

freepages.genealogy.rootsweb.ancestry.com/~ewyatt/_borders/Tex
as%20Slave%20Narratives/Texas%20G/Grant,%20Lizzie.html
(retrieved 18 August 2012).

"General Orders No. 135 (U.S. War Department)." (2014) In *Ohio
Civil War Central*, Retrieved September 14, 2014, from Ohio
Civil War Central: ohiocivilwarcentral.com/
entry.php?rec=1192

Greene, Lorenzo J. Greene, Antonio F. Holland and Gary Kremer.
"The Role of the Negro in Missouri History, 1719-1970."
Official Manual, State of Missouri, 1973-1974.
law.wustl.edu/staff/ taylor/manual/manual.htm
(retrieved 2 August 2012)

"History and Genealogy, Westmoreland County, Virginia:
James E. DeAtley (Deatly)," rivahresearch.com/
westmorelandcty/vitals/resources/family
(retrieved 16 June 2012)

home.usmo.com/~momollus/FranCoCW/54EMM.htm (retrieved
11 Nov 2012)

listverse.com/2011/01/25/10-fascinating-interracial-marriages-in-history/ (retrieved 25 Jan 2013)

"Memory Book" hosted by the Smithsonian Institution's National Museum of African American History and Culture. Africanamerican.si.edu/Programs/Memorybook (Arthur Jackson)

"Missouri Death certificates," Missouri Secretary of State. s1.sos.mo.gov/records/archives/archivesdb/deathcertificates/

news.google.com/newspapers?id=09dNAAAAIBAJ&sjid=x4oDA AAAIBAJ&dq=deatley%20oak%20grove&pg=7340%2C2971 342 (retrieved 28 Apr. 2013)

news.google.com/newspapers?id=xW1WAAAAIBAJ&sjid=FuQD AAAAIBAJ&pg=6472%2C2048823 (retrieved 28 Apr 2013)

"Organization Index to Pension Files of Veterans Who Served Between 1861 and 1900." fold3.com (NARA microfilm publication T289)

"Pinpointing DNA Ancestry in Africa: Most African Americans hail from just 46 ethnic groups, research shows." Heywood, Linda, Ph.D., and John Thornton, Ph.D. http://www.theroot.com/articles/culture/2011/10/tracing_dna_ not_just_to_africa_but_to_1_tribe.html (retrieved 14 Dec. 2015)

rivahresearch.com/westmorelandcty/vitals/resources/ families/DeatleyJames.html, courtesy Francesca Henle Taylor, Genealogy Volunteer, Westmoreland County, Virginia (retrieved 16 June 2012)

rivahresearch.com/westmorelandcty/vitals/resources/cemetery/locu sthillcemetery.html (retrieved 16 June 2012)

rootsweb.ancestry.com/~wvkanawh/Early/abtkan.html
(retrieved 16 June 2012)

skyscraperpage.com/cities/?buildingID=553 (retrieved 1 Feb 2015)

"Slave Surnames: Where Are They From?"
msualumni.wordpress.com/2009/06/25/slave-surnames-where-
are-they-from/ (retrieved 28 Aug 2012)

sos.mo.gov/archives/provost/ (retrieved 4 Dec 2012)

sos.mo.gov/images/Archives/Provost/F1897.5.pdf
(retrieved 4 Dec 2012)

"United States Civil War and Later Pension Index, 1861-1917,"
index. familysearch.org/pal:/MM9.1.1/N4T7-ZZG
(retrieved 21 Sep 2014)

"U.S. Colored Troops and the Plight of the Refugee Slave,"
usgennet.org/usa/mo/county/stlouis/ct.htm
(retrieved 14 Sept. 2014)

U.S. Department of the Interior, Bureau of Land Management,
General Land Office Records online database
(retrieved 25 Jan 2013)

usgennet.org/usa/mo/county/stlouis/ct.htm (retrieved 14 Sept 2014)

usgennet.org/usa/mo/topic/afro-amer/slavesinmo.html
(retrieved 2 August 2012)

"US law abolishing transatlantic slave trade takes effect."
blog.oup.com/2012/01/slave-trade/ (retrieved 15 Jan 2015)

vahistorical.org/research/genealogy.htm (retrieved 2 August 2012)

"Washington: The 'Blackest Name' in America,"
huffingtonpost.com/2011/02/21/washington-blackest-name-
america_n_825884.html (retrieved 20 Sept. 2014)

wvculture.org/history/histamne/jacksonw.html
(retrieved 16 Mar 2013)

wvculture.org/history/slavery.html (retrieved 2 August 2012)

Wilson-Kleekamp, Traci L. *How Do I Put All the Information
Together?* African American Genealogy: Part 5 of 5 Part
Series. Missouri State Archives online presentations.
sos.mo.gov/archives/presentations/default.asp?ap=aagene5
(retrieved 11 Nov 2012)

en.wikisource.org/wiki/1990_Census_Name_Files_dist.all.last_(1-
100) (retrieved 20 Sept. 2014)

en.wikipedia.org/wiki/Anti-miscegenation_laws_in_the_
United_States (retrieved 25 Jan 2013)

en.wikipedia.org/wiki/Enrolled_Missouri_Militia
(retrieved 11 November 2012)

en.wikipedia.org/wiki/History_of_slavery_in_West_Virginia
(retrieved 11 November 2012)

en.wikipedia.org/wiki/Iowa_people (retrieved 9 Jan 2015)

en.wikipedia.org/wiki/Ioway_Reservation (retrieved 9 Jan 2015)

en.wikipedia.org/wiki/United_States_Colored_Troops
(retrieved 27 Jan 2015)

Acknowledgements

I'm thankful to my Grandpa Roy Jackson for sharing with me over our *many* years together his memories and details about his grandparents, Arthur and Ida Jackson. I know it may not be easy to accept the reality that his Grandpa Jackson was black given the prejudice ingrained in his youth (he's 97 in 2015). I can only hope it might give him some relief to know for certain the family secret that his Grandma Jackson surely tried to impart to him on her deathbed in 1948. To Arthur and Ida's descendants, we are better knowing and owning this unique truth. Thank you for your contributions: Betty (Jackson) Allen; Mary (Johnson) Bentley [now deceased]; Susan (Bentley) Breckenridge; Virginia Lee Jackson (1941); Marcia (Levine) Ogren; Dorothy (Johnson) Rittermeyer [now deceased]; and, Alice (Bentley) White.

To the descendants of Richard Ludlow and Lucinda Edwards (Deatley) Jackson, Sr., I hope that this scholarly, in-depth exploration about your ancestors is acceptable to you. Discovering that one's ancestor(s) were slaveholders presents a conflict. I, too, have ancestors who were slaveholders. It's a fact of their lives and their times that we must admit, accept, learn from, forgive, and move forward in grace. Thank you, especially, to Dr. Jabez North Jackson's grandson, Jabez Jackson "Jim" MacLaughlin [now deceased], and his daughter, for corresponding with me. I resonate with a granddaughter of Dr. Jackson, Sally (Harris) Wolfe, who said, *"It's so nice to feel the far reaching arms of the heritage the Good Lord provided. We shall all understand one day how we all interconnect and I for one have found all my family near, far and really extended to be a great blessing and gift from above!"* I exchanged genealogical finings about Virginia (Jackson) Thomas with her descendants: Jere Herring, Fred Thomas, and Bob Thomas. And, I enjoy my acquaintance with one of Dr. Jackson's great grandsons, who also lives in Kansas City, Tom Platt.

My long-time friend, James A. Tharp, is always encouraging of my varied research and publishing projects. And, I'm lucky to have continued collaboration with him on several ventures. James is astute and I respect his knowledge, wisdom, and opinions. Of course, his willingness to do look-ups when I'm in a pickle must not go without a nod, wink and handshake. And, luckily for me, James usually goes overboard when in hot-pursuit of an answer. I must also recognize his book, *Colleges of Medicine, Dentistry and Pharmacy, Kansas City, Missouri*, which took years to research and produce, and was useful in providing unique details about the Kansas City doctors in the Richard and Lucinda Jackson, Sr., family.

As a veteran archivist myself, I value the dedication of three respected professionals in their field for their assistance with this product: Claire Prechtel-Kluskens (Projects Archivist, Archives I Research Support Branch (RD-DC), National Archives and Records Administration, Washington, D.C.) and, Beth L. Rowe (Regional Documents Librarian and Head of Documents and Microforms Section at the University of North Carolina at Chapel Hill) kindly and diligently discovered (and amended their catalogs for) the 1850 and 1860 Agricultural and Manufacturing U.S. Census Schedules for Kanawha County, Virginia, which are filmed and filed with West Virginia counties. And, Jennifer McGillan, (Archivist, Archives & Special Collections Augustus C. Long Health Sciences Library, Columbia University Medical Center, New York, New York) provided detailed research into 1872-1873 graduation catalogs, trustees minutes and faculty minutes documenting John W. and James P. Jackson's education at a critical time in this Jackson family's *histiogeneography*.™

Cheryl Lang and Kirsten Grubbs, adept and admired librarians at the Midwest Genealogy Center of the Mid-Continent Public Library System, Independence, Missouri, untiringly assist with queries they field . . . always with a smile and "can do" attitude.

County courthouse and historical society staff and volunteers provide invaluable access services to researchers beyond providing safety, security and preservation responsibilities.

Thank you to all who contributed directly and indirectly to this work, with specific applause to: Francesca Henle Taylor (Westmoreland County, Virginia, genealogy volunteer) for her extensive postings, particularly about one of her county's most prestigious 18th century residents, James E. Deatley; Sue Lampe (volunteer researcher) and Steve Claggett (volunteer and author) with Four Rivers Genealogical Society and Washington Historical Society, Washington, Franklin County, Missouri; Holt County Historical Society, Mound City, Missouri; and, Vicki Book, Holt County, Missouri, Recorder of Deeds, who has also personally focused research and education about Holt County's African American heritage.

A glance at the bibliography yields a wealth of information that has been assembled on this topic, both in print and electronically as websites and searchable databases. In addition to the aforementioned institutions, I'm indebted to the Kansas City Public Library's Missouri Valley Special Collections department; the State Historical Society of Missouri, Columbia, Missouri; and, the Library of Congress, Washington, D.C., for their monumental digitization projects, particularly with regard to searchable historic images and 19th century newspapers.

Ancestry.com and National Geographic's Geno2.0 DNA projects provide 'futuristic' services I never could have imagined when I started my genealogical pursuits in 1980. These scientific and genetic advances mesh perfectly with old-fashioned historical and genealogical research that helps to connect with our deep ancestry across time and space.

Could Harrison A. Trexler have known that his seminal 1919 work, *Slavery in Missouri*, would be of such tremendous interest and use to this *histiogeneography*™ 100-years-later? His grandsons, Jim and Sam Trexler, should be proud. I also found Dr. Diane Mutti Burke's, *On Slavery's Border*, brilliant and enlightening to Arthur Jackson's experience as a young slave on a small Missouri farm.

And, I have been inspired by internationally known author, speaker, presenter and professional genealogist, Kathleen Brandt, for the solid research advice she shares with the world through her a3genealogy.com portal. Then too, my friends and colleagues in the Midwest Afro-American Genealogical Interest Coalition (M.A.G.I.C.), particularly Reggie James, Audreay McKinney, Mrs. Corrine Nunn Patterson, and Bill and Annette Curtis, exemplify a dedication to African American genealogy, research, education, publication and display. I hope they may see their influences sprinkled throughout this *histiogeneography.* ™

Now that I put this first edition "to bed," I have already embarked on a quest to trace the lineages of these forbearers.

Will the next edition pinpoint more precisely Arthur Jackson's parentage and ancestors?

I'm calling on them now for assistance.

About the Author

David W. Jackson was graduated magna cum laude with a B.S. in Historic Preservation / Archives Studies from Southeast Missouri State University in 1993. He is director of The Orderly Pack Rat, an independent historical research and consulting firm and publishing house he founded in 1996.

Jacksons's 20+year professional career included Archives and Education Director for the Jackson County (Mo.) Historical Society; and, as an archivist for Unity School of Christianity, Unity Village, Missouri.

In 2009, he co-founded the Gay and Lesbian Archive of Mid-America (GLAMA), jointly maintained and operated by the Kansas City Museum and LaBudde Special Collections of Miller Nichols Library at University of Missouri-Kansas City.

He is an 1859 Guild member of the Jackson County (Mo.) Historical Society; life member of the Four Rivers Genealogical Society (Washington, Mo.) and Holt County (Mo.) Historical Society; and, is an active member, recording secretary, newsletter editor and website contributor for the Midwest Afro-American Genealogical Interest Coalition (M.A.G.I.C.).

Jackson is author of numerous books, newspaper columns, and periodical articles.

Through The Orderly Pack Rat (orderlypackrat.com) he continues to consult, research, write and publish on local history/heritage/historic preservation matters.

BORN A SLAVE

Index

BORN A SLAVE

CPSIA information can be obtained at www.ICGtesting.com
Printed in the USA
LVOW10s1702040316

477823LV00010B/178/P